STRIKE THROUGH
THE MASK

ELIZABETH RENKER

STRIKE THROUGH THE MASK

Herman Melville and the Scene of Writing

THE JOHNS HOPKINS UNIVERSITY PRESS

Baltimore and London

© 1996 THE JOHNS HOPKINS UNIVERSITY PRESS
All rights reserved. Published 1996
Printed in the United States of America on acid-free paper

Johns Hopkins Paperbacks edition, 1998
9 8 7 6 5 4 3 2 1

THE JOHNS HOPKINS UNIVERSITY PRESS
2715 North Charles Street
Baltimore, Maryland 21218-4319
The Johns Hopkins Press Ltd., London

Library of Congress Cataloging-in-Publication Data will be found at the
end of this book.
A catalog record for this book is available from the British Library.

ISBN 0-8018-5230-7
ISBN 0-8018-5875-5 (pbk.)

FRONTISPIECE ILLUSTRATION:
Herman Melville (1819–1891), engraving,
The Bettmann Archive.

For
EDITH MCCONVILLE RENKER
May 15, 1921–May 26, 1993

> The mother's face,
> The purpose of the poem, fills the room.
> They are together, here, and it is warm.
>
> WALLACE STEVENS
> "The Auroras of Autumn"

Contents

Illustrations

Acknowledgments

I am grateful to the Ohio State University College of Humanities for providing generous research assistance for the completion of this project. The American Antiquarian Society's provocative 1992 summer seminars in the history of the book, led by Michael Winship, were invaluable. John T. Irwin always said the right thing at the right time. Larzer Ziff's friendship and advice offered sustenance at crucial points. Paul Metcalf's conversation energized me. Liz Prelinger answered my questions about foreshortening. Jim Bracken of the Ohio State University Libraries eased the research task. The anonymous readers for the Johns Hopkins University Press engaged the manuscript extensively and shrewdly, and I benefited from their comments. And Ken Hewes claimed throughout the years of composition that he still found it interesting.

I cite and describe Melville manuscripts with the generous permission of the Houghton Library, Harvard University and the Gansevoort-Lansing Collection, Rare Books and Manuscripts Division, the New York Public Library, Astor, Lenox and Tilden Foundations. Chapter 3 appeared in an abbreviated version as "Herman Melville, Wife Beating, and the Written Page" in *American Literature* 66 (March 1994) and appears here by permission. Chapter 1 appeared, in a slightly altered version, in *Arizona Quarterly* 51.2 (summer 1995).

Note on Texts
and Manuscripts

P age references to *Typee, Omoo, Mardi, Redburn, White-Jacket, Moby-Dick, Pierre, Israel Potter, The Piazza Tales and Other Prose Pieces, 1839–1860, The Confidence-Man, Clarel, Correspondence,* and *Journals* are to volumes 1–10, 12, and 14–15, respectively, of the Northwestern-Newberry Edition of *The Writings of Herman Melville,* edited by Harrison Hayford, Hershel Parker, and G. Thomas Tanselle (Evanston and Chicago: Northwestern UP and Newberry Library, 1968–93). Parenthetical references in the text and in the endnotes cite these volumes as cited in the list of abbreviations. The last two volumes of the Northwestern-Newberry edition, one devoted to Melville's published poems and one to *Billy Budd* and other late manuscripts, were still pending when this project was completed. References to *Battle-Pieces and Aspects of the War* are taken from the first edition (New York: Harper, 1866). Citations of other poems by Melville, unless otherwise specified, are from *Collected Poems of Herman Melville,* edited by Howard P. Vincent (Chicago: Hendricks House, 1947). References to *Billy Budd* are taken from the 1986 Viking Penguin edition, *Billy Budd and Other Stories,* edited by Frederick Busch, which reprints the 1962 reading text by Harrison Hayford and Merton M. Sealts Jr.

I describe and quote Melville manuscripts and papers by permission of the Houghton Library, Harvard University and the Gansevoort-Lansing Collection, Rare Books and Manuscripts Division, the New York Public Library, Astor, Lenox and Tilden Foundations.

Introduction

*One adequate look at that face conveyed to most
philosophical observers a notion of something not before
included in their scheme of the Universe.*

—Melville, *Pierre*

In his 1850 review of Nathaniel Hawthorne's *Mosses from an Old Manse*, Herman Melville writes that fine authors are portrait painters whose textual faces are characterized by a "lurking something,"[1] a resistant quality whose nature he will not or cannot define. The concealment, troubled perception, and obscured vision connoted by the word "lurking" inform Melville's enduring association of faces with "lurking" forces. In this volume I am concerned with the persistent power with which Melville figures disturbing confrontations with faces: the terrifying tattooed faces of the Typees, the inexplicably missing face of Moby-Dick, the appalling pale face of Plotinus Plinlimmon, the mute white faces of women in "Fragments from a Writing Desk" and "The Tartarus of Maids," the disguised and perhaps nonexistent face of the Confidence-Man. Melville's repeated figuration of faces is symptomatic of the terms of his material and conceptual engagement with the process of writing, and, more specifically, with the chronic frustrations and blocks that characterize his engagements with the page. The configurations of Melville's scene of writing are constitutive of the terms of his fiction and poetry in ways that render their importance primary to understanding the body of his work.[2]

The terms Melville himself invokes to talk about his project as a writer center on the idea of telling the truth. Thus he writes in "Hawthorne and His Mosses" that Shakespeare merits renown as the profoundest of thinkers because of

> those deep far-away things in him; those occasional flashings-forth of the
> intuitive Truth in him; those short, quick probings at the very axis of reality;—
> these are the things that make Shakespeare, Shakespeare. Through the mouths of
> the dark characters of Hamlet, Timon, Lear, and Iago, he craftily says, or
> sometimes insinuates the things, which we feel to be so terrifically true, that it
> were all but madness for any good man, in his own proper character, to utter, or
> even hint of them. Tormented into desperation, Lear the frantic King tears off the
> mask, and speaks the sane madness of vital truth. (244)

Although this essay takes Hawthorne as its subject, its discussion of the problems facing the American genius clearly refers to Melville himself, who was in the process of composing *Moby-Dick* at the time.[3] Thus, when he describes Shakespeare and Hawthorne as masters of "the great Art of Telling the Truth," he simultaneously describes his conception of his own project, to which he unmistakably refers with the remark, "You must have plenty of sea-room to tell the truth in" (246). A few years later, he again figures authorship as an attempt at truth-telling in the newly embittered tone of *Pierre* (1852), in which the hero's desire to tell the truth ultimately produces both failure as a novelist and self-destruction.

In Melville's terms, the "great Art of Telling the Truth" required speaking "craftily," since, as quoted in the passage above, "it were all but madness for any good man, in his own proper character, to utter, or even hint" of the things we feel "to be so terrifically true." As early as 1849, Melville lamented that an author could never be frank with his readers: "What a madness & anguish it is, that an author can never—under no conceivable circumstances—be at all frank with his readers."[4] He wrote to Hawthorne that "Truth is the silliest thing under the sun. Try to get a living by the Truth—and go to the Soup Societies. . . . Truth is ridiculous to men."[5] By the time of *The Confidence-Man* (1857), the "good man" who cannot speak "in his own proper character" becomes Francis Goodman, one of the Confidence-Man's personae. His designation as "Frank" (thus "frank good man") rewrites Melville's blocked desire "to be frank with his readers" under the sign of a charlatan, an embodiment of the impossibility of "frankness" in writing. "For I hold it a verity," Melville writes in 1849, "that even Shakespeare, was not a frank man to the uttermost."[6]

The paradoxical problem of telling the truth that can't be told is also given structural expression in Melville's work in his predilection for impostors as narrators and protagonists. Tommo in *Typee*, Typee in *Omoo*, Taji in *Mardi*, White-Jacket in *White-Jacket*, and Ishmael in *Moby-Dick* are all narrators who operate under assumed names; a merely partial list of protagonist-impostors in works written in the third person includes Plotinus Plinlimmon in *Pierre*, Babo in "Benito Cereno," and the Confidence-Man; and, if we use the term *impostor* slightly more loosely, to signify one who on occasion or unintentionally deceives others about his identity, we might also include Pierre (whom Steel, Flint & Asbestos accuse of being "a swindler"), Israel Potter in *Israel Potter* (who assumes a string of identities and disguises), and the narrator of "The Piazza" (who withholds his identity from Marianna).

Melville also had a penchant for authorial pseudonyms. "The Encantadas," for example, was published under the name "Salvator R. Tarnmoor," and "Hawthorne and His Mosses" under the byline "By a Virginian Spending July in Vermont" (neither description applied to Melville); even his first known piece of fiction, "Fragments from a Writing Desk" (1839), was published under the initials "L.A.V." "Bartleby, the Scrivener," "Benito Cereno," "The Lightning-Rod Man," "The Bell-Tower," and many of his other magazine pieces were published anonymously.[7] When English publisher Richard Bentley was unenthusiastic about Melville's new proposal for a novel to follow *Moby-Dick*, blaming poor sales on Melville's too-rapid publication of successive books, Melville proposed publishing *Pierre* "anonymously, or under an assumed name:—'By a Vermonter' say," or, he added with alacrity, "By Guy Winthrop."[8]

What is most important, for my purposes, about Melville's predilection for impostors, taken in the context of his expressed desire for a truth that cannot be spoken frankly, is the way it points to a constitutive problem of inexpressibility and deflected communication at the core of his fiction.[9] He conceived of his books, in a well-known phrase, as "botches"—books that were neither the kind that would sell nor "what I feel most moved to write," but an unsuccessful combination of the two.[10] He associated popular books with apparent meanings suited to the superficial skimmer of pages, and unpopular books with deep truths suited to "men who *dive,*" thought-divers who come up with bloodshot eyes.[11] "So far as I am individually concerned, & independent of my pocket, it is my earnest desire to write those sort of books which are said to 'fail,' "[12] he wrote in 1849, but even those books, he lamented, had to be written secretly, to disguise and manage the truth, as Solomon did, to suit the limitations of the audience.[13]

In other words, a problem that Melville blamed on the limitations of his readers, as in the remark I've quoted above ("What a madness & anguish it is, that an author can never—under no conceivable circumstances—be at all frank with his readers"), displaced what was more profoundly a frustration with his own writing as such. It would be "madness" to speak the things that are terrifically true ("it were all but madness for any good man, in his own proper character, to utter, or even hint" of the things we feel "to be so terrifically true"), but it was also "madness" that he could not do so. Placing those two propositions of Melville's side by side does not leave much room for writing in a calm, silent, grass-growing mood—precisely the frame of mind that Melville himself said could never be his.[14]

Melville's irruptive faces emerge concomitant to his conflicted desire for truth-telling, simultaneously and insistently figuring moments of blockage, suspension, and fear. These faces stage "within" Melville's texts the scene of blocked writing constitutive of those texts. When I speak here about writer's block, I do not mean that Melville was unable to produce—which would be nonsensical in the case of a writer who published more than nine novels and four volumes of poetry—but rather that he chronically experienced the page as an obscuring, frustrating, resistant force against whose powers of blankness he battled as he wrote.

These irruptive faces also change from one text to the next, as Melville's engagements with the scene of writing change. So while, on the one hand, Melville repeatedly figures faces in his texts, often to great thematic effect, his relation to faces also exceeds the thematic; here I use the term *thematic* to designate Melville's manipulation of a chosen topos to explore and vary consciously controlled and defined symbols, although the term can carry much broader designations in literary studies.[15] As Melville's faces create powerful side effects that transcend individual novels and tales, they delineate in a sustained fashion the terms of his relation to his own scene of writing.

The material thing confronting Melville as he wrestled with "the angel—Art" was a page, blank or in various stages of inscription.[16] The struggle he recounts in the late poem "Art," in which the quoted phrase appears, is specifically the struggle to embody the "unbodied scheme" in "form" (1. 2, 3). The poem figures his scene of writing as one of physical struggle and confrontation, here metaphorized in the biblical terms of Jacob's wrestling match. The persistent thematization of faces that I argue is a central structure in his work is also confrontational: the irruptive face as Melville figures it visually confronts and arrests the narrator, a character, the author, or the reader. The confrontational aspect of these facial scenarios is fostered, I argue, by his physical struggle to produce writing on the confrontational surface of the page.

His confrontation with the material page is one to which the manuscript of "Art" itself attests, just one among many such examples found in Melville's manuscripts. The poem is, materially speaking, composed of several layers of paper: a page heavily scrawled in pencil; another piece of paper pinned over the top part of the first page, obscuring a section of the previous draft but carefully allowing a precise part of it—half of line 5—to peek through; a second pinned-on sheet following this half-line; and a third sheet pinned on top of the second.[17] The extensive material manipulations that constitute this manuscript are themselves a crucial part of the process about which the poem speaks.

Indeed, writing was a struggle for Melville: his handwriting was illegible; he found spelling impossible; and, among other physical ailments, he suffered from eye, back, and head trouble that made the activity painful. In 1849 he complained to Evert A. Duyckinck of the "vile small print unendurable to my eyes which are tender as young sparrows," and in 1851 he wrote, "I steal abroad by twilight, owing to the twilight of my eyes."[18] Having set out on a journey in 1856 to escape the strains of authorship under which he seemed to be breaking down, he reported to his brother Allan from Liverpool, "Concerning my enjoyment of the thing, it is rather solitary business, poking about the world without a companion. Still, my health is benefited. My hip & back are better, & also my head."[19] The operative association for Melville (and his family) between his writing and physical suffering is emblematized by his donation of funds given to him for the publication of *Clarel* to the New York Society for the Relief of the Ruptured and Crippled. Its association with mental suffering is similarly suggested by his attempt to sell Arrowhead, his home in Pittsfield, Massachusetts, to the Insane Asylum Commission as a site for a new institution.[20]

His physical engagement with the written page was a violent one that disfigured its surface, filling up every available white space with writing as well as cross-outs, revisions, carets, circles, and other manipulations. He cut passages out and pasted them elsewhere with sealing wax; he attached them to each other with pins; he wrote on both sides of the page; he turned the paper upside-down and wrote some more. His consuming relation to the written page in general was also characteristic of his relation to the written character in particular. He characteristically abbreviated his written marks, condensing words, eliding or combining characters, even fusing strokes of the pen that are conventionally formed as discrete units (for example, at the end of one letter and the beginning of another). When he was writing at white heat, his hand became increasingly rough and more and more abbreviated and elided.[21]

Melville's relation to his writing was a material relation whose materiality he desired to efface. He wanted to render the very page confronting him transparent, to dissolve mere paper and type into the "Truth" in terms of which he conceived of his goals as a writer.[22] In response to Hawthorne's praise for *Moby-Dick,* Melville figured the "unspeakable security" that Hawthorne's letter produced in him as a mutual dissolution:

Whence come you, Hawthorne? By what right do you drink from my flagon of life? And when I put it to my lips—lo, they are yours and not mine. I feel that the Godhead is broken up like the bread at the Supper, and that we are the pieces. Hence this infinite fraternity of feeling. Now, sympathizing with the paper, my angel turns over another page. You did not care a penny for the book. But, now and then as you read, you understood the pervading thought that impelled the book—and that you praised.[23]

The image of two men who drink the same liquid becomes in the next sentence the dissolution of the two men into one another, a perfect and secure transparency of selves in which both mutually penetrate the material ("the book") to apprehend the transcendent ("the pervading thought").[24] The subsequent identification of both men as "pieces," ostensibly of the Godhead, leads to a metonymic association with pieces of paper and a page two sentences later. In what is perhaps the letter's most intriguing sentence, his reference to "my angel," Melville conjures the muse figure who will also appear as an angel in other texts, including *The Confidence-Man* and "Art." In the former, the angel falsely promises a "Bright Future" in China Aster's dream (*CM* 212); in the context of that novel, this moment clearly signifies Melville's own history of authorship, as I discuss in chapter 4. In the latter, the angel is a confrontational figure to be wrestled with at the scene of writing. In the letter in question Melville presents the angel as a figure who controls the material text, in this case presumably by turning the page over.[25] Wrestling with the angel who turns the page implies a struggle located specifically at the site of the materials of writing. Melville's repeated figurations of the "angel" in the context of the production of writing suggest that the angel who is "sympathizing with the paper" on this occasion does not always do so. In light of Melville's other invocations of this figure, the angel here appears uncharacteristically cooperative.

This letter to Hawthorne presents the sole documented instance in Melville's career in which he achieved such a profound level of satisfaction with one of his own texts. Indeed, the gratification of producing writing that achieves dissolution of "the book" and of "pieces" of paper into transparency is so powerful for Melville that he cannot stop himself from writing: "I can't stop yet. If the world was entirely made up of Magians, I'll tell you what I should do. I should have a paper-mill established at one end of the house, and so have an endless riband of foolscap rolling in upon my desk; and upon that endless riband I should write a thousand—a million—billion thoughts, all under the form of a letter to you." Writing pages that seem to effect the desired dissolution of "the book" into its "pervading thought" fosters Melville's desire to write endlessly. At the same time, the satisfaction he expresses in this letter by way of metaphors of a sympathetic angel and an endlessly generative scene of paper production turns to hellish frustration elsewhere in his writing: the sympathetic angel becomes the oppositional figure in "Art" and the paper-mill becomes the "Tartarus" whose invocation of Melville's own "house" and "desk" he no longer embraces.

It is concomitant to Melville's desire to dissolve the words on the page into transparency that the repeated figuration of impenetrable faces irrupts, blocking Melville at the surface of a "botch" marred by bad spellings, cross-outs, write-overs, and other errors. This confrontation, finally, is what I take to motivate his metaphorics of the face as an always impenetrable text. Ahab's well-known desire to "strike through the mask" of the dead, blind wall he maniacally confronts figures a desire to strike through a white surface marked with hieroglyphic lines, his figure for the whale's brow. The mask that Ahab wants to strike through is made of "pasteboard," a stiff board composed of paper whose resonance for the author is starkly literal. Striking through the pasteboard mask carries a profoundly material connotation for Melville's own relentless striking through and crossing out and rewriting in an effort to find a satisfactory relation to his own white page. Unfortunately, no manuscript of *Moby-Dick* is known to survive, but the metaphorics of Melville's relation to his writing in general shed light on why he figured his feeling of satisfaction with *Moby-Dick* as feeling "spotless"[26]: as if the "wickedness" and consummate achievement of the book had produced perfectly transparent writing.

By the time of the composition of *Mardi*, Melville's third novel, his wife, Elizabeth Shaw Melville, and his sisters had become his copyists, producing fair copies from which they omitted punctuation, at Melville's direction, so he could add it himself.[27] Punctuation marking in particular has a puncturing quality in the relation it expresses between the page and the writer's hand. In a letter to Duyckinck in December of 1849, after the disappointing reception of *Mardi*, Melville wrote: "Hereafter I shall no more stab at a book (in print, I mean) than I would stab at a man.—. . . . Had I not written & printed 'Mardi,' in all likelihood, I would not be as wise as I am now, or may be. For that thing was stabbed *at* (I do not say *through*)—& therefore, I am the wiser for it.—But a bit of note paper is not large enough for this sort of writing—so no more of it."[28] His figuration of *Mardi* as a text that can be stabbed *at* but not *through* suggests, at one level, that it was philosophically too thick to be demolished by its critics; at another level, the stabbing also suggests a constitutive inability to penetrate the surface of the text, for himself as well as for other aggressors: a blocked "striking through," like that which was to return in Ahab's cry. Billy Budd's speech impediment, a "lurking defect" (*BB* 349) whose nature, as Barbara Johnson points out, is a linguistic one,[29] is what Melville calls "a striking instance" that Satan reminds us, "I too have a hand here" (*BB* 302). The embedded presence of "art" in Claggart's name renders salient his position as master-at-arms, stressing, for present purposes, the importance of the idea that it is "arms" he controls (*BB* 313). That Claggart then frustrates Billy into self-destructive striking is consistent with the signifying scenario of writing and violence that I've described here, and return to in depth in chapter 3.

While it is possible, from one standpoint, to say that Melville's contested confrontation with the page was an effect of, and secondary in importance to, his concern with the epistemological condition of humankind, since the page confronted him with another surface in a world of tormenting surfaces (imagining for a moment how my argument might be conversely reimagined by way of generations of Melville scholarship), I find such an analysis finally unsatisfying because it fails to attend to the intense primacy for Melville of the particular surface that he stared at and labored over. In other words, his confrontation with the written page is not so much a metaphor for the epistemological struggle that anguished him—a confrontation that recalled, say, Ahab's confrontation with the white whale—as it is *constitutive of* the persistent facial confrontations in his fiction.[30] And as such it is finally this face that "lurks" in the impenetrable faces to which Melville gives many other forms.

Abbreviations

WORKS BY MELVILLE

BB	*Billy Budd*
BP	*Battle-Pieces and Aspects of the War*
C	*Clarel*
CM	*The Confidence-Man*
IP	*Israel Potter*
J	*Journals*
JM	*John Marr and Other Sailors*
L	*Correspondence*
M	*Mardi*
MD	*Moby-Dick*
O	*Omoo*
P	*Pierre*
PT	*The Piazza Tales and Other Prose Pieces, 1839–1860*
R	*Redburn*
T	*Typee*
WJ	*White-Jacket*

OTHERS

EI	*Enter Isabel: The Herman Melville Correspondence of Clare Spark and Paul Metcalf*, ed. Paul Metcalf
EWW	*The Endless, Winding Way in Melville: New Charts by Kring and Carey*, ed. Donald Yannella and Hershel Parker

STRIKE THROUGH
THE MASK

save me apart of his smoking before he could divide
the other — he & & & continuing his illustrations by
.... the fleshy part of my arm in his teeth
& intimating that by the whole gesture that the
people who lived as in that direction would like
nothing better than to pick that me in just such a
manner — Having assured himself that we were fully
enlightened in this particular, he proceeded to
another branch of his subject, which I have no doubt
he would have preffaced with a "Secondly" had he
been anything else than the illiterate barbarian
that he was. Ah! tippii', onolake! There we
being .... — there we ...... — chockoo — there we
cockoo — there we we we we! — ....
tholoma' ...., would imply " Oh, tippii'! Is'nt
it a fine place though! no danger I starve here
I tell you — .... plenty of breadfruit —
plenty of water, plenty poee pudding Oh plenty of
every thing — the heaps, heaps, heaps! — All this
was borne accustom by marginal gestures & a
.... of regard motions, which
any ...... might have apprehended.
As he continued his harangue however, this those
like man ...... in emulation of our more
polished orators, chosen to branch at rather ....
into his subject, enlarging perhaps upon the moral
reflections that it .... & proceeding in
a stream of unintelligible gibberish, in the .....
of which he seemed ...... of a man with his
mouthful of chesit spluttering, chirking & spitting the
..... at us in every direction. Such a harsh discharging
...... was heard before. All this and some
seemed to be ..... upon a .... pressure
...... — I can defend me with
such another outbreak! It gave me
rheumatic pains in my joints in my body — What
it all meant it could not ...... of me conjecture

Chapter One

Melville's Spell
in *Typee*

~

L et me begin with a well-known story. Published as an autobiographical travel narrative in 1846, *Typee,* Melville's first book, provoked a
controversy among readers and reviewers. English publisher John
Murray's Colonial and Home Library, the series in which *Typee* was
published, specialized in the real-life experiences of travelers in
exotic places, and promised accuracy and fidelity to facts. But the taint of fiction that was taboo in Murray's series clung to Melville's manuscript. Readers
doubted that "Herman Melville" was a real person, and that his account of his
experience in the Marquesas Islands was true. British readers in particular were
incredulous that any common sailor could write so well. Murray, who worried
from the start about the authenticity of both the author and the tale, repeatedly
begged Melville to substantiate the truth of the narrative somehow, even after
"Toby," one of the book's main characters, fortuitously appeared, "happy to
testify to the entire accuracy of the work, so long as I was with Melville."[1]

Although today we know that "Herman Melville" was a real person who
had shipped as a common sailor to Polynesia and jumped ship in the Marquesas Islands, we also know that the authenticity debate over the book was well
founded. Herman's brother Gansevoort, acting as his agent in London, assured
Murray that the author of *Typee* had "never before written either book or
pamphlet, and to the best of my belief has not even contributed to a magazine
or newspaper."[2] But Melville had already published at least several letters and
one piece of fiction in the local press. Furthermore, as Charles R. Anderson

Illustration 1. Page [20] from the *Typee* manuscript, in Herman Melville's hand, showing the
spellings "Tippii," "Tipii," "Kiri Kiri," and "poe poe" (see lines 12, 15, 23, and 13, respectively). By
permission of the Gansevoort-Lansing Collection, Rare Books and Manuscripts Division, the
New York Public Library, Astor, Lenox and Tilden Foundations.

demonstrated in his groundbreaking *Melville in the South Seas* (1939), *Typee* was a substantially embellished version of the "facts," converting Melville's "relatively slight contact with primitive life" during a four-week sojourn in the Marquesas into Tommo's extensive interaction during a four-month captivity,[3] a premise that rendered *Typee* an authoritative source for subsequent generations of ethnologists. Anderson also showed that Melville borrowed heavily from previous travel narratives, even in constructing allegedly "first-person" observations, and argued that almost all of Melville's recorded "experiences" in *Typee* were in fact derived from the travel literature he read upon his return home. Melville frequently copied not only the subject matter for his chapters and their arrangement but also entire phrases and figures of speech. Anderson concludes that he must have worked with his source books open in front of him, and that he "might have written *Typee* without ever having seen the Marquesas Islands."[4] Hershel Parker similarly concludes: "All in all, the evidence seems to show that Melville's last-minute cobbling was not inspired by his publisher but by his own desire to eke out his brief impressions from his four weeks among the Typeeans (rather than the four months he was claiming), plundering sourcebooks for passages which could be rewritten as his own experiences."[5] Thus Melville's written account of his experience in the Marquesas violated what Nina Baym calls the "implicit genre contract" with his readers to tell the truth, a truth that contemporary admirers of *Typee* adamantly defended.[6]

Although Melville's use of sources in *Typee* is well known among Melville scholars, the implications of this writing practice have not been adequately grasped. Literary criticism of this first novel has concentrated on the conflict among European, American, and Polynesian cultures to which Melville was an eyewitness. Although different moments in the history of criticism approach this conflict in different terms—in some cases, invoking contrasting notions of "civilization" and "the primitive"; in others, exploring Melville's role as impassioned critic of the Euro-American destruction of Polynesia or, alternatively, as complicit tool of imperialism[7]—the underlying focus on cultural conflict as such remains constant. Melville's position (sometimes differentiated from, and sometimes equated with, Tommo's) within a range of cultural discourses about missionary activity, "the primitive," imperialism, Manifest Destiny, Indian removal, and so on have long occupied the discursive center of the book for literary critics. Milton R. Stern's overview of *Typee* criticism is right to stress its "depressingly repetitive" character.[8]

Although a conflict among cultures is indeed the conflict Melville recounts in *Typee*, the tradition of readings I have described largely reproduces Melville's own terms, merely disagreeing over which side of the debate to assign him to and which side deserves our moral valuation—fluctuations useful mostly for what they reveal about literary studies at a given historical moment. The problem with this critical tradition is that its attention to the cultural conflict Melville explicitly addresses has largely blinded us to the importance of the conflict the text struggles so hard to repress: the fact that this "first-person" account of experience disingenuously copies from other books.

The crucial implications of this repressed conflict have been obscured by the discomfort Melville scholars have felt in the face of the specter of plagiarism. Anderson and others, for example, writing in the critical style of their time, argue that Melville recast his borrowed material "to secure greater artistic unity and effect" or to make the material "his own."[9] Their investment in this position is meant to secure the status of Melville's "authorship" and to absolve him of any blame for a practice that a less favorably inclined party might call plagiarism.[10] Indeed, when reading accounts of Melville's use of sources, one cannot escape vigorous pronouncements about how definitively he was *not* a plagiarist. Writing in 1949, Howard P. Vincent summarizes Anderson's findings this way: "Anderson showed how carefully and how deftly Melville adapted many details from travel books to insure accuracy and authenticity for his own narratives of travel," and he summarily concludes, "Melville transformed his borrowings with such skill that the charge of plagiarism is inadmissible."[11] Melville's second novel, *Omoo* (1847), was also heavily "borrowed," and Gordon Roper's Historical Note to the Northwestern-Newberry edition of that text (1968) remarks: "Melville's extensive borrowings from his source books were not those of a plagiarist. He had been in the islands, and had seen native life with his own eyes and reacted to it in his own way. He had been there only a short time, it is true, but what he experienced he experienced vividly and particularly; what he lacked was the broader knowledge which longer residence had given such an observer as Ellis."[12]

Defenses like Vincent's and Roper's suggest most forcefully the felt presence of the "charge" rather than its dismissal. Harrison Hayford and Walter Blair's Introduction to the Hendricks House edition of *Omoo* (1969), which supplements and extends Anderson's account, points out that "his [Melville's] claims about the truth of *Omoo* were by no means candid," and that

> he had not plagiarized, merely, for he had always rewritten and nearly always improved the passages he appropriated. Yet he had composed his books in a way he had not really acknowledged, and in a way that even his most suspicious contemporary critics had never dreamed.
>
> But we believe that even Anderson understated the pervasiveness of these fictional procedures in *Omoo*.[13]

Their formulation that Melville "had not plagiarized, merely," usefully displays the critical hesitancies about this issue: the word "merely" changes the sense of the claim from "he had not plagiarized" to "he had plagiarized, but he had also done more than that," an important and more accurate inflection of the "plagiarism" issue than the other defenses I've cited.[14]

The contemporary version of the argument that Melville made the borrowed material "his own" is well represented by John Samson—another critic writing in the style of his time—in *White Lies: Melville's Narratives of Facts* (1989). Samson claims that Melville carefully chose the passages he lifted, intricately deconstructing the ideological foundations of each as he revised it for inclusion in his own text. Samson's approach is meant to bolster his ultimate argument that Melville was politically forward-thinking and engaged in a deliberate and conscious critique of his sources as representatives of "white" ideology.[15] Melville's reliance upon sources is rendered fully justified in this scheme because it is construed as an integral part of his ideological critique. Samson and Anderson represent the same position because both act as advocates for Melville, whether for his artistic genius or his correct politics, who seek thereby to redeem his writing practices, redemptive gestures common in source studies of Melville's work.

The most serious flaw in these redemptive gestures with respect to *Typee* in particular is that they avoid and obscure the fact that Melville borrowed so much of his first novel *as such*. The scholar's discomfort with "plagiarism" produces the scholar's need to find ways to justify Melville's use of sources, and therefore—and this argumentative turn is a crucial one—to dismiss the ultimate importance of the sources to Melville's final product. But by dismissing the ultimate importance of the presence of source-texts, scholars also dismiss a crucially constitutive component of Melville's relation to his own text and to its production. We cannot dismiss, ignore, or otherwise justify away Melville's copying from the books open in front of him without distorting his relation both to his writing practice and to the text that practice produced.

Melville's writing practice in *Typee* is one that the author himself is disturbed by, and that he wanted and needed to disavow. He famously concludes his Preface to *Typee*, "trusting that his anxious desire to speak the unvarnished truth will gain for him the confidence of his readers" (xiv). The author's equivocation is clear: he claims not that he *does* speak the truth but only that he desires to do so. He also reveals that the issue of truth-telling provokes his anxiety.[16] This anxiety, I argue, centers in his own awareness of his extensive copying from sourcebooks. Hayford and Blair's formulation that "he had composed his books in a way he had not really acknowledged" points usefully to the author's anxiety and disavowal to which I want to call attention. This anxiety shapes the terms of the text, particularly its terrifying facial tattoos.

When I refer to the "presence of writing" in *Typee* that provokes Melville's anxiety, I mean to designate two compelling senses of this phrase. First, I mean the presence during composition of printed texts from which Melville secretly copies to construct his "first-person" account. The presence of writing in this sense interferes with the premise of autobiographical "experience" at the heart of *Typee*. Second, the "presence of writing" signifies Melville's own handwriting, the marks on the page that must efface themselves in order to deliver the pure realm of sound and experience they promise to conjure. The transparent transmission of such a pure realm is impossible, of course, as poststructuralism and particularly deconstruction have long stressed within our own historical moment; but my focus at present is less the impossibility of that transparency in a philosophical sense than the particular anxiety that the interfering ineffaceability of writing provokes for this particular author in this particular text, a situation exacerbated by Melville's notoriously bad handwriting and spelling. The presence of writing in the two senses I have sketched, and Melville's anxious disavowal of that presence, stand at the core of the narrative's anxieties. Furthermore, these anxieties are in fact closely related, since Melville's heavy "borrowings" from printed sources are one kind of nagging indication that *Typee* is made of written marks and not of the world of experience and sound to which he so wishfully appeals.

Part of *Typee*'s project was the representation of a foreign language. Melville invented his own orthography: "In the Polynesian words used in this volume—except in those cases where the spelling has been previously determined by others—that form of orthography has been employed, which might be supposed most easily to convey their sound to a stranger. In several works descriptive of the islands in the Pacific, many of the most beautiful combinations of vocal sounds have been altogether lost to the ear of the reader by an over-attention to the ordinary rules of spelling" (xiv). Melville's claim to represent the lost sounds of Polynesia is part of his project to represent his subject truly and without distortion.[17] But readers of *Typee* and *Omoo* familiar with the languages Melville renders have long been puzzled and disturbed by his orthography, rather than impressed with its naturalness. Robert Louis Stevenson, for example, was aghast at Melville's bad ear and "grotesque misspelling," and Anderson refers to his "usual phonetic inaccuracy."[18] The effect of Melville's Marquesan orthography on readers familiar with the "beautiful . . . vocal sounds" in question has dramatized the non-aural nature of his combinations of letters, rather than the non-written nature he wants to claim for them.

Melville was a chronically frustrated speller.[19] For example, he habitually misspelled words like "accont" (for *account*), "acknoledge" (for *acknowledge*), and "pont" (for *point*), as well as "ie" words in general ("beleive," "cheifly," "acheivment"). Moments of spelling frustration erupt in his correspondence in response to words he has just penned: "(how the devel [*sic*] do you spell it?)"; "(I spell the word right from your sheet)"; "(what a devel [*sic*] of an unspellable word!)"; "(How is it spelt?)"; and "Pardon me, if I have unintentionally translated your patronymick into the Sanscrit."[20] Although American spelling practices were not fully standardized by this time, during the course of the nineteenth century spelling moved toward increasing standardization. Melville reported to John Murray in 1849 that his American printers had instructed him to spell according to Webster.[21] Spelling by the book—and Melville ordered at least three copies of Webster's *American Dictionary of the English Language* in 1847 and 1848[22]—is presumably one of the kinds of alterations to his writing practice resulting from the difficult logistics of readying *Typee* for the press.

Leon Howard stresses that the editorial additions and attentions to Melville's first manuscript are important "because they affected the character of the book and perhaps its author's later habits of writing."[23] Murray had felt it necessary to employ Henry Milton, the reader of the manuscript, to revise Melville's text, and Milton spent seventy-seven hours revising part 1 and ninety-one and one-half hours revising part 2. For his extensive labors he was paid just over half the amount Melville himself was paid for the manuscript.[24] But since the manuscript of *Typee* does not survive—with the exception of the sixteen leaves, covered on both sides, constituting a working draft of chapters 12–14, only one of which had been found by the time the Northwestern-Newberry edition was produced—we can only speculate about exactly what Melville's manuscript looked like before it was revised.[25] Looking back on his experience publishing his first book, Melville assured Murray in July 1846 that his new manuscript (*Omoo*) "will be in a rather better state for the press than the M.S.S. handed to him by my brother. A little experience in this art of book-craft has done wonders."[26]

Among Melville's various problems producing manuscript, I mean to stress for the moment the importance of his spelling difficulties, at present for the terms of *Typee* in particular, although they certainly resonate throughout his writing in ways scholarship has overlooked. The most compelling relevance of spelling for Melville was its difficulty and its resistance to self-evidence; it constituted one of the material obstacles intruding upon his scene of writing. By "material" here I mean the physical object that is a word, as opposed to the transcendent meaning to which the object-word can be construed as a trans-

parent window—a crux at the center of Melville's writing and his writing difficulties. In addition to the obtrusiveness of his spelling frustrations, we can see
in Melville's misspelling important effects of meaning. On this matter I disagree
with critics and editors who believe that Melville's spelling should be corrected
in the service of producing a more adequate text. Norman Eugene Jarrard's
edition of the published poems, for example, concludes that "legitimate interest
in such spelling errors is non-literary."[27]

In *Typee*, Melville's confrontation with what was for him the endlessly
frustrating problem of how to spell words becomes an explicit part of his
writing process by way of his orthographic project. His chronic problem with
spelling usually had no occasion for explicit mention in his published works,
but in his first novel the need to represent a foreign language introduced the
subject of spelling as such as a pertinent one. While his characteristically errant
spellings of standardized words would be regularized during the publishing
process, his Marquesan orthography was not subject to conventions of Western spelling. His spellings were meant to reproduce "beautiful combinations
of vocal sounds" that "the ordinary rules of spelling" might destroy, and
these were "sounds" about which Melville, as a "first-person" observer, was an
authority.

In practice, of course, his intention to naturalize writing is self-defeating
on two counts. First, Melville's relation to spelling as part of the practice of
writing was not at all comfortable and so did not flow naturally. And second,
the promise to render spelling a transparent window to sound is an impossible
attempt to bypass the writtenness of writing, to naturalize and thereby dissolve its mediating presence. Since letters do not have a transparent relation to
sound, the purity of sound reproduction to which Melville appeals is already
marred by writing since it must be constituted by it. The "easy" conveyance of
sound Melville claims as his orthographic goal accords perfectly with the narrative's pretensions to "genuineness" and pure experience, since, in reproducing
Polynesian sounds unmediated by the "ordinary rules of spelling," he attempts
to dispel forms of writing that could only interfere with a true experience of the
Marquesas. The pretense of dissolving writing into sound, of dispelling spelling
and in its place restoring "beautiful combinations of vocal sounds . . . altogether lost to the ear of the reader," is part of Melville's more thoroughgoing
and anxious need to disclaim the writtenness of the text.

The beautiful vocal sounds he claims to restore are inescapably words, and
his relation to these words blocks any claim to transparent writing in a way that
was, I maintain, compelling to the author himself. Manuscript leaves from the
extant draft reveal, for example, that spellings are not always consistent: many

trees selected for the purpose. I am the absolute &
most symmetrical that the vale afforded.— As one
denominated in the language of the natives the "ti
end now placed this ꆛ This was the building, to
which Mehevi was conducted us. Thus far we had
been accompanied by a troop of the natives of both sexes,
but as soon as we approached its vicinity the females
singled themselves out from the crowd & standing aloof
permitted us to pass on. The interdicts & prohibitions
of the taboo were likewise extended to this edifice &
enforced by the same dreadful penalty that secured the
Hoolah Hoolah ground from the unmanly pollution
of a woman's presence. ⊕ On entering the house we
were struck with the aspect of four or
five old wretches on whom decrepid his home of tatooing seemed
to have obliterated every trace of humanity.— Owing to the
continual process of tatooing, which only terminates among
them upon after all the figures sketched upon
their limbs have been blended together, an effect produced
however only in cases of extreme longevity, the bodies of these
men were of a uniform dull green color; the hue which
the tatooing gradually assumed as the individual advances
in age. Their skin had a frightful scaly appear-
ance which united with its singular color gave them the appearance of
ance this their flesh lay upon them in huge folds
like the out lapping pleats of the rhinoc-
erous— The head was completely bald & they presented
no vestige of a beard. ꆛ These repulsive looking creatures seemed
to have lost the use of their lower limbs altogether, sitting
upon the floor crosslegged in a state of torpor.
— They never heeded us in the least, scarcely appear conscious of our presence. while Mehevi seated us upon the
mats & Kori Kori gave utterance to some of his unintelligible gibberish ꆛ In a few moments a boy entered
with a wooden trencher of poi-poi & I was obliged
again to submit to the officious intervention of
my indefatigable servitor. Various other dishes
followed, the Chief manifesting the most
hospitable importunity in pressing us to partake

of the spellings eventually published as the "natural" ones were different at this stage of composition, and some were in a clear state of transition within the draft from one spelling to another. "Kory-Kory" is usually "Kori Kori" at this stage, although in one case it appears to be "KoKiri" and in another "Kiri Kiri"; "Happar" is "Hapaa," or sometimes "Haapaa"; "kokoo" is "cuckoo"; "Marheyo" is "Maheyo"; "Typee" is "Tipii" or sometimes "Tippii"; and "Fayaway" is "Faawa" or perhaps "Faaua." We can see "Faawa" changing to "Fayaway" at one point in the draft as Melville overscores the former with the latter. The final spellings "Typee" and "Kory-Kory" don't appear at all. It is thus clear from the extant draft that what became the spellings in the first English edition, which in turn became the copy-text for the Northwestern-Newberry edition, were determined only after Melville tried many other forms of these words. (See illustrations 1, 2, and 3.)[28]

On the inside of the folded and sewn paper cover of the manuscript, Melville experiments with different spellings of the name that appears in copy-text as "Marheyo"; here, he writes in a vertical column "Marheyoo," "Mh," "Mar," "Marheeyo," and "Marheyo." Several different combinations of letters can approximate one particular combination of sounds, since the letters themselves bear no essential relation to the sounds they "reproduce,"[29] and here we see Melville working through, in the case of one particular word in his Marquesan orthography, the practical problems of spelling arising from that condition. In the body of the manuscript, Melville chooses "Maheyo."[30] These examples illustrate both the lack of transparency in Melville's Polynesian words—since the "form of orthography . . . which might be supposed most easily to convey their sound to a stranger" was a product of experimentation and change—and suggest how variations in Melville's spellings produce effects only detectable in their written form, since presumably all these variant spellings "sound" the same way. These purely written differences—say, between "Fayaway" and "Faaua"—thus mark the presence of writing in a text that disclaimed its own writtenness.

In Bette S. Weidman's transcription of part of leaf 10, we find Melville wrestling with acknowledging the writtenness of Toby's words:

> As I cannot remember the words made use of by Toby on this occasion, I shall accordingly relate his adventure in my own language tho' in the same putting the words in his mouth.

Illustration 2. Page [5] from the *Typee* manuscript, in Herman Melville's hand, showing the spellings "Kori Kori" (line 31) and "poi=poi" (line 33), paragraph symbols, and other textual marks. By permission of the Gansevoort-Lansing Collection, Rare Books and Manuscripts Division, the New York Public Library, Astor, Lenox and Tilden Foundations.

companion and asked Alarmedly " What it can all
this mean Toby ? " " oh nothing, ~~getting~~ said he —
getting the fire ready I suppose " — " Fire ! " exclaimed
I — " what fire ? " — " Why, the fire to cook us, to be
sure, what else indeed would the bloody cannibals
be kicking up such a row about, if it were not for that? "
" Oh Toby, have done with your jokes, this is no time for
them, something is about to happen I feel confydant "
" I think there is myself, " said Toby " Why, what do you
suppose the devils ~~on~~ have been feeding us ~~it~~ for
in this kind of style, ~~for~~ the last three days, unless
it ~~were~~ for something that you are afraid to talk about?
Look at that Kori Kori then, how ~~he~~ has been stuffing you
with his confounded mushes; just the same ~~kind of~~
~~stuff they give to swine before they kill them~~ nay
they treat swine before they kill them? Depend upon it
~~will~~ we will be taken this blessed night, & there is the fire
we ~~will~~ roast by." " This ~~language of my companion~~ whether
to be taken in earnest or otherwise, was not at all
Calculated to allay my apprehensions; & I shud=
dered, when I reflected, that we were indeed in
at the mercy of a tribe of cannibals, ~~at at~~
and that the ~~horrible~~ contingency to which Toby had
alluded, was by no means removed beyond the bonds
of possibility. — " There, I told you so, they are coming
for us " exclaimed my companion the next moment as
the forms of ~~four natives~~ were seen, mounted the steps
& approaching toward us — They came on warilely, nay
stealthfully, and glided along through the gloom that
surrounded us, as tho' about to spring upon some
object they were fearful of disturbing before they should
make sure of it — Gracious Heaven ! the horrible
thing of reflections that crowded upon me at that
moment — A cold sweat stood upon my brow &
spell bound with terror I awaited my fate. —
Suddenly the silence was broken by the well remembered tones
of "Mehevi" & at the kindly accents of his voice
my fears were immediately disappeated. " Tomo,

> Though I can not recall to mind anything like the precise phraseology
> employed on this occasion still for the sake of unity I shall permit my companion
> to rehearse his own adventure in the language that most readily occurs to me.

Weidman's transcription reveals that Melville tries to get this moment right twice: he strikes out the first sentence quoted, and both are entirely absent from the published text, in which Toby merely "was sufficiently recovered to tell me what had occurred" and begins speaking.[31] The conflicted admission that these words of dialogue are not the recalled and experienced voice of Toby, but, rather, Melville's own written words, is one finally eliminated. The problems of invented dialogue (like Toby's in this example) and invented spelling (Melville's orthography rather than "pure" sound) further intersect in the tension evident throughout the narrative between Tommo's ability to understand the Typees' language and his inability to do so. Thus he frequently prefaces a long paraphrase of native speech with a paradoxical disclaimer about his ignorance of the language. Tommo tells us the meanings of the Typees' words despite what is to him their opacity, a gesture that makes present to his audience what is not present to him. Tommo's position as translator thus restages Melville's position as autobiographer, since Melville presents to his audience as first-person accounts what are present to him not as "pure" sound but as printed pages.

Early on, the narrator both acknowledges and disclaims his own printed sources:

> Of this interesting group [of islands], but little account has ever been given, if we
> except the slight mention made of them in the sketches of South-Sea voyages . . .
> [;] all that we know about them is from a few general narratives. Among these,
> there are two that claim particular notice. Porter's 'Journal of a Cruise of the U.S.
> frigate Essex, in the Pacific, during the late War,' is said to contain some
> interesting particulars concerning the islanders. This is a work, however, which I
> have never happened to meet with; and Stewart, the chaplain of the American
> sloop of war Vincennes, has likewise devoted a portion of his book, entitled 'A
> Visit to the South Seas,' to the same subject. (6)

He also acknowledges "interesting accounts" of Tahiti by Ellis (6). According to Anderson, these texts were in fact Melville's chief sources in *Typee:* Captain David Porter's *Journal of a Cruise Made to the Pacific Ocean, in the U.S. Frigate Essex, in the Years 1812, 1813, and 1814* (1815), Charles S. Stewart's *A Visit to the*

Illustration 3. Page [7] from the *Typee* manuscript, in Herman Melville's hand, showing the spellings "Kori Kori" (line 13) and "Tomo" (line 38), paragraph symbols, and circle transversed by two lines that marks insertion of text. By permission of the Gansevoort-Lansing Collection, Rare Books and Manuscripts Division, the New York Public Library, Astor, Lenox and Tilden Foundations.

South Seas, in the U.S. Ship Vincennes, During the Years 1829 and 1830 (1831), and, to a lesser extent, William Ellis's *Polynesian Researches* (1829).[32] Ellis would become what Hayford and Blair call his "major prompt-book" in *Omoo*.[33] The narrator of *Typee* defensively acknowledges having read Stewart and Ellis but does not acknowledge his reliance upon them, and he disclaims having read Porter altogether. Meanwhile, his awareness in the Preface of how unnamed "others" spell Polynesian words shows a familiarity with previous accounts of the region. The American Revised Edition of *Typee* deleted the reference to Porter and Stewart entirely; this deletion was apparently one of the "two or three slight alterations" that Melville sent to Wiley and Putnam, his American publishers, before the wholesale revisions of July 1846.[34] Howard argues that Melville omitted this passage because his claim "may have been true when he began writing his book but was certainly false by the time he had finished it."[35] Whether Melville deleted this passage after he borrowed heavily from these sources or merely thought better of even mentioning them, this deletion marks Melville's ambivalence and vacillation about acknowledging the sources he copied from. Around the same time he is deleting the fib about his sources, he adamantly defends, to Murray and others, "the truth of my narrative *as I sent it to London.*"[36]

Anderson and Hayford and Blair point out that Melville's quirky spellings and inaccuracies about Polynesia are in many cases attributable to the sources from which he copied. In this sense Melville's orthography as a textual site for the presence of his engagement with written words as such overlaps with the presence of writing constituted by his reliance on printed text. Hayford and Blair correctly point out that Melville's claim to have been governed by sounds in devising his orthography has been too uncritically accepted, and that the many words he borrowed from books would have been seen, not heard. Thus those who fault Melville's "ear" overlook the crucial fact that the sources of distortion were non-aural.[37] Hayford and Blair's observation that critics "have sought no more precise explanation of his spelling practices" than that of his "poor ear" still holds true; Hayford and Blair themselves have produced the most useful work to date on this subject.[38]

Thinking about Melville's orthography in the light of these important suggestions produces valuable results. While Stewart and others incline toward the spelling "Taipi," for example (the orthography that prevailed in the nineteenth century and that remains standard today),[39] Melville unconventionally rendered the word as "Typee," presumably a later orthographic choice than the "Tipii" that usually appears in the body of the extant draft. On the cover of the draft the later spelling, "Typee," is written in what appears to be Melville's hand.[40] A French official who visited the Marquesas around the same time as Melville notes that he spelled the word "Typee" "bizarrement."[41] Early in the novel, the narrator reports of "the dreaded Typees" that their "very name is a frightful one; for the word 'Typee' in the Marquesan dialect signifies a lover of human flesh" (24). Anderson is puzzled by the "unspeakable terrors" (24) Melville aligns with the word:

> In the first place, the word "Typee" in the Marquesan dialect did not signify "a lover of human flesh." The Abbé Boniface Mosblech in his Marquesan-French dictionary gives the word "Taipi" as meaning "ennemi" or "peuple ennemi." This in itself is puzzling, for no people would take upon themselves voluntarily the name of enemy. . . . Whatever the meaning, there was nothing in the word "Typee," etymologically at least, to inspire anyone with unspeakable terrors.[42]

The image of the word's terrors as "unspeakable" is apt, since part of the narrative investment in it is a function of its spelling. The written form "Typee" echoes and bears the mark of the disavowed Porter, who also uses this unconventional orthography.[43] Melville's description also echoes Stewart's comment that the "very name [of the Taipiis] seemed to be a watchword of terror" among the Teiis,[44] so this moment in Melville's text is doubly constituted by written sources.

Writing is materially embedded in the word "Typee" not only as Porter's orthographic mark in particular, but also in the form of "type," a sign for the presence in the narrative of Melville's printed source texts in general as well as of Porter's text in particular.[45] That the word "Typee" carried the resonance of printed text is substantiated by James Russell Lowell's witticism about proofreading: "This having to do with printers is dreadful business. There was a Mr. Melville who I believe enjoyed it, but for my part I am heartily sick of *Typee*."[46] Lowell invokes the word *Typee* as a pun for *type* (*type*, of course, refers to the small blocks featuring a raised letter or other character used to print), and expresses his irritation with the latter by way of Melville and the former. The "*Typee*" he is sick of is not Melville's book, but rather everything associated with "printers" and the "business" of book production.

The presence of "type" in "Typee" for Lowell is clear; its presence for Melville is one we can best see by considering his approach to spelling Polynesian words in general. When Tommo and Toby are initially welcomed into Typee valley, a name exchange takes place. The narrator introduces himself to the Typees as "Tom" because he thinks his "real name" would be difficult for them to pronounce. "But I could not have made a worse selection; the chief could not master it: 'Tommo,' 'Tomma,' 'Tommee,' every thing but plain 'Tom'"

(72), he laments. The Marquesan version of "Tom" adds to that single syllable a second syllable of "mo," "ma," or "mee." (The spelling "Tomo" also appears in the draft; see illustration 3.) Melville's orthography in general conforms to this structural pattern, concluding an otherwise recognizable or partly recognizable English word with "ee." Thus "franee" means French and "botee" means boat. This model suggests that "type" is a seed word as present in "Typee" as "Tom" is in "Tommo."

Melville's spelling of the island's staple breadfruit dish also orthographically embeds the presence of writing. While orthographies generally rendered this word as "popoi" or "poipoi,"[47] Melville writes "poee-poee." (In the draft, "poi=poi" appears on one occasion [p. 5; see illustration 2] and "poipoi" on another [p. 9]; "poee-poee" never appears.) Stewart, to whom I have already pointed as one of Melville's primary sources, is another exception to conventional spellings, and writes simply "poe" (1: 261). In the extant draft, Melville writes "poe poe" on one occasion.[48] (See illustration 1.) In what was presumably a later change, Melville does not adopt Stewart's spelling as such, but doubles the word and adds a final "e"—"poe" becomes "poee-poee." According to the orthographic structure by which "Tommo" embeds "Tom" and "Typee" embeds "type," "poee-poee" embeds the word "poe," this time not only Stewart's spelling but also Edgar Allan Poe, whose *Narrative of Arthur Gordon Pym* (1838) is an unacknowledged fictional source for *Typee*. Even more so than the travel narratives he had open in front of him as he wrote, Melville particularly needed to mask any suggestions of fiction because of the narrative's pretensions to factual accuracy.

Like *Typee*, Poe's *Pym* recorded a factual/fictional account of a sailing expedition from Massachusetts to the South Seas that made extensive use of source-texts. John T. Irwin has called attention to the way that *Pym* thematizes its own status as writing, especially in Pym's confrontation with characters hewn out of the black granite landscape.[49] While Melville's letters and journals offer no explicit indication that he read Poe, Poe's appearance as an unnamed raven-haired writer and peddler of tracts in *The Confidence-Man* is a late gesture of explicit acknowledgment (*CM* 195). *Typee* also describes poee-poee as similar to "bookbinders' paste" (73), an image whose bookishness for Melville is reinforced by the fact that he lifts this metaphor from Stewart.[50] Melville's "poee-poee" is thus a word inspired both by Stewart's "poe" and by Poe, and at the same time a disfiguration of both. Like the doubleness in the word "Typee," which signifies both as a spelling indebted to Porter and as a word denoting "type," "poee-poee" signifies both as a spelling indebted to Stewart and as a word denoting the name of another printed source (Poe). Thus the disfigured presence of printed sources lurks within the "beautiful vocal sounds" in the interest of which Melville disavows ordinary spelling.

In addition to appearing once in the extant pages of the draft, the spelling "poe-poe" also appears once in the first English edition, but the Northwestern-Newberry editors regularize this spelling to "poee-poee" in accordance with the American and American Revised editions, "since the shorter form might not be given the intended pronunciation by English readers."[51] It is of course impossible to tell if the spelling "poe-poe" here was Melville's (either a slip of the pen or a deliberate choice) or a compositor's error; but it is clear, as I note above, that the spelling "poe poe" also appears on one occasion at a different moment in the extant draft, substantiating this spelling as one Melville himself used. The appearance of "poe poe" in the copy-text suggests the potentially quite meaningful effects of Melville's spelling and spelling irregularities. The editors' decision to emend it in the interest of "pronunciation" exemplifies both the way in which editorial regularization and emendation can erase those effects and the persisting notion that Melville's orthography in *Typee* is primarily aural in nature.

The identic hinge that inheres in Melville's orthographic final letter *e* is a point of fluctuation particularly connected to Melville's own written identity. His patronymic was originally spelled without its final *e: Melvill*. His mother, Maria Gansevoort, added the final letter after her husband Allan, Melville's father, died in 1832.[52] Nevertheless, Melville still occasionally wrote his name with this original spelling.[53] In one such case, a letter to Murray in 1848 about the *Typee* controversy, Melville signed his letter "Herman Melville" but wrote within it: "Will you still continue, Mr Murray, to break seals from the Land of Shadows—persisting in carrying on this mysterious correspondence with an imposter shade, that under the fanciful appellation of Herman Melvill still practices upon your honest credulity?"[54] Here Melville divides himself into two, "Herman Melville" and "Herman Melvill," and raises the specter of himself as an impostor, in this case an imposture constituted by an entirely written difference (since the final *e* is silent) between "Melville" and "Melvill." His letter to Murray associates this form of self-disfiguration—the absence or presence of a final *e*—with both his own written identity and with the "imposture" issue in *Typee*. This signature effect continues to be important for Melville in subsequent writings. Philip Young points out that Daniel Orme, the protagonist of the late tale of that title, is Melville's self-portrait, and that the name "Orme" is Melville's pun for "or me." "Orme" also appears in "Pebbles" in *John Marr and Other Sailors* (1888) as "Orm."[55] Melville wrote "Orme. Orm" at the top of one page of the manuscript.[56] This fluctuation in the spellings of Orme/Orm is important for its registration of Melville's attraction to the absence or presence of a final *e* as a signature effect. It is of course interpreting the final *e* in the word "Typee" as silent that enables Lowell's reading of the word as "type."

The same graphic device, as we have seen, disfigures the presence of source texts in the "combinations of vocal sounds" in type/Typee. Melville was in fact particularly invested in the word "Typee" as the title of his narrative. Murray had published the book under the title *Narrative of a Four Months' Residence Among the Natives of a Valley of the Marquesas Islands; or, A Peep at Polynesian Life.*[57] Melville wrote to Murray:

> From the first I have deeply regretted that it did not appear in England under the title I always intended for it—"Typee". . . . "Typee" is a title *naturally suggested by the narrative itself*, and not farfetched as some strange titles are. Besides, its very strangeness & novelty, founded as it is upon the character of the book—are the very things to make "Typee" a popular title. The work also should be known by the same name on both sides of the water.—For these and other reasons I have thought that in all subsequent editions of the book you might entitle it "Typee"— merely prefixing that single but eloquent word to the title as it now stands with you. If you try out the revised edition with the Sequel—that would be the time to make this very slight but most important alteration.—I trust that Mr Murray will at once consider the propriety of following this suggestion.[58]

Typee is a title "naturally suggested by the narrative itself," but embedded in that notion of "naturalness"—as is the case with the "beautiful vocal sounds" whose primary nature is non-aural—is the felt presence of type.

The felt presence of type that speaks to Melville's anxieties about his specifically printed sources is one conjoined with the narrative's anxiety about its own status as handwriting on paper. These scenarios are discrete, in that one speaks to his relation to printed sources and printed text and the other to his production of manuscript, but also mutually significant in that both point to the written nature of his text, at odds with its pretensions. Melville's heavy "borrowings" are one kind of nagging indication that *Typee* is made of written marks and not of the world of experience and sound to which he so wishfully appeals. Although Tommo describes Typee as an island where "parchments and title deeds there were none" (202), Melville's figurations of Typee nonetheless point to the compelling presence of paper, ink, and writing. Tappa, a cloth of dazzling whiteness made from the bark of the paper mulberry tree, is widely known to resemble paper.[59] Indeed, Melville's "tappa" is also known as "paper cloth,"[60] and samples of decorated Polynesian tappa on display at the Whaling Museum in Nantucket visually—and starkly—resemble inked paper of the kind Melville wrote the *Typee* draft itself on. His description of tappa manufacture echoes stages of paper production: fibers of the "cloth-tree" are soaked, soft-ened, and beaten with a mallet (147). Melville returns to the subject of paper production in a more explicit and sustained way in the 1855 tale "The Paradise of Bachelors and the Tartarus of Maids," which I discuss at length in chapter 3. The ubiquity of tappa in *Typee* (and indeed at times it feels like this substance is everywhere Tommo turns) is thus heavily loaded with the material presence of text.

We find another form of writing paper in the bodies and faces of the natives themselves, which are "human canvas" (218) inked with tattoos by "Karky the artist" (219). Tattooing as an "art" in *Typee* represents an activity of the hand and its implements that figures the act of writing. Karky works with a set of instruments and inks that resemble writer's tools, "short slender stick[s]" dipped in "coloring matter," "terminat[ing] in a single fine point" and "like very delicate pencils" (217, 218). Tommo also describes Karky on several occa-sions as a "painter" (219) and as "A Professor of the Fine Arts" (217). Karky's painterliness is pertinent—and requires attention since I've just claimed that he figures writing—because the particular inflection of writing it summons is not one of writing as "authorship" but of writing as penmanship, as a design produced by the hand that thus shares an affinity with painting and drawing. I'll provisionally define "authorship" as calling a particular ("original") ar-rangement of words into being, with the sanction of Melville's comment in a late unpublished manuscript that "authorship . . . implies origination."[61]

Penmanship manuals and advertisements by writing masters in antebel-lum America frequently refer to penmanship as an "art"; the common phrase "the art of writing" in the period signifies penmanship. "Writing masters" also engaged in other "arts" like painting and cutting silhouettes.[62] These manu-als also frequently either pair or analogize "writing" and "penmanship" with "drawing." The title of James French's 1854 volume *The Art of Pen Drawing*, which contains "examples of all the usual hands," and Rembrandt Peale's *Graphics: A Manual of Drawing and Writing* (1835) provide two examples. Peale treated writing and drawing as aspects of the same skill.[63] The business cards of writing master Christopher C. Fellows of New Hampshire advertised "Beauties of Writing," "Teacher of Writing & Painting," and "C. C. Fellows, Writing, Drawing & Painting Academy."[64] Instructions for ornamental penmanship de-scribe manipulations of the hand and arm as well as of the implements of writing (such as the nib of the pen) in order to achieve a variety of beautiful effects. Penmanship specimens displayed at the entrances to writing shops and on the title pages of manuals were often elaborate pen-drawings in which the flourishes and basic strokes of handwriting were used to form fish, eagles, angels, geese, swans, and other designs.[65] Penmanship was an art, and for it the hand needed to be trained and the proper tools used.

Conceptions of penmanship in the antebellum North were hovering at a crux between the ornamental and the practical, between writing as a design whose flourishes should be beautiful and writing as an occupation that should be "plain, bold, and rapid," stressing speed and endurance over beauty. "Mercantile penmanship" becomes a catch phrase in the early part of the century, and training in "rapid business writing" is similarly widely advertised.[66] Some manuals speak to both conceptions of penmanship simultaneously, conjoining, for example, "writing, drawing, and book-keeping" or advertising "a handwriting at once beautiful and practical." Ray Nash notes that during the first half of the nineteenth century, handwriting became a regular subject in American schools, including the rising commercial schools and business colleges. By the early nineteenth century, a good business hand had become the prime objective in teaching handwriting.[67]

As early as 1832, Melville's mother Maria was scrutinizing his correspondence and insisting that he improve his handwriting through assiduous practice: "His last letter was much praise'd, for its superiority over the first, the hand writing particularly, he must practise [sic] often, & daily," she wrote to her brother Peter, with whom Melville was staying at the time.[68] Howard emphasizes the vocational imperative behind Maria's insistence that Melville improve his handwriting, and attributes to his "youthful failure" to do so his "disqualification" from employment as a copyist. Melville and his friend Eli James Murdock Fly both sought jobs in a tough economy, out "West" and in New York; while Fly obtained a situation in New York in 1840 "where he has incessant writing from morning to Eve," Melville went to sea, presumably unable to gain employment like Fly's because of his bad handwriting.[69] Ironically, although Melville's handwriting failed to meet Maria's standards, which were in turn directed at employment, Melville nonetheless became a "writer," one who eventually needed to put his own copyists to work in order to produce his texts. Leo Marx inaugurated a tradition of reading "Bartleby, the Scrivener" as an autobiographical account of Melville's refusal to write against his heart and for the market.[70] If Bartleby is a self-portrait, and I agree with Marx that he is, then we must also recognize the extent to which the tale suggests that Melville saw the activity of copying as fundamental to his own processes of composition. It is crucial to distinguish copying in this context from generating "original" text, the work of an "author" as Melville himself defined it. For Melville, copying means both repeatedly copying out versions of a manuscript in progress (an exhaustive and labor-intensive process for him and his copyists) and also copying text generated by others. It is the latter that is Bartleby's writing labor, an

observation that should radically revise decades of reading Bartleby's prefer-
ence "not to" as a desire to renounce authorship.

The scene of writing that Karky the "Professor of the Fine Arts" conjures is
not that of the writer as "author" but of the writer as penman. Indeed, Tommo
can relate to the products of Karky's hand only as design, since he is never able
to determine what, if anything, tattooing means. Tommo is given a "choice of
patterns" for his facial tattoos: "I was at perfect liberty to have my face spanned
by three horizontal bars, after the fashion of my serving-man's; or to have as
many oblique stripes slanting across it; or if, like a true courtier, I chose to
model my style on that of royalty, I might wear a sort of freemason badge upon
my countenance in the shape of a mystic triangle" (220). Melville makes a
variety of designs on his manuscript. He writes in an ornamental hand on the
cover page and in his chapter titles,[71] and he marks his text with frequent
designs including paragraphing symbols, wavy lines, diamonds, oblong boxes,
concentric circles around dots, a circle transversed by two lines with each
resulting wedge then marked with dots and underlined in its entirety, and a
circle transversed by three lines and then enclosed within a square. Some of
these designs mark blocks of text to be moved and places where text is to be
inserted (see illustrations 2 and 3).

From Tommo's perspective, Karky is a flourishing practitioner of the "art
of writing," a role for which Melville's cramped and nearly illegible handwriting—a problem throughout his writing life—disqualified him. He opens an
1881 letter to his sister Kate with uncharacteristically large writing and sweeping flourishes, and comments, "Dont [*sic*] be alarmed by these beautiful flourishes of mine; I have been recently improving my penmanship by lessons from a
High Dutch professor who teaches all the stylish flourishes imaginable."[72] At
moments like this one Melville is explicitly aware of penmanship and of his
customary hand's deficiencies from the standpoint of "beautiful flourishes." Yet
although Melville's atrocious penmanship disqualified him from employment
as a copyist, a secret scene of copying is at the heart of the genesis of *Typee* and
Omoo. The chapter on tattooing in *Omoo*, "The Tattooers of La Dominica," was
itself borrowed largely from Langsdorff.[73] Karky's "art of writing" that ultimately so terrifies Tommo is thus a particular employment of the hand that
resonates for Melville as penmanship; and penmanship is in turn associated
with its vocational applications of copying, of reproducing someone else's
"words" rather than "originating" the words themselves. Although from the
standpoint of employment Melville was disqualified from working as a copyist,
the scene of writing *Typee* is predicated upon employments of the hand as
copyist that Melville is simultaneously engaged in and disavowing.

The plot of *Typee* in fact localizes Melville's anxiety about his scene of writing in that which terrifies the narrator most: facial tattoos. Although critics often read cannibalism as the primary threat in Typee,[74] the fear of facial tattooing effectively usurps the primacy of cannibalism as the force motivating Tommo's fear. Thus as Tommo and his mates are about to go on shore leave, the captain warns them:

> Plenty of white men have gone ashore here and never been seen anymore. There was the old *Dido,* she put in here about two years ago, and sent one watch off on liberty; they never were heard of again for a week—the natives swore they didn't know where they were—and only three of them ever got back to the ship again, and one with his face damaged for life, for the cursed heathens tattooed a broad patch clean across his figurehead. But it will be no use talking to you, for go you will, that I see plainly; so all I have to say is, that you need not blame me if the islanders make a meal of you. (34–35)

While the overt thrust of the captain's warning is the threat of cannibalism ("if the islanders make a meal of you"), and thus of joining the ranks of the "white men who have gone ashore here and never been seen anymore," the specter the captain paints most clearly is not that of the white men who are never seen (because they have been eaten), but of the white man who is seen all too vividly: the sailor who returns to the ship "with his face damaged for life" because it has been tattooed.

The spectacle of the sailor whose face is damaged for life is the image that begins to haunt Tommo during an otherwise edenic sojourn in the valley. When Karky begins to insist that Tommo have his face tattooed, a demand the other Typees soon join him in pressing upon their white visitor, Tommo's disgust and fear are overwhelming. Although he had begun to enter comfortably into the life of the Typees, and even the mysterious leg ailment plaguing him had disappeared, the prospect of facial tattooing fills Tommo with "utter abhorrence" and "unconquerable repugnance," and he is "fairly driven to despair" by it (219–20). It is at this point in the narrative that he realizes he must escape. He says of Karky's insistence, "This incident opened my eyes to a new danger; and I now felt convinced that in some luckless hour I should be disfigured in such a manner as never more to have the *face* to return to my countrymen, even should an opportunity offer" (219; emphasis in original).

The subordination of the threat of cannibalism to the fear of facial tattooing that operates in the captain's warning now recurs to motivate developments in the plot. Tommo's fear of disfiguration by facial tattooing that dominates chapter 30 and explicitly resolves him to escape ("in some luckless hour I should be disfigured") now generates the narrative production of the cannibal banquet in chapter 32. His opening reflections in the chapter on the misery he feels because of the threats to his face prepare the narrative ground for the "last horrid revelation": "From the time of my casual encounter with Karky the artist, my life was one of absolute wretchedness. Not a day passed but I was persecuted by the solicitations of some of the natives to subject myself to the odious operation of tattooing. Their importunities drove me half wild" (231). He reports that now he "began bitterly to feel the state of captivity in which [he] was held" (231), and the painful malady in his leg returns. It is at this point that he makes the frightful discoveries of three smoked human heads kept hidden in the house of his hosts, and of the cannibal banquet that follows a skirmish with some Happar warriors. But whereas in chapter 27 the narrator had mitigated the horror of the Typees' cannibalism (this "only enormity in their character is not half so horrible as it is usually described," he explains, pointing out that it is practiced upon the bodies of slain enemies alone [205]), the attacks upon his face "augment" (232) the aspect of cannibalism into something intolerably horrifying.

Here pressing on the slippery critical tendency to elide Tommo the character with Melville the author becomes useful, since what I am suggesting is that Tommo and his fears at the level of the plot both brandish and hide Melville's own.[75] Tommo's fears of both cannibalism and facial tattooing signal his fear of consumption by an alien culture: the literal consumption of his body threatened in the first case becomes the metaphorical consumption of his identity in the second,[76] the particular resonance of "the fearful apprehensions that consumed me" (232). "A fact which I soon afterwards learned augmented my apprehension. The whole system of tattooing was, I found, connected with their religion; and it was evident, therefore, that they were resolved to make a convert of me" (220), to absorb his identity into their own culture.

The fear the narrative invests in the prospect of facial tattooing by an alien culture is one that participates in similar fears expressed in other American captivity narratives popular at the time. Horace Holden's *A Narrative of the Shipwreck, Captivity & Sufferings of Horace Holden & Benjamin H. Nute* (1836), for example, recounts the author's experience as a captive among the Pelew Islanders of Polynesia, including the forcible tattooing of his entire body. His captors "were exceedingly anxious to perform the operation upon our faces; but this we would not submit to, telling them that sooner than have it done we would die in resisting them," Holden writes (103). The best-selling *Captivity of the Oatman Girls* (1857) would later recount Olive Ann Oatman's forcible facial tattooing with the mark of a slave while in captivity among the Mohave Indians.[77] The repulsive tattoos displayed in these narratives were simultaneously objects of cultural fascination, a fascination that fed the increasingly popular

American exhibitions of people who claimed to have been forcibly tattooed, by Indians or other "heathen" captors. A white man tattooed on his face and body in Micronesia was exhibited in a New York circus in 1851 in one instance of what would become a side show craze as the century progressed. Freak shows and dime museums all over the United States displayed tattooed men, women, couples, families, Indians—even a tattooed Great Dane and a tattooed cow were put on display.[78] The forced submission to alien marks of identity that often characterized the companion tales to these increasingly popular displays invests Melville's tale at the level of the plot.

What I am suggesting is that Tommo's fear of cultural consumption, which participates in and also certainly helped to generate the cultural scenarios discussed above, coexists with and gives deflected form to Melville's anxiety about the scene of writing. While it is not clear to ethnologists what purpose tattooing served in Marquesan culture,[79] it is more important for understanding Melville's relation to his own narrative to consider what "purpose" Melville's *representation* of Marquesan tattooing serves in the logic of his textual Typee. Considered from that vantage, tattooing is most notably two things: one, it is a system of writing; and two, it is a system of writing that threatens the identity of the narrator with alien marks.[80] As Mitchell Breitwieser points out, underlying Tommo's fear of tattooing is a "fear of reversed parts," the fear that "the writer may be written upon."[81] In this respect it is particularly useful to return to the captain's warning, quoted earlier, which specifically brandishes a tattooed "figurehead," here meaning "face" in the usage of the time. This moment in *Typee* marks the earliest instance of an incipient structure for Melville, for whom the word *figurehead* was deeply loaded with career anxieties. Melville's attraction to figureheads as symbols of his writing career became explicit as early as *Redburn,* and persisted through the late poem "The Figure-Head" in *John Marr and Other Sailors.*[82]

The anxiety about disfiguration of his figurehead—"I now felt convinced that in some luckless hour I should be disfigured in such a manner as never more to have the *face* to return to my countrymen," as quoted above—is in a deep sense Melville's anxiety about the relation between his own text and his source texts. By using the term *anxiety* in such a context I do not mean a Bloomian anxiety of influence, a sublimated agon of figuration, but an anxiety about overtly copying whole chunks of text from other authors. The fearful tattooed faces in *Typee* delineate the disfiguration by his own hand of the disavowed printed pages open before him, a disfiguration that grotesquely conflates the copying activity of his hand and the printed source-page.[83] The project of recovery Melville claims for the text is in fact predicated upon the sufficient mutilation of his printed sources so that, for example, his pages conjure the Typee landscape that Tommo saw rather than the pages of Stewart's text that Melville saw, and from which his descriptions of Typee are at times lifted.[84]

The presence of these texts for Melville as he composed was so strong that, as Anderson points out, he "almost habitually leaned upon his authorities even in matters with which he certainly must have had a first-hand acquaintance. For some reason, he preferred to work from the descriptions of previous authors, which he found ready to hand . . . sometimes even retaining the exact phraseology of his original." Anderson was baffled by Melville's extensive copying from sources: "Just why he followed his sources so closely, even in phraseology[,] it is hard to say. Perhaps, in *Typee* especially, he was conscious of his own inexperience as a writer."[85]

Melville's "anxious desire" to conjure a world of true experience is one impossibly predicated upon effacing the writing out of which his text is constituted. In order to hear the sounds of Typee, Melville's spelling must be rendered transparent; in order to tell the truth, his printed sources must disappear. While readers of *Typee* hotly disagreed over the extent to which *Typee* did or did not conjure an "authentic" world, Melville's "anxious desire," generated by the impossibility of those effacements, reinscribes the presence of writing in *Typee* in the ways this chapter has explored. In the captain's warning, what should never again be seen emerges, uncontrollably and in mutilated form, at odds with the captain's own premises. Tommo's terrified confrontation with facial tattoos stands in, for Melville, for the anxious visual scene of writing, in which the object that should not be seen is the one seen all too vividly.

Chapter Two

Fear of Faces:
From *Moby-Dick*
to *Pierre*

~

Why do faces frighten Pierre? Lucy implores him early in the narrative: "Tell me once more the story of that face, Pierre— that mysterious, haunting face, which thou once told'st me, thou didst thrice vainly try to shun" (37). The "haunting face" whose story, as the novel opens, has already been told, and whose image the hero has already repeatedly tried to escape, is the force whose pressure presides over the events of the novel. In a scenario that compulsively repeats itself, Pierre cries, "I shudder at thee! The face!—the face! . . . the face steals down upon me" (41). After Pierre's first vision of Isabel's face at the sewing-circle, he begins to feel "the terrors of the face" (49), and although the referent of "the face" here is presumably the face of Isabel, the phrase calls attention to terrors that exceed her face in particular. And in fact hers is not the only face that haunts the hero.[1] The face of his father in the chair-portrait unsettles him with its ambiguous smile. The aloof face of Plotinus Plinlimmon taunts him through his window at the Church of the Apostles. And the two portrait-faces he views at the conclusion of the tale, the Cenci and the Stranger's Head, push him into his final despair. The consistent use of the article ("the face") rather than a personal pronoun ("her face") reinforces the elevation of the term to a status beyond that of an individual countenance.

Pierre senses the oneness of these nominally discrete faces in his exhilarated and terrified moments of epiphany. When he confronts his father's portrait-face, he discovers its "supernatural" unity with "the face" of Isabel: "And now, by irresistible intuitions, all that had been inexplicably mysterious to him in the portrait, and all that had been inexplicably familiar in the face, most magically these now coincided; the merriness of the one not inharmonious with the mournfulness of the other, but by some ineffable correlativeness, they reciprocally identified each other, and, as it were, melted into each other, and thus interpenetratingly uniting, presented lineaments of an added supernaturalness" (85). Pierre then "start[s] to his feet with clenched hands and outstaring eyes at the transfixed face in the air" (85). This "transfixed face in the air" is neither the portrait-face of his father nor the remembered face of Isabel but, rather, the "supernatural" face to which both are subordinate. While the reciprocal identification of these two particular faces with one another is in part a function of their alleged father-daughter relationship, the "transfixed face in the air" toward which both point represents a "supernatural" power that exceeds the particularities of genealogical intrigue.

This scene is recalled late in the novel when Pierre perceives an unnerving likeness between his father's chair-portrait and the Stranger's Head at the gallery, both of which resemble Isabel. To Pierre "this face was in part as the resurrection of the one he had burnt at the Inn. Not that the separate features were the same; but the pervading look of it, the subtler interior keeping of the entirety, was almost identical" (351). His nominal suspicion is not that the stranger is related to his father, but rather that Isabel could be the daughter of either. At the level of the plot, this restaging of Pierre's earlier confrontation with his father's portrait throws into question the presumed blood relationship the earlier scene helped to establish, for which Pierre has lost everything in the meantime. But while this face, too, participates in the novel's anxieties about family relations, it also "resurrects" the "transfixed face in the air" whose "subtler interior keeping" exceeds questions of family. The persistent force of faces in *Pierre* is related to a genealogical nightmare but not explained by it.

The haunting and persistent faces of *Pierre* are provoked by the institution of a destructive regime of writing. Pierre and the narrator are characterized by competing modes of vision, and what is finally at stake in those competing modes of vision is competing visions of the written page: as a realm of invisible depth or of visible and superficial marks. The force of the page that provokes crises of vision for both Pierre and the narrator ultimately becomes particularly associated with Plotinus Plinlimmon. After exploring these phenomena, I argue that the powerful faces of *Pierre* emerge from its relation to Melville's previous novel, *Moby-Dick,* as the oppressive materiality of writing takes over Melville's relation to his own pages.[2] This turn also accounts for *Pierre*'s link between haunting faces and a genealogical nightmare: as Melville's page becomes oppressively visible, it carries with it destructive domestic and family scenarios that invoke the scene of textual production in the Melville household (which I explore at length in chapter 3). In my assessment it is the invisibility of Moby-Dick's face that is most importantly lost in *Pierre;* that invisibility is what sustains the metaphysical quest that subsequently goes bankrupt in *Pierre,* as faces/pages emerge from invisible "depth" to haunt the hero in the visual field.[3]

The proliferating faces of *Pierre* appear concomitant to the institution of a regime of writing, as the "transfixed face in the air" inaugurates a series of events that shackles Pierre to his writing desk. During the course of the novel, he undergoes a transition from the unemployment of a gentleman to employment as an author. The haughty Mary Glendinning remarks, "Now, Pierre, if you were in any profession, or in any business at all; nay, if I were a farmer's wife, and you my child, working in my fields; why, then, you and Lucy should still wait awhile [to be married]. But . . . you have nothing to do but to think of Lucy by day, and dream of her by night" (56). Although we learn later that Pierre had been a celebrated author during his early life of leisure, his prior status as author is one that falls under the sign of leisure and gentlemanly unemployment, a model that contrasts starkly with the devastating employment into which he is led by "the terrors of the face." It's also the case that Pierre is not identified as a youthful author until the "terrors of the face" have already inaugurated a regime of writing by casting Pierre out of Saddle Meadows and into his city life; in this respect it is more important that the issue of authorship emerges at a particular stage in the narrative than that it is chronologically out of order.[4]

Pierre is obsessed with reading and writing. Pierre constantly demands pen and paper. Notes are frequently written and received. Mrs. Glendinning writes to Lucy. Pierre receives letters from Isabel, from Wonder & Wen, Peter Pence, Donald Dundonald, from Steel, Flint & Asbestos, from Glendinning Stanly and Frederic Tartan; he writes to Lucy, to Glen, to Dates, to Delly Ulver. In his initial overwhelmed response to Isabel's revelation, he writes to Lucy, and when he attempts to reread his own note before sealing it, "he could not adequately comprehend his own writing, for a sudden cloud came over him" (93). This cloud passes and reading is accomplished, but a crisis of legibility portends.

This crisis is further delineated in Isabel's note of introduction to Pierre, which is "stained, too, here and there, with spots of tears, which chemically acted upon by the ink, assumed a strange and reddish hue—as if blood and not tears had dropped upon the sheet" (64–65). Isabel later remarks, "How blest I felt that my so bitterly tear-mingled ink—that last depth of my anguish—would never be visibly known to thee, but the tears would dry upon the page" (159).

Isabel's presumption about the invisibility of her tears moves Pierre: " 'Ah, there thou wast deceived, poor Isabel,' cried Pierre impulsively; 'thy tears dried not fair, but dried red, almost like blood; and nothing so much moved my inmost soul as that tragic sight' " (159). The visibility of the tears that Isabel presumes will be invisible materializes a problem that preoccupies the novel: visibility on the page versus the invisibility of "depth" and the crucial relation between those realms. The amalgam that leaves its mark on the page is a mixture of ink with an invisible force, the "depth of anguish" in tears. Isabel is "deceived" in believing that her "depth of anguish" would "never be visibly known"; it is the materialization of those "depths" as marks on the page that constitutes Pierre's "tragic sight." The mixture of tears and ink produces a color ("red") that is also a homonym for a visual act ("read"). Pierre's "moved" reading of Isabel's note, whose "depth of anguish" touches his own "inmost soul," is a response to that amalgam and the consequent visual presence (red/read) of what should not be seen.

Isabel's "tears" are further materialized as marks on the page later when Pierre is revealed as the author of a sonnet entitled "The Tear," which recasts Isabel's teary "depth of anguish" as a literary text. An admirer of Pierre's literary compositions finds "a dot (*tear*), over an *i* (*eye*)" in "a small fragment of the original manuscript" (263; emphasis in original), and begs to preserve it, although the tear later "disappears" when the scrap is caught in a rain. "The Tear" is not only a tear dropping from a human eye and a dot hovering over the character *i* but also a rip in a piece of paper (not "tear" rhyming with "cheer" but "tear" rhyming with "chair"). The fragmentary nature of the piece of "The Tear" in question itself suggests a rip in material text. Isabel's tears become visible on a torn sheet, "so completely torn in two by Pierre's own hand" (65); the dot/tear on a fragment of text disappears in the rain. The visibility of Isabel's tears as "red" marks on a page becomes the visibility of a written character (dot-tear) in a text called "The Tear." Her tears emerge into visibility from a state of presumed invisibility; the dot undergoes a watery disappearance from a state of inky visibility. The novel construes the visibility of Isabel's marks as "tragic sight," I suggest, because the cross from invisible depth to visibility on the page to which these parallel scenarios speak threatens to convert the "invisible" force behind the production of writing into mere marks on a page that can be torn and erased, transforming "depth of anguish" first into written marks—a dot over an *i*—and finally into a blank piece of paper.

The trajectory from invisible depth to visibility on the page and the cross from one to the other structure oppositions constitutive of the novel's outcome. The narrator meditates on different ways of looking at things: "But according to what view you take of it, it is either the gracious or the malicious gift of the great gods to man, that on the threshold of any wholly new and momentous devoted enterprise, the thousand ulterior intricacies and emperilings to which it must conduct; these, at the outset, are mostly withheld from sight" (175). I want to linger on "the thousand ulterior intricacies and emperilings to which [an enterprise] must conduct," which "are mostly withheld from sight," because of the frequency with which structurally similar images appear in the novel.

Book 11, for example, opens with the metaphor of a seemingly endless row of billiard balls: "Strike at one end the longest conceivable row of billiard balls in close contact, and the furthermost ball will start forth, while all the rest stand still; and yet that last ball was not struck at all. So, through long previous generations, whether of births or thoughts, Fate strikes the present man" (182). The "thousand ulterior intricacies and emperilings to which [an enterprise] must conduct" in the first figure and the endless row of billiard balls in the second echo later in the narrator's description of what Pierre can't see: "While Pierre was thinking that he was entirely transplanted into a new and wonderful element of Beauty and Power, he was, in fact, but in one of the stages of the transition" (283).

I also place under this structural rubric one of literary criticism's favorite images in *Pierre*, that of the empty sarcophagus. As Pierre begins to work on his novel and to see through the "first superficiality of the world, he fondly weens he has come to the unlayered substance," but "far as any geologist has yet gone down into the world, it is found to consist of nothing but surface stratified on surface. To its axis, the world being nothing but superinduced superficies. By vast pains we mine into the pyramid; by horrible gropings we come to the central room; with joy we espy the sarcophagus; but we lift the lid—and no body is there!—appallingly vacant as vast is the soul of a man!" (285). These layers are like the intricacies, rows, and stages in the previous figures. Pierre does not see the depth or extent of the layers; he mistakes his superficial penetration of the first layer for definitive contact with "unlayered substance." Although he comes to see, as the narrator does throughout, the superficiality of his early writings, he does not yet see how his new writing project is fundamentally also a superficial one.

What the narrator construes as Pierre's chronic misperception of depth and extent also characterizes Pierre's vision of the face that steals down upon him: "What is it that thou has veiled in thee so imperfectly, that I seem to see its motion, but not its form? It visibly rustles behind the concealing screen. Now, never into the soul of Pierre, stole there before, a muffledness like this! If aught really lurks in it, ye sovereign powers that claim all my leal worshipings, I conjure ye to lift the veil; I must see it face to face" (41). The object of Pierre's Ahabian address, "thou," is "the face, the face." What's odd here is that he demands to see "the face, the face" "face to face." The face is a "screen" and a "veil" that conceals another face, and he wants the face behind the visible face to reveal the "muffled" and secret knowledge that "rustles behind" the face he sees. He expresses a similar desire when, "with this nameless fascination of the face upon him, during those two days that it had first and fully possessed him for its own" (51), he explains, "For me, thou hast uncovered one infinite, dumb, beseeching countenance of mystery, underlying all the surfaces of visible time and space" (52). The face he does see does not satisfy him, but "uncovers" another face ("countenance") that constitutes a posited definitive ground.

Thus Pierre imagines not that faces will open out endlessly upon layers of faces—as Isabel does when she tells Pierre that "a second face, and a third face, and a fourth face peep at me from within thy own" (117–18)—but that the face just beyond the one he sees constitutes the "unlayered substance" he yearns to see "face to face." This face "underlies" all the surfaces of his vision, providing a definitive bottom even as it connotes infinity and mystery. That is, the *structure* of Pierre's vision of the "countenance of mystery" is not infinite, as in my examples of the narrator's language; rather, the "countenance" is infinite in its meaning although it nevertheless constitutes the ultimate ground beneath all surfaces. Pierre's desire for and assertion of a definitive ground—located just behind the visible plane—stands in fundamental contrast to the narrator's vision of deferred, receding, and sometimes bottomless structures. In some cases, such as the figure of billiard balls, the narrator posits an originary although distant and obscured point, but in other cases, such as the sarcophagus figure, the narrator's posited layers are essentially bottomless. At this point it is important to note both the structure of stratification and the narrator's equivocation about its ground, an equivocation to whose consequences I will return.

The structure of a posited but illusory ground in fact informs all the faces that obsess Pierre in that all suggest but withhold secret knowledge. In its resemblance to his father's face, Isabel's face seems to reveal her illicit paternity; the father's expression in the portrait seems to reveal his fornication with the Frenchwoman; Plinlimmon's face seems to possess knowledge of the true nature of Pierre's relationship with Isabel. When Pierre shudders, "Ay . . . the face knows that Isabel is not my wife! And that seems the reason it leers" (293), the content of its knowledge "that Isabel is not my wife" sounds deceptively definitive. Knowing that Isabel is not Pierre's wife could mean knowing that Isabel is really his sister (thus knowing of Pierre's deception); knowing that Isabel, while not his wife, is his lover (thus knowing of Pierre's fornication); or knowing that

Isabel is both his sister and his lover (thus knowing of Pierre's incest). Pierre's conception of what Plinlimmon's face "knows" thus posits a ground behind Plinlimmon's face, but this ground too is an equivocal one.

To understand the consequences of these insistent figures of extent and depth against which Pierre's vision is brought up short, we need to return to the passage quoted earlier, which tells us that "the thousand ulterior intricacies" are "mostly withheld from sight," just as rows and stages and layers are unseen in the subsequent examples. The "either . . . or" that introduces this passage under the sign of contrasting vision ("according to what view you take of it, it is either the gracious or the malicious gift of the great gods") plays out later in the passage in other terms: "That all-comprehending oneness, that calm representativeness, by which a steady philosophic mind reaches forth and draws to itself, in their collective entirety, the objects of its contemplations; that pertains not to the young enthusiast. By his eagerness, all objects are deceptively foreshortened; by his intensity each object is viewed as detached; so that essentially and relatively every thing is misseen by him" (175). The competing views now belong to competing viewers: the "steady philosophic mind" and the "young enthusiast." The "young enthusiast" is Pierre, whose vision is characterized as "misseeing" and juxtaposed with the kind of vision that is entire and all-comprehending. All-comprehending vision perceives the entireties, intricacies, and "emperilings" that Pierre misses; it sees what is "mostly withheld from sight," the chains of intricacies, rows, stages, and layers in the previous examples, and thus becomes associated with the narrator.

Pierre's "misseeing" falls under the sign of "foreshortening." For present purposes it is important to note that this term invokes a technique of visual perspective in drawing and painting that creates the illusion of depth on a two-dimensional surface and brings "deep" objects forward within the visual field by shortening an object's lines. Webster's 1847 *Dictionary* defines the verb "foreshorten": "In *painting*, to represent figures as they appear to the eye when viewed obliquely. Thus, a carriage-wheel, when viewed obliquely, appears like an ellipse. Human figures painted on a ceiling are sometimes so foreshortened that the toes appear almost to touch the chin. So, also, in standing near a lofty building, the parts above are *foreshortened*, or appear shorter to the eye than they really are, because seen obliquely from below." In the narrator's assessment, Pierre's vision creates a "deceptive" sense of depth that misses the presumably nonillusory layers that the all-embracing vision perceives in the entirety of their endless unfolding. The conflict between Pierre's "foreshortened" and "misseen" depth and the all-seeing with which it is contrasted is thus fundamentally one of dimension, and its painterly terms invoke, and reject, the illusions of a two-dimensional field in which true depth does not exist. Read with the narrator's persistent critiques of Pierre's vision in mind, we can hear that it is the implied shallowness of what Pierre believes to be depth that renders it inadequate for the narrator; its detachment fails to place objects within the terrain of (potentially infinite) recession to which Pierre is currently blind.

But the narrator's terms for critiquing Pierre's vision themselves betray equivocation. Later in the passage about Pierre's "foreshortening," the narrator remarks:

> Not that the impulsive Pierre wholly overlooked all that was menacing to him in his future, if now he acted out his most rare resolve; but eagerly foreshortened by him, they assumed not their full magnitude of menacing; nor, indeed,—so riveted now his purpose—were they pushed up to his face, would he for that renounce his self-renunciation; while concerning all things more immediately contingent upon his central resolution; these were, doubtless, in a measure, foreseen and understood by him. Perfectly, at least, he seemed to foresee and understand, that the present hope of Lucy Tartan must be banished from his being. (176)

The "foreshortened" vision introduced just prior to this passage is still at issue ("eagerly foreshortened by him"); in another depth opposition, here the narrator contrasts Pierre's "foreshortened" vision with a "full magnitude of menacing." Images of vision and depth center the passage: "overlooked," "foreshortened," "magnitude," "riveted," "pushed up to his face," "measure," "foreseen," "foresee." Pierre's foreshortened vision becomes converted into foresight ("foreseen," "foresee"), suggesting a link between the spatial phenomenon of the former and the temporal phenomenon of the latter.

The nominally chronological "foresight" in this passage takes its greatest force from the presence within that word of "sight," placing it further within the visual signifying realm of the word "foreshortening." That nominally temporal phenomena are here underwritten by spatial phenomena furthers the novel's broader disruption of conventional chronology, evidenced, for example, in the narrator's rejection of chronological narrative at the start of book 17—"I write precisely as I please"—and in the destabilization of time in Plinlimmon's pamphlet. Nominally temporal words and categories, like "foresight" in this passage, are also under the pressure of the novel's agonizing spatialization.

The narrator's insistence upon the limits of Pierre's vision and the syntactically mangled fashion in which he describes them (predicated upon negative, subjunctive, and conditional propositions that render the passage virtually unreadable) point me to the next stage in my argument. The narrator's ostensi-

bly coherent contrast between the two modes of vision I have been discussing—
Pierre's foreshortened vision, whose limitations Pierre himself cannot (yet) see;
and the all-encompassing vision implicitly aligned with the narrator himself—
ultimately verges on incoherence in a way that speaks to a conflict within the
novel's own terms. Pierre's foreshortened, illusory notion of depth is opposed
to the "full magnitude of menacing"; the language of magnitude here seems to
suggest an extent far greater than that Pierre perceives. But at the same time, "all
that was menacing" is what Pierre "overlooks," which suggests not that he
doesn't see far enough but rather that he *looks past the menace.*

This implication is repeated in the suggestion that if the unidentified
"they" were to assume "their full magnitude of menacing," they would not
recede farther into the vast distances whose stratifications Pierre misses but
rather "push up to his face." The active and benign gesture earlier attributed to
the "steady philosophic mind" that "reaches forth and draws to itself, in their
collective entirety, the objects of its contemplations" is a gesture aggressively
turned on Pierre in this later image, an aggression that resonates not only in the
image of "pushing" but also in the passage's distorted logic, syntax, and punctuation. Robert Penn Warren characterizes Melville's versification as violent, an
incisive observation that applies to the language of *Pierre* as well.[5] What I mean
by calling this equivocation a conflict within the novel's own terms is that the
novel displays a fundamental uncertainty about, and does not resolve, whether
what Pierre "missees" is in fact receding at an infinite temporal and spatial
depth, or located right beneath his face. Pierre wants to posit the visual object
of desire just behind what he sees, but to ascribe to it a deep meaning; the
narrator wants to posit it in a deep terrain of recession. But even within the
narrator's equivocation we hear that the vision he posits as superior to Pierre's
still "draws to itself"—an image within whose projection of extent and depth
we hear the activity of a hand writing on a two-dimensional surface.

The nature of the danger lurking in Pierre's foreshortened vision—a danger perceived, importantly, by the narrator, who imagines it "pushed up to his
face"—is one we can also hear in the narrator's refusal to reproduce Pierre's
letter to Glen: "Not here and now can we set down the precise contents of
Pierre's letter, without a tautology illy doing justice to the ideas themselves." He
goes on to identify "the dread of tautology" as "the continual torment of some
earnest minds" (227). Tautology is Melville's emblem for an increasingly crucial
problem in his relation to his writing. Eric Sundquist first demonstrated the
importance of Melvillean tautology to "Benito Cereno," citing this moment in
Pierre as an anchor for his claims about that text;[6] tautology is also crucial in
The Confidence-Man, an argument I make at length in chapter 4. Here tautol-

ogy threatens in the prospect of "setting down the precise contents of Pierre's letter." Although the other frequent notes in the novel are reproduced in full, this one is merely paraphrased, a sign that the status of this note is of somehow more intense consequence.

The moment of anxious "dread" here importantly belongs not to Pierre but to the narrator himself. The tautology that threatens is one whose form, by definition, defies conceptual penetration: representing Pierre's letter would mean representing Pierre's letter. That is, the reproduction of the letter's visible form—its letters laid out on a page—threatens to block the transmission of "the ideas themselves" that it is meant to contain, thus "illy doing justice" to them. The "tragic sight" of Isabel's note is the sight of marks on the page that alchemically materialize the "invisible" force behind them. "The Tear" enacts a full materialization of the "depth" of tears into paper that can be and is torn and written characters that can be and are erased. In the present instance, rendering the marks on the page visible would threaten the "ideas themselves" with a thorough blockage that goes under the opaque sign of tautology. The paraphrase produced instead of the letter itself staves off the immediate danger of tautology without resolving the broader threat it poses. Thus the crisis impending in the early reproduction of Isabel's note—that depths of anguish will become mere marks—finally comes home to the narrator's own relation to his text. His anxiety about tautology emerges within and despite his insistence upon his own vision of depths opposed to Pierre's "misseeing."

It is text itself that comes to stand in the anxious space in which competing visions of depth are posited. The extent to which Pierre's vision is oppressively flattened out against his own desire for invisible depths is legible in his feeling of imprisonment by his writing and in his trouble with seeing the page. "His incessant application told upon his eyes" so that he sometimes "blindly wrote with his eyes turned away from the paper;—thus unconsciously symbolizing the hostile necessity and distaste, the former whereof made of him this most unwilling states-prisoner of letters" (140). The "letters" to which he is prisoner, like the "letter" to Glen that provokes the narrator's dread, are marks on a page whose transcendental motivations and projections are under duress as Pierre struggles to compose his "great, deep book" (341). Here again we can feel the power of tautology whose operations imprison words at the surface of the page that they do not penetrate as a metaphysical "space" of meaning.

The narrator further comments on the tautological nature of text when he tells us that Pierre "did not see" that books are "the mutilated shadowings-forth of invisible and eternally unembodied images in the soul; so that they are but the mirrors, distortedly reflecting to us our own things; and never mind what the mirror may be, if we would see the object, we must look at the object itself, and not at its reflection" (284). Text is a mirror that gives us back "our own things," a tautology that Melville will return to and pursue in *The Confidence-Man*. In *Pierre*, text falls under the sign of mutilation, distortion, and mirrors, all invoked as obstructions that prevent us from "seeing the object" of desire. The "object itself" desired and unseen here is "invisible and eternally unembodied"; it falls on the side of invisibility opposed to the "tragic sight" of visible text. And text, including the narrator's own text, stands opposed to that desired but invisible realm.

Pierre's crisis of vision central to the novel's plot empties out the world "within" (136) to which he dedicates himself, as he comes to see everything as merely another surface. He simultaneously comes to perceive the narrator's mode of vision against which his own vision has been implicitly and explicitly criticized throughout the novel. But although Pierre comes to see the possibility of seeing what the narrator sees, both are ultimately left in a space of crisis as they confront the anxiety provoked by the obtrusion of a confrontational flat surface in the space of posited depth. The false bottom of Pierre's illusory depths is pulled out over a yawning abyss of stratifications; but that realm then threatens to empty out all depth and push right up into Pierre's/the narrator's face; and in this particular instance, I do mean to conflate their otherwise discrete positions. Assessed by way of the contradictory effects within the terms of the novel that I identify above, of both endlessly unfolding depths and of relentless flattening, Pierre's eviscerating vision and the narrator's dread of tautology both fall on the side of a crisis of two dimensions. The narrator's focus on the illusory depths of foreshortened vision and Pierre's gradual realization of his illusions speak to a flattening out into the dimensions of the page exerted *against* the narrator's desire for depths greater than those Pierre sees.[7]

"For the more and the more that he wrote, and the deeper and the deeper that he dived, Pierre saw the everlasting elusiveness of Truth; the universal lurking insincerity of even the greatest and purest written thoughts" (339). Pierre's attempts to dive deeply are brought up short against the "lurking" force associated here and elsewhere in Melville's work with the written page. In Pierre's address to the face quoted earlier, he demands to see "the face" "face to face," a demand he prefaces with the phrase, "If aught really lurks in it" (41). His desire there to see what's just beyond the face he sees is also the desire not to see the "lurking" force I have identified as the flat surface of the page, since this lurking "form" ("I seem to see its motion, but not its form" [41]) has the power to obliterate the metaphysical countenance Pierre desires.

Michael Fried reads foreshortening in the paintings of Thomas Eakins as a

projection within the vertical space of the canvas of a "horizontal" plane associated with the "space" of writing/drawing,[8] an insight that has enabled me to see
the fundamentally different terms of the contest of vision in *Pierre*. This contest
of vision is one predicated upon the horizontal plane of the page, and that sets
at odds a vision of text as endlessly "deep" and a contrasting vision of text as
two-dimensional. The former vision invites the language of and desire for
penetration; the latter repels it. Pierre's trajectory of ruin associated with authorship is one in which he moves from seeing the invitation of depth to
realizing the repulsion from surface.

It is Plotinus Plinlimmon who ultimately embodies the lurking force associated with the space of the page, an identification that accounts for his central
and disturbing power in the novel.[9] The page most literally associated with
Plinlimmon is the title page of his pamphlet, *Chronometricals and Horologicals,*
whose triangular design (210) reads two ways. First, its shape suggests Mount
Greylock, to which the novel is dedicated; not only does Plinlimmon's name
echo the name of a mountain in Wales, Plynlimon, as William Dillingham
reveals,[10] but his air of "non-Benevolence" (290) echoes Greylock's questionable benignity in the dedication ("I here devoutly kneel, and render up my
gratitude, whether, thereto, The Most Excellent Purple Majesty of Greylock
benignantly incline his hoary crown or no"). Second, the triangularity of Plinlimmon's title page suggests a pyramid, a figure central to the sarcophagus
passage quoted earlier as a form with a questionable inside.[11] Plinlimmon's title
page redraws both of those three-dimensional triangular forms (mountain and
pyramid) into the two dimensions of the page.

While the graphics of the title page suggest a pyramid and a mountain
rendered in two dimensions, the content of the title page presents the pamphlet
as an architectural structure: "(Being not so much the Portal, as part of the
temporary Scaffold to the Portal of this new Philosophy.)" (210). This structural metaphor stresses the pamphlet's uncertain interior: doctrinally, since it is
the first of a series of lectures that might not exist; architecturally, since it is only
part of a scaffold temporarily associated with a portal; and materially, since the
copy of the pamphlet that Pierre reads is torn and missing its conclusion.

This uncertain interior echoes the structure of the Church of the Apostles,
the "literal" architectural structure that Plinlimmon inhabits. The church is an
elaborate two-part edifice, a stone building connected by brick colonnades to a
taller, modern brick addition behind it. A small flagstone courtyard lies between the brick and stone buildings, flanked by the colonnades. It is across this
courtyard that Pierre sees Plinlimmon's face. The central space of the church's
design is thus an "inside" that is not inside and that does not contain anything;

this provisional central space also recalls the inside of the pyramid whose "central room" is empty (285). Plinlimmon's title page thus aligns him with vacancy and simultaneously with a conversion of three-dimensional forms (pyramid, mountain, church) into the two-dimensional space of the page.

Plinlimmon himself, the pamphlet's ostensible author and the "leader" of the Church of the Apostles, is figured as bloodless: he has "no family or blood ties of any sort" (290), and is preternaturally pale. His bloodlessness also connotes an internal vacancy, a vacancy I ascribe to his identification with the page. It is in these terms, too, that I understand why the graphics of Pierre's title page are shaped like an eagle (247). In *Mardi*, Babbalanja castigates critics, and remarks "Oh! that all round the domains of genius should lie thus unhedged, for such cattle to uproot! Oh! that an eagle should be stabbed by a goose-quill!" (599). *Mardi* imagines a goose-quill pen as the force that stabs the aspiring eagle/author. *Pierre* recasts this drama of deflation: Pierre's successful youthful effusions are associated with the eagle by way of the eagle-shaped title page; Plinlimmon's text is associated with the two dimensions of the written page. The kind of writing associated with Plinlimmon is like the deflating force of the goose-quill that stabs the eagle. And, indeed, Plinlimmon presides over a dramatic change in Pierre's writing.

As Pierre struggles to write, it is Plinlimmon's face that arrests him, looming high in the tower: "Only through two panes of glass—his own and the stranger's—had Pierre hitherto beheld that remarkable face of repose,—repose neither divine nor human, nor any thing made up of either or both—but a repose separate and apart—a repose of a face by itself. One adequate look at that face conveyed to most philosophical observers a notion of something not before included in their scheme of the Universe" (291). Plinlimmon's face-to-face confrontation with Pierre across the quadrangle positions each man behind a pane of glass. These "panes" are rectangular forms in the vertical plane like that rectangular form Pierre agonizes over in the horizontal plane, the page in various stages of inscription. That Pierre projects the rectangular, horizontal space of the page outside his room is also suggested by the quadrangular space of the courtyard that appears to him as a "black gulf" outside his window. "From the lofty window of that beggarly room, what is it that Pierre is so intently eying? There is no street at his feet; like a profound black gulf the open area of the quadrangle gapes beneath him" (271). Here Pierre displaces outside his window, in a downward direction and in the horizontal plane, the "black gulf" he confronts as he struggles to write.

A similar upward displacement occurs when he gazes at Plinlimmon behind his window pane in the vertical plane. I have already claimed that Pierre's fear of faces is provoked by the obtrusive force of the page, and that it is Plin-limmon in particular who comes to embody that force. I situate the verticaliza-tion of Plinlimmon's face with respect to the elevated status of all the novel's haunting faces in the air or at a height. Isabel's face "steals down" upon him from the "high secrecies" of a tree (41). The chair-portrait "before which Pierre had many a time trancedly stood" is "hung, by long cords" (71) in Pierre's chamber-closet. At the gallery of paintings, the portraits of the Cenci and the stranger's head are "hung at a good elevation in one of the upper tiers" (351).

The imprisoning force of the page associated metonymically throughout the novel with faces is also associated with its walls, including the "tower face" (291) of Plinlimmon that Pierre sees from his room; the "unwindowed wall" of Pierre's title page (249); and the prison in which he dies. The "stone cheeks of the walls" of Pierre's cell (360), a figure that renders walls as faces, become Isabel's haunting face a few pages later when, at the novel's conclusion, her last words "came gasping from the wall" (362). The oft-remarked conflation of Isabel with the prison itself in the last paragraph literalizes the novel's confla-tion of faces and walls. The chronic figurations of both haunting faces and imprisoning walls in *Pierre* verticalize and elevate the text at which Pierre looks down on his desk, rendering it an impenetrable wall through which passage becomes impossible (thus it is "unwindowed").

Thus Plinlimmon, the "tower face" who walls up before Pierre's gaze, functions as an exteriorized and verticalized page. This link in fact resonates in the minimal difference between the words "pane" and "page," a substantial association for Melville that we can see at work elsewhere in his writing. He restages the face-off between Pierre and Plinlimmon in "The Two Temples," written sometime in 1853 or 1854 but not printed during Melville's lifetime.[12] Here the first-person narrator, who has been denied admission to a church service, sneaks up inside the church tower from which he wants to look down over the congregation through "a curious little window high over the orchestra and everything else" (*PT* 304):

> As I drew nigh the spot, I well knew from the added clearness with which the sound of worship came to me, that the window did indeed look down upon the entire interior. But I was hardly prepared to find that no pane of glass, stained or unstained, was to stand between me and the far-under aisles and altar. For the purpose of ventilation, doubtless, the opening had been left unsupplied with sash of any sort. But a sheet of fine-woven, gauzy wire-work was in place of that. When, all eagerness, and open book in hand, I first advanced to stand before the window, I involuntarily shrank, as from before the mouth of a furnace, upon suddenly feeling a forceful puff of strange, heated air, blown, as by a blacksmith's bellows, full into my face and lungs. (*PT* 305)

In place of the missing "pane of glass," the narrator finds "a sheet of fine-woven, gauzy wire-work" that has the effect "of casting crape upon all I saw. Only by making allowances for the crape, could I gain a right idea of the scene disclosed" (*PT* 306). The paperlike quality of the material that substitutes for the missing "pane"—fine-woven, gauzy, crape-like—suggests its association with a "page" of paper. Crape, a gauzy woven fabric embossed on the surface, was sometimes used as a facial disguise (Hawthorne's minister's black veil is made of crape), and Melville characteristically wrote on embossed paper.[13]

The conflation in Melville's description of "fine-woven, gauzy wire-work" and the effects it creates of "casting crape" recall, both historically and within the terms of Melville's texts, the process of paper production that he also invokes in *Typee* and "The Paradise of Bachelors and the Tartarus of Maids."[14] The papermaking machinery that helped to revolutionize printing in America operated by passing an endless revolving wire band or web through a vat of pulp, which was distributed across the wire, then couched, pressed, and dried.[15] The "wire-work" and the "heated air" into which the narrator looks in "The Two Temples" present a verticalized version of the narrator's encounter with literal papermaking machinery in "The Tartarus of Maids." In "The Tartarus of Maids," the paper pulp passing before the gaze of the narrator is described as a "thin, gauzy vail" (*PT* 333); in "The Two Temples," also written after Melville's 1851 visit to the Carson mill in Dalton, Massachusetts, upon which "The Tartarus of Maids" appears to have been based, the narrator encounters a "sheet of fine-woven, gauzy wire-work" that conflates a sheet of paper and the screen from which it emerges through the drying action of steam. In chapter 3 I discuss how the narrator's gaze upon paper production in "The Tartarus of Maids" provokes his writing anxiety; at present I'll merely note that the narrator of "The Two Temples" approaches the "sheet" eagerly, with "open book in hand," but finds himself repelled by "a forceful puff . . . full into my face and lungs." In "The Two Temples" the papery sheet not only acts as a site of blockage characteristic of the Melvillean scene of writing, but also renders the window itself facelike by dressing it with a facial veil, a connection enhanced by the window's "circular" shape (306). The "strange, heated air, blown, as by a blacksmith's bellows, full into my face and lungs" is a resistant force associated with the narrator's approach to the window through which he cannot clearly see, figuring not only the repellent force of the page but also its resistance to visual penetration.

Pierre associates a "pane" with Plinlimmon's face, and, in turn, with the page. When Pierre can no longer bear Plinlimmon's leer, he covers his window with muslin, "and the face became curtained like any portrait," a conflation of the window itself with the face upon which it looks, which is actually in the distance. But the muslin does not perform its office: "Pierre knew that still the face leered behind the muslin" (293). The "muslin" suggesting papery cloth barely conceals the face behind it, thus both enacting Pierre's earlier desire to "see" the lurking "form" that "visibly rustles behind the concealing screen" (41) and insisting that the content of that sight is not what Pierre desires. Both the "screen" associated with the face in *Pierre* and the "fine-woven, gauzy wire-work" of "The Two Temples" resonate with a visual confrontation with paper, a resonance we can hear all the more clearly when we remember that Pierre's troubles with his eyesight make his page look "fretted with wires" (340).

Plinlimmon's face is brought from the spatial depth of his own window forward into the space of Pierre's window, a pushing forward that simultaneously enacts a spatial flattening from three into two dimensions. This flattening is represented by turning the window through which Pierre sees Plinlimmon's face in the distance into the window as a frame within whose two dimensions that face is contained as a portrait-face, a two-dimensional space of representation.[16] This threatening flattening out (and indeed Pierre feels the threat as presently as before the face was covered with muslin) enacts a "pushing up" into his face like that the narrator imagined earlier. It is Plinlimmon's embodiment of the "non-Benevolence" of the lurking force of the page that renders his repose "neither divine nor human," but rather "a face by itself": something whose force is nonhuman, nontranscendental, and whose pressing claims upon both Pierre and the narrator have not previously been accounted for. It's also the case that *Pierre* is Melville's first work written in the third person, and this shift introduces what is for Melville a new kind of narrative distance that is also a new position of observation: a newly configured position for the observation of the page itself.[17]

Earlier, I claimed that Pierre's attempts to dive deeply are brought up short against the "lurking" force associated in *Pierre* and elsewhere in Melville's work with the written page. To lurk, according to the *OED*, is "to lie in ambush; to remain furtively or unobserved about one spot." The fear of something of questionable visibility suggested by Melville's frequent reference to "lurking" forces is also implicit in his persistent use of the word "looming": according to the *OED*, the word *loom* is, among other denotations, a "seaman's term for the indistinct and exaggerated appearance or outline of an object when it first comes into view, as the outline of land on the horizon, an object seen through the mist or darkness, etc." It also means "to appear indistinctly; to come into view in an enlarged and indefinite form." Denotatively, both words suggest problems of visibility as something unseen threatens to come into view; the "lurkings" and "loomings" that are chronic figures for Melville are both furtive and vaguely threatening, seen only dimly and incompletely.

Melville figures lurking and looming forces throughout his writing career, a merely partial list of which includes the "lurking something" he attributes to textual faces in "Hawthorne and His Mosses"; the "lurking" force Pierre identifies with "the face" ("If aught really lurks in it" [41]); the "floating" (290) face of Plinlimmon that looms before Pierre; the looming white phantom of the whale (to which I will turn presently); and the pyramids, which Melville associates both with Plinlimmon and with Moby-Dick and that appear in their full looming splendor in Melville's journal. When he visited the pyramids in January 1857, he described feelings of terror: "Pyramids still loom before me— something vast, indefinite, incomprehensible, and awful" (*J* 76). He recounts the story of an old man who tried "to go into the interior—fainted—brought out. . . . Too much for him; oppressed by the massiveness & mystery of the pyramids. I myself too" (*J* 75). Revisions in the journal suggest this was material Melville was working and reworking rather than "pure" diary, so the chronic and powerful fear he describes ultimately feels both like an affective response and like one whose motivation was strategic, with an eye toward a future writing project of some kind.[18] In either case, he treats pyramids as impenetrable surfaces "looming" before him, a word choice especially resonant in its echo of the "Loomings" that begin *Moby-Dick*. A pyramid is also a looming, gigantic blind wall, like the whale-wall with its hieroglyphic brow.[19]

All these lurkings and loomings, I maintain, are projections into a vertical space—in the case of the pyramid, onto a landscape, and in the case of Plinlimmon's face, into the rectangular space of a pane of glass—of the horizontal space of the white page that Melville saw at some level of awareness as he wrote,[20] and toward which his relation changed during the course of his career. It is in these terms that I understand the furtive, threatening, and indistinct visualization of both his lurking and looming forces. Ultimately, I attribute Plinlimmon's enormous power in this text to what I take to be his identification with the material space of the page, and in this regard Plinlimmon is less the author of the pamphlet—in fact we are told he did not write it (290)—than he is the pamphlet itself, part of the novel's conversion of three dimensions into two.

During the state in which Pierre is unable to look on paper, he has a "baseless vision" that opens with sweeping pastures of amaranth, a small white flower that multiplies so uncontrollably that the pastures in June "show like banks of snow," rendering them sterile (342, 343). This scene of sterile whiteness is followed by a vision of Enceladus, the mutilated heaven-assaulter. The scene of the white page from which Pierre turns his eyes becomes his vision of a sterile white field, a vision that "displaced the four blank walls, the desk, and camp-bed" (346), an explicit indication within the terms of the text that Pierre displaces the scene of writing into images in which that scene powerfully lurks. In the late poem "Pontoosuce," amaranth appears as a screen for a dangerous lurking force ("in very amaranths the worm doth lurk," l. 52). Here in *Pierre* amaranth is also a screen for a lurking force that is explicitly the white page.

The confrontation with "the phantom" Enceladus, introduced under the sign of a spectral vision of the white page, dramatizes the narrator's earlier fears about tautology, as the white page becomes a "mirror" that gives Pierre back only his own face: "That moment the phantom faced him; and Pierre saw Enceladus no more; but on the Titan's armless trunk, his own duplicate face and features magnifiedly gleamed upon him with prophetic discomfiture and woe" (346). This "phantom" force associated with the page also recasts the looming white phantom Moby-Dick, whose presence in *Pierre* is distilled to the level of the written inscription on the Memnon Stone, in which a plaintive force "seemed to lurk" (134). Its "half-obliterate initials—'S ye W'" (133)—inscribe the presence of the Sperm Whale, as mere written marks, in Pierre's confrontation with this "huge stumbling-block" (132).

Earlier, I claimed that Pierre's fear of faces begins even before the beginning of the novel proper. In one sense, what comes before *Pierre* begins is *Moby-Dick,* and the suggestion that the haunting face predates the beginning of *Pierre* speaks in part to the persistence of facial scenarios in Melville's writing in general, and to the immediate proximity of *Moby-Dick* in particular.[21] What's most crucially lost in *Pierre* is the invisibility of Moby-Dick's face, as the indistinctness of the furtive, looming form of the page is converted to oppressive visibility. As the two-dimensional space of the page emerges from invisible "depths" into the field of vision, the metaphysical quest of *Moby-Dick* is rendered bankrupt.

Moby-Dick is insistently interested in the whale's tauntingly absent face. "Physiognomically regarded, the Sperm Whale is an anomalous creature" (345), Ishmael writes. The whale is a physiognomical puzzle because, having no face, he lacks exactly that text the physiognomist would read.[22] "For you see no one point precisely; not one distinct feature is revealed; no nose, eyes, ears, or mouth; no face; he has none, proper" (346). The extent to which this missing face is not only an occasion for Ishmael's ongoing philosophical reflection (most notably in the chapters "The Battering-Ram" and "The Prairie") but also a source of discomposure becomes clear at the conclusion of "The Tail": "But if I know not even the tail of this whale, how understand his head? much more, how comprehend his face, when face he has none? Thou shalt see my back parts, my tail, he seems to say, but my face shall not be seen. But I cannot completely make out his back parts; and hint what he will about his face, I say again he has no face" (379).

The tone of philosophical reflection that dominates "The Tail" begins to give way in this concluding section to agitated desire for the face the whale deliberately withholds. Both the ultimate significance of that face and the inter-diction upon seeing it render it like the face of God, whose words the whale echoes: "And he said, Thou canst not see my face; for there shall no man see me, and live" (Exodus 33:20); "And I will take away mine hand, and thou shalt see my back; but my face shall not be seen" (Exodus 33:23); "I will show them the back, and not the face, in the day of their calamity" (Jeremiah 18:17). James Barbour comments that the whale, like God, "exists beyond our ability to know,"[23] and in this sense its face is a posited but absent site of ultimate significance, as is "the face" for Pierre. It is upon the missing text of the whale's face in particular that the desires of Ishmael and Ahab converge. Ishmael's frustrated yearning to see the whale face to face intersects with Ahab's desire to "strike through the mask!" (164) behind which he imagines that "some un-known but still reasoning thing puts forth the mouldings of its features" (164).

In *Pierre,* written immediately following *Moby-Dick* and published the next year, the face whose absence was so taunting at last appears, with a ven-geance, as tormenting faces now confront Pierre everywhere: "Escape the face he could not" (49). The "terrors of the face" threaten Pierre because "he felt that what he had always before considered the solid land of veritable reality, was now being audaciously encroached upon by bannered armies of hooded phan-toms, disembarking in his soul, as from flotillas of specter-boats" (49). His vision of the "transfixed face in the air" occurs as "forth trooped thickening phantoms of an infinite gloom" (85). The "hooded" and trooping "phantoms" that the face conjures in *Pierre* recall Ishmael's "endless processions of the whale, and midmost of them all, one grand hooded phantom, like a snow hill in the air" (7).

The echoes of *Moby-Dick* in *Pierre* and the transformations between the two work out Melville's changing and increasingly agonizing relation to his pages as oppressive, impenetrable spaces whose visible presence confronts him as he writes. It is in these terms that I understand why the whale is a wall, according to the accounts of both Ahab and Ishmael. Ahab asks, "How can the prisoner reach outside except by thrusting through the wall? To me, the white whale is that wall, shoved near to me" (164). For Ishmael, "the Sperm Whale's head is a dead, blind wall," and this faceless mass "presents an almost wholly vertical plane to the water" (336, 337). This dead, blind, vertical plane is also one in which, Ishmael further comments, "I do not think any sensation lurks" (337). Like Ahab, Pierre wants to strike against the obstructions walling up before him. In response to the revelation of his half-sister, he cries, "I will lift my hand in fury, for am I not struck?" and "Thou Black Knight, that with visor down, thus confrontest me, and mockest at me; Lo! I strike through thy helm and will see thy face, be it Gorgon!" (65–66). This visored helmet is like the "concealing screen" in the face of whose "lurkings" Pierre cried, "I conjure ye to lift the veil; I must see it face to face" (41).

Ishmael's descriptions of the whale as a "dead, blind wall" appear in "The Battering-Ram," and although the title presumably describes that dead, blind wall itself and "whatever battering-ram power may be lodged there" (336), "battering-ram" power is exerted not only by the wall but also against it: "The severest pointed harpoon, the sharpest lance darted by the strongest human arm, impotently rebounds from it," Ishmael comments (337). Webster (1847) describes a battering-ram as "a military engine used to beat down the walls of besieged places." The title of the chapter thus connotes not only the whale-wall that the harpoons and lances besiege but also the violent force of arm by the harpoons and lances that it provokes in response. That the battering-ram activities of arm are impotent before the whale-wall foregrounds the whale's resistance to penetration, a resistance that further suggests that the depth of this space is pressingly at issue. In fact, the arm's operations of dissection, of literally penetrating whale bodies, are chronicled throughout the novel, as Sharon Cameron has rightly stressed,[24] but such operations are crucially thwarted in the case of Moby-Dick, whose space thus remains impenetrable.

Moby-Dick's physical volume speaks to its great depth, a depth that Ishmael associates both with the whale's literal movements and with its meaning. Like the "large book" whose "multitude of pages" astonishes Queequeg in "A Bosom Friend" (49), the size of material text suggests the scope of its metaphysical subject, a scope that leads Ishmael to conclude in "Cetology" that the book of the whale can only be "the draught of a draught" (145). The bookish attributes of Ishmael's whale come to the fore in *Pierre*, in which, although there is no white whale, there is Pierre's "great, deep book" (341). This materialization of text, by which I mean not a whale metaphorized as a book, but a book as such with attributes of what was formerly the whale, can be understood in conjunction with the haunting visibility of the once-missing face.

Ishmael insists that whales are books, and their physical "volume" is the only "practicable" basis for categorization (140); thus, too, he demands, "Give me a condor's quill! Give me Vesuvius' crater for an inkstand!" as his "chirography expands into placard capitals" (456). But even as Ishmael asserts the compatibility between a physically large book and a physically and metaphysically large subject, his confidence threatens to collapse. At the end of chapter 41, entitled "Moby Dick" and thus marked with the name of the volume itself, we learn that Ishmael cannot explain "what the White Whale was" (187), since "all this to explain, would be to dive deeper than Ishmael can go. The subterranean miner that works in us all, how can one tell whither leads his shaft by the ever shifting, muffled sound of his pick? Who does not feel the irresistible arm drag?" (187). Ishmael's inability to "dive deep" enough is figured in terms of a pen as "pick," a figure that associates writing across a page with digging depths. Here Ishmael's desire to dive deep enough begins to flatten out against the material surface of the page on which the pen can write but through whose phantom subterranean space it cannot satisfyingly "pick"—a problem that gives rise to the "arm drag" whose power cannot be resisted. Significantly, the space imagined in this moment of "arm drag" is not subaqueous (thus figuring the watery realms that are Ishmael's subject) but "subterranean," as the space to be penetrated hardens before the arm's tools. This miner's "pick" is the writerly version of the harpoons and lances "darted by the strongest human arm" in "The Battering-Ram," which also rebound from an impenetrable wall.

This moment of "arm drag" constitutes the overlooked but compelling context for the emergence of the crisis of the next chapter, "The Whiteness of the Whale," which meditates upon the "elusive something in the innermost idea of this hue" that makes its bearers "transcendent horrors" (189). The whiteness that surfaces here in such overwhelming force is the whiteness of the page that overpowers the writing arm at the end of the preceding chapter. My reading thus differs with a long tradition of identifying both Moby-Dick and whiteness in transcendent terms.[25] The arm drags as the "pick" fails to penetrate the surface of the page and fails to render accessible its "subterranean" depths. "The Whiteness of the Whale" both posits that the meaning of whiteness is fearful because "transcendent" and at the same time fears that it is not; its frenetic effort to establish the transcendent meaning of "innermost" whiteness, like the efforts of the "subterranean miner" in the previous chapter, posits a space of meaning within the white page whose resistance provokes the attempts to "pick" and pierce through it. "It was the whiteness of the whale that above all things appalled me," Ishmael comments. "But how can I hope to explain myself here; and yet, in some dim, random way, explain myself I must, else all these chapters might be naught" (188).

The fear that he cannot explain the "transcendent" meaning of the whale's whiteness threatens to render his writing "naught"; and here Ishmael's fear that writing is "naught" echoes Ahab's fear that there's "naught" beyond the mask of the whale/wall: when he proposes, as quoted earlier, that "some unknown but still reasoning thing puts forth the mouldings of its features from behind the unreasoning mask" (164), he suggests that a face lurks behind the mask, and goes on to propose that that face is accessible by "striking through" the obstructing surface that covers it. But he simultaneously proposes that there might be nothing behind the mask after all: "Sometimes I think there's naught beyond" (164). Ahab's equivocation about what if anything lurks behind the visible plane echoes in Pierre's belief that the face he needs to see is just behind the "screen" or "veil" of the face he sees, and that there might in fact be nothing there: "If aught really lurks in it, ye sovereign powers that claim all my leal worshippings, I conjure ye to lift the veil; I must see it face to face" (41). Ishmael's "picking" and "diving" and the "irresistible arm drag" those activities provoke are thus related to Ahab's desire to "strike through the mask" of the whale's blind white wall: the space that can't be penetrated by harpoons and arms.

Another invocation of arm drag emerges in "The Counterpane," when Ishmael feels "a supernatural hand" placed in his. The "nameless, unimaginable, silent form or phantom, to which the hand belonged" (26) invokes the whale in general and the "phantom" Moby-Dick in particular,[26] and associates the whale's phantom presence with a peculiar heavy consciousness of the hand. The dissected sperm whale body is a "vast white headless phantom" (308) whose blubber is compared to a "counterpane" (307) and whose aura is construed as a "ghost" (309). The ghostly white mass associated with a blubbery "counterpane" thus recalls the eponymous counterpane of chapter 4. There, Ishmael's foregrounded arm and hand—"My arm hung over the counterpane" (26)—are "frozen"; he says, "I lay there, frozen with the most awful fears, not daring to drag away my hand, yet ever thinking that if I could but stir it one single inch, the horrid spell would be broken" (26). Ishmael has been sent to bed early on the longest day of the year, doomed to spend sixteen hours there, and this tale about his childhood is an encrypted representation of the scene of writing whose configurations for Melville are crucially domestic in ways I elaborate in chapter 3. Anticipating my extended argument, I will merely note that the nightmarish confinement in his room away from a resented woman (the stepmother who "was all the time whipping me" [25]), as he "with a bitter sigh got between the sheets" (26), resonates with Melville's confinement in his room with his "sheets" of paper. Parker suggests that *Moby-Dick* is influenced by Melville's "fantasy of escaping from the lonely, cramped, frigid conditions in which he was writing—from winter in an isolated Berkshire farmhouse full of

women, where even Malcolm was probably still in petticoats."[27] In "The Counterpane," Ishmael experiences a paralyzing form of "arm drag" associated with
confinement in his room, with writing, and with trying to penetrate the whale.

Just as the whale's battering-ram power also characterizes attempts to
besiege it, the blindness of the impenetrable whale-wall ("you must now have
perceived that the front of the Sperm Whale's head is a dead, blind wall" [336–
37]) speaks to a corollary blindness in those who confront it. The whale as a
blind wall thus participates in the novel's anxiety about vision and visibility, an
anxiety that in fact resonates strongly in the question hovering over the bulk of
the novel: when will Moby-Dick be seen? Even after he is first sighted—very
close to the end of this very long book—the terms of the novel continue to focus
on the emerging and submerging visibility of the whale from the horizontal
plane of the ocean's surface. The last three chapters of the novel—the only
chapters in which Moby-Dick actually does appear—center on the ways in
which he becomes visible and the kinds of marks he makes on or through the
ocean's surface. Thus these chapters chronicle his "visible jets" (547), "ever-
contracting circles" (551), "vertical thrusts" (550), "horizontal attitudes" (551),
glidings, swells, soundings, and other kinds of visible motions played against
his "still withholding from sight the full terrors of his submerged trunk" (548).

The "arm drag" of the subterranean miner is here reconfigured as "suddenly the waters around them slowly swelled in broad circles; then quickly
upheaved, as if sideways sliding from a submerged berg of ice, swiftly rising to
the surface. A low rumbling sound was heard; a subterraneous hum; and then
all held their breaths; as bedraggled with trailing ropes, and harpoons, and
lances, a vast form shot lengthwise, but obliquely from the sea" (567). I have
argued that the terrifying whiteness of Moby-Dick invokes the writer's page; the
whale, figured as it often is in terms of hiddenness or part-visibility, here
becomes the "subterraneous" force whose depths the writer's pen-pick seeks to
plumb. When Moby-Dick comes crashing through, he does so bearing the
marks of the pick/shaft/pen whose blocked attempts to dig depths produce
"arm drag": "the tall but shattered pole of a recent lance projected from the
white whale's back" (548). When suddenly "Moby Dick burst into view" the
"torn, enraged waves he shakes off" (558). These "torn" waves render the horizontal watery plane papery, as, in *Pierre*, "The Tear" is both a watery phenomenon and a rip in material text that ultimately speaks to the visibility of marks on
the page.

It is against the body of this white mass, appearing now vertically, now
horizontally, that so many "loose harpoons and lances, with all their bristling
barbs and points" (559) have been caught, twisted, corkscrewed, and destroyed.

Moby-Dick rushes at the ship with "his blank forehead" (570) as "all the seamen now hung inactive; hammers, bits of plank, lances, and harpoons, mechanically retained in their hands, just as they had darted from their various employments" (571). The overbearing looming white form of the whale's blank forehead, this "solid white buttress" (571), stops the mechanical activities of the hands and paralyzes them into inactivity. In so doing, it recalls the impotence of arm invoked in "The Battering-Ram."

The "untraceable evolutions" of Moby-Dick "so crossed and recrossed, and in a thousand ways entangled the slack of the three lines now fast to him, that they foreshortened, and, of themselves, warped the devoted boats towards the planted irons in him" (558–59). Irwin has explored Moby-Dick's multi-layered association with hieroglyphic writing; here I want to stress that the crossing and recrossing of lines in this passage specifically invoke the working and reworking of lines of handwriting.[28] It is by way of this identification that I understand the "foreshortening" of lines that pulls the boats toward the "irons" planted in the whale's body. As the invocation of written lines on the white page becomes most palpable within the nominal plot, the three "dimensions" of the scene begin to flatten out as the boats and the "irons" close in upon one another's space because of the foreshortened "lines."

The foreshortening that draws the boats closer within the scene also collapses the dimensions of the scene itself, and, in this sense, what "bursts bodily into view" is Melville's own "lines," his engagement with the space of the page out of which the endless depths of *Moby-Dick* are conjured. It is on that "torn" space that "lines" of handwriting effect the foreshortening that Melville invokes in the revealing ways I have shown in both *Pierre* and *Moby-Dick*. When Ahab determines to "take the whale head-and-head,—that is, pull straight up to his forehead" (558), we can hear the aggressive kind of pushing straight up to the face that we find in *Pierre*. This pulling straight up to his forehead and the concomitant drama of foreshortening just described figure in terms that will become all the more forceful in *Pierre* as the antagonistic power of the material text with which Melville wrestled. The conflict in *Pierre* between endless depth and relentless flattening, which provokes the narrator's own anxieties even as he mocks Pierre, thus reconfigures *Moby-Dick:* the conflict between writing and diving deep becomes agonizingly spatialized, and material text increasingly obtrudes as that which exerts rather than defeats "confines," to use Ahab's language (164).

When Ahab says, "all the things that most exasperate and outrage mortal man, all these things are bodiless, but only bodiless as objects, not as agents" (564), he equivocates about precisely the materiality of the exasperating and outraging forces in question. We are left to ask to what extent and in what way—exactly—these "things that most exasperate and outrage" are "bodiless." Ahab's slippery formulation about bodiless "objects" speaks to the "phantom" status of the page, whose material dimensions and features fail to account for its power in a way that satisfies Melville. What comes "crashing through" the heartlessly immense surface of the sea is the whale as a white page, a page whose association with "depth" comes under further pressure in the claustrophobic domestic ruins of *Pierre*. It is to Melville's outrages and exasperations with that confining space that I now turn.

Chapter Three

Wife Beating and the Written Page

~

n 1975, *Proceedings of the Massachusetts Historical Society* published an
article bringing to light some newly discovered letters, dated May 1867,
that suggest Herman Melville physically and emotionally abused his
wife. One letter reveals that Elizabeth Shaw Melville's minister proposed
a feigned kidnapping to get her out of the house and away from her
husband.[1] In 1981, twelve commentators responded to this discovery in a
monograph published by the Melville Society. Several of them believed the new
information to be crucial to Melville studies, while others dismissed its importance. Beyond this monograph—and despite its aim to put the new evidence
"quickly . . . in the widest possible scholarly and critical perspectives"[2]—the
discovery has received astonishingly little sustained attention.[3]

The 1867 letters, one written by Elizabeth's half-brother, Samuel S. Shaw,
and one by Elizabeth herself, were both found in the papers of Henry Whitney
Bellows, the minister of the All Souls Unitarian Church in New York City from
1839 to 1882. Elizabeth and Herman were members of this church and rented a
pew there beginning in 1849.[4] Samuel Shaw's letter is a response to what was
apparently Bellows' suggestion that the Shaws arrange to "kidnap" Elizabeth,
with her covert participation. Shaw writes: "If I understand your letter it is
proposed to make a sudden interference and carry her off, she protesting that
she does not wish to go and that it is none of her doing." Although Shaw rejects
the kidnapping plan, he stresses the necessity of getting his sister out of the
house in response to unspecified "ill treat[ment]."[5] He cites Elizabeth's "belief
in the insanity of her husband" and complains of "the present lamentable state
of things"; he also refers to Herman and Elizabeth's domestic situation as "a
cause of anxiety to all of us for years past," reporting that even "the Melvilles
also, though not till quite recently, have expressed a willingness to lend their

49

assistance."[6] The second letter, from Elizabeth herself, thanks Bellows for his interest and writes—apparently indicating that she has decided not to leave—"whatever further trial may be before me, I shall feel that your counsel is a strong help to sustain, more perhaps than any other earthly counsel could. I think you will be glad to know that your long talk with me has been a very great comfort, both for its appreciative sympathy, and for other reasons. I lay to heart your encouraging words, and pray for submission and faith to *realize* the sustaining power of the Master's love, and to approach his Table in the very spirit of his last command."[7] In her work on wife beating and battered women's resistance, Linda Gordon argues that marital violence has often been aimed at forcing a wife to stay when she threatens to leave;[8] this makes one think hard about the circumstances surrounding Elizabeth's decision, and about the "further trial" she envisioned.

Samuel Shaw's letter explains that Elizabeth would have acted to extricate herself from the domestic situation "long ago if not for imaginary and groundless apprehensions of the censure of the world upon her conduct." He reports that she has "a most exaggerated dread" of how "the eyes of the world" would look upon her "case."[9] Ensuring the credibility of the "case" clearly concerns both Elizabeth and Samuel, and his rejection of the kidnapping scheme, and in fact of any scheme to make Elizabeth look as if she has not herself decided to leave Herman, is predicated upon such concerns:

> But if *we* are to seem to be the real putters asunder of man and wife and she is merely to acquiesce I do not think it could be managed better than by having her at our house and by keeping her there and carefully preventing her husband from seeing her, and telling him and everybody that we had made up our minds not to let her return.
>
> But this might embarrass our subsequent relations with Mr. Melville and really injure my sisters [sic] case because if he should commence legal proceedings it would throw suspicion over her motives in acquiescing in a separation.
>
> It may well be said Here is a case of mischief making where the wifes [sic] relations have created all the trouble. "She says *now* that her husband ill treated her so that she could not live with him but why did she not say so before. She goes to Boston and by dint of argument and remonstrances and bad advice of all sorts is at last persuaded into thinking herself a much injured woman." &c &c &c
>
> And her very patience and fortitude will be turned into arguments against her belief in the insanity of her husband. (Samuel S. Shaw to Henry Whitney Bellows, 6 May 1867, Kring and Carey 14; emphasis in original)

The hypothetical resistance to Elizabeth's charges that her half-brother imagines suggests that it was not unlikely for such charges brought by wives to meet these kinds of suspicion. The fact that Shaw was himself a lawyer[10] presumably informs his assessment of the situation. In fact, women who brought wife beating charges to court in the nineteenth century met with little success.[11] In addition, white, native-born women like Elizabeth appear to have been less likely than black and immigrant women to complain to police about wife beating, which may indicate that they were more likely to fear the stigma of dealing with police and courts.[12] Elizabeth apparently dreaded publicizing her "trial." Furthermore, the intervention of family and friends was the primary informal means for the regulation of wife beating in the period, far more effective than any formal means.[13]

The grievances abused women did bring against their husbands were often indirect indications rather than direct charges of physical violence. They charged abusive men with related offenses that were clearer and more actionable violations of prevailing norms, including intemperance, bad language, and nonsupport, rather than with physical abuse as such. The temperance movement in particular insisted on the implicit connection between intemperance and wife abuse. In fact, "drinking" became a code word for male violence by about 1850.[14] According to Gordon, indirect accusations of the kinds listed above gave women a clearer claim on the community's protection than did their often-unsuccessful charges of wife beating per se. Only after 1930 did the women in her study begin to complain directly rather than indirectly about physical abuse.[15] Both Samuel and Elizabeth's oblique language about Herman's "ill treat[ment]" and "insanity," combined with indications that he drank heavily,[16] thus assume especially ominous overtones in conjunction with all the available evidence.

The additional evidence of Melville's wife abuse is largely anecdotal. Its primary source is Eleanor Melville Metcalf, his oldest grandchild, the daughter of his youngest daughter, Frances (1855–1938); when Herman died (1891), Eleanor was nine years old. In addition to her memories of him, she reports having learned about him and about the family history primarily from her grandmother, Elizabeth (1822–1906), from her parents, Frances and Henry B. Thomas, and from her great-uncle Samuel Shaw;[17] thus she presumably knew a great deal indeed about the Melvilles' domestic circle.

It was Eleanor's cooperation with Raymond M. Weaver, who contacted her in 1919, that made possible Weaver's groundbreaking book, *Herman Melville: Mariner and Mystic* (1921); her subsequent cooperation with the Melville scholars who followed him fueled the Melville revival of the 1920s. In *Herman Melville: Cycle and Epicycle* (1953), she mentions "such men as Harry Murray, Charles Olson, Francis Matthiessen, and many others, [who] come to the house seeking Melville."[18] Eleanor granted Weaver complete access to what he describes as "all the surviving records of her grandfather: Melville manuscripts, letters, journals, annotated books, photographs, and a variety of other material," including the "undiscovered" manuscript of *Billy Budd*.[19] The word "surviving" here is especially weighty, since many family letters and records had been destroyed, by Melville himself and by others.[20] Reports that family papers were deliberately burned have horrified and enticed Melville scholars for generations.

Anecdotal evidence of Melville's wife abuse at last emerged in print in the Melville Society monograph, obliquely entitled *The Endless, Winding Way in Melville: New Charts by Kring and Carey,* edited by Donald Yannella and Hershel Parker, with an introduction by Walter D. Kring. The monograph reprinted Kring and Jonathan S. Carey's 1975 article announcing the discovery and presented responses to it by William Braswell, Paul Metcalf, Leon Howard, Elizabeth S. Foster, Edward H. Rosenberry, Tyrus Hillway, Joyce D. and Frederick J. Kennedy, G. Thomas Tanselle, Edwin Haviland Miller, Edwin S. Shneidman, and Robert Milder. Paul Metcalf, Eleanor's son and Herman's great-grandson, reports having been told by Charles Olson that Herman came home drunk on brandy, beat Elizabeth up, and threw her down the stairs. Metcalf is right to point out both that this story has not been verified and that it is also possible that worse may be true.[21] In *Call me Ishmael* (1947), Olson writes of Melville's "ill" behavior between 1851 and 1856: "He remained periodically violent to his wife, and strange with his mother."[22] Although Olson never revealed his source, his text effusively acknowledges Eleanor and Henry K. Metcalf, "for they have made all Melville's things mine, indeed have made me a member of their family,"[23] and the record does indicate that Eleanor told others that Melville struck his wife.[24] Paul Metcalf has further suggested that his mother's central involvement in the Melville revival caused what he believes to have been her nervous breakdown at the time, as she was "forced to wrestle with a new conception of her grandfather" in that "the 'beast' was now becoming a 'Great Man.'"[25] Frances herself remarked of her father as late as 1928, "I don't know him in the new light." Olson claimed that Eleanor and all the Melville women hated Herman, who said of his mother late in life, "She hated me."[26]

Braswell reports more family oral history, for which Weaver was the source: when Melville took a voyage to the Holy Land after completing *The Confidence-Man,* "some members of the family hoped he would get lost and never return."[27] This is presumably the kind of story that Eleanor is reputed to have told Weaver with the expectation that he would suppress it.[28] Clare Spark points out that Eleanor objected to Jay Leyda's inclusion in *The Melville Log* of letters indicating that Herman's father Allan died a "Maniac!"[29] When Paul Metcalf began to take a serious interest in Melville in the 1950s, he quickly found himself on the verge of what he calls the "forbidden territory" of Herman and Elizabeth's marital difficulties. "It became clear that she [his mother Eleanor] was privy to information—dirt, as we would call it—that she had no intention of sharing with me—being convinced (and from her point of view, rightly so) that I would probably misuse it." His mother suppressed family "dirt" to "defend at all costs" the good names of Herman and Elizabeth, and "her method was to suppress any information that might be subject to derogatory interpretation."[30] She wanted Paul to be proud of Melville's literary accomplishments, but his drinking and wife abuse were not to be discussed.[31]

Walker Cowen's *Melville's Marginalia* points to a corollary suppression by the Melville women. Cowen notes the frequency of misogynous markings and annotations among the marginalia, and suggests that many of these markings were deliberately erased. He believes that Melville's daughters or granddaughters, or perhaps Elizabeth herself, "attempted to remove the traces of embarrassing marginalia." Many of the erasures, he concludes, "reveal that Melville spent a lifetime thinking about women in spite of the rather limited use he made of them in his fiction." He goes on to suggest that the "misogynous nature of the markings" indicates that Melville was "too much bothered by the subject to trust himself to write about it."[32] The erasures note "unpleasant aspects of women in general"; others "censure wives in particular and criticize family life from the point of view of one held captive by, but alienated from the family circle."[33]

Although Eleanor would not tell Paul any "derogatory" stories, he believes that she passed such information along to "*responsible* ears."[34] Henry A. Murray is widely reputed to have known the "dirt"; perhaps Howard P. Vincent and Olson knew as well. Olson referred to Murray in 1947 as "the other true biographer."[35] Harrison Hayford notes that "it was the general belief all during my Melville lifetime that he [Murray] had Melville materials and knowledge which he was withholding for inclusion in his biography."[36] According to Donald Yannella, both Murray and Vincent denied having been privy to any such information.[37] In Lewis Mumford's 1929 biography—one that effusively thanks Melville's daughter Frances, Eleanor, Weaver, and Murray for their help and information—Mumford writes of Melville's life in the wake of *Pierre*, "When harassed by external circumstances, one wants to attack the universe: but, like Ahab, one finds that the universe will not get in one's way: so one takes revenge on the first creature that crosses one's path. Too likely it will be a creature one holds dear: the animus is not directed against that one, but it strikes as if it were. An explosion: a blow: a raised hand: an uncontrollable outburst of vituperation—then drink, remorse, repentance, the ugly vanity of it all."[38] In his correspondence with Jay Leyda in 1947, Hayford complained, "It just makes me think what a general fuck-up the whole Melville business has been, including Murray who in my calendar qualified as one of the criminals of the century to have sat on this stuff all these years. . . . Scholars for nearly a generation now have stewed around in ignorance that he could have enlightened." In his recent gloss on this letter, Hayford completely retracts his description of Murray as "one of the criminals of the century" and remarks that "it might take a like psychologist [as was Murray[39]] to explain why I myself have published so little of what I 'know'—not that I am sitting on primary documents, which I've never done,"[40] certainly a cryptic and provocative allusion in the middle of a discourse on the "secrets" Murray withheld. Spark reports that Murray admitted in a 1987 interview with her that he was in possession of "family secrets" and that he intended to divulge them before his death.[41]

One long-kept secret in Murray's possession, which eventually came to light through the work of another scholar, was the evidence that Melville's father had an illegitimate daughter, suggesting a powerful autobiographical context for *Pierre*. But this is clearly not the only family secret in which Murray was invested, and was not a secret at all by the time of Murray's 1987 (and Hayford's 1990) comments; Murray himself had published the findings in 1985.[42] Paul Metcalf believes that the "secret" in Murray's possession may have been the secret of Melville's wife abuse.[43] Murray died in June 1988;[44] if he did divulge any such secrets, they have not yet been made public. Forrest G. Robinson's 1992 biography of Murray does reveal that his surviving unfinished manuscript of the Melville biography, more than one thousand pages long, identifies Melville's "disastrous" marriage as "the incommunicable grief, the ever-gnawing pain that he, apostle of chivalry, could never confess to anyone." Robinson believes that Murray was unable to complete and publish the biography because of the extent to which he was "brought up short by what he learned of his subject, especially of his failures in later life as a husband and father." Robinson refers without elaboration to Melville as a "sometimes violent husband and father." He also identifies Melville's "fractious discontent with marriage" as one of the multiple sites of Murray's "personal identification" with Melville, an identification that consumed Murray.[45]

Edwin S. Shneidman suggests that when the Melvilles' eldest son, Malcolm, committed suicide in September of 1867 by shooting himself in the head—four months after the kidnapping plan was discussed—he was perhaps wielding the weapon that was meant to be used "if his father, whether in an intoxicated or crazy state, ever again physically abused his mother."[46] Shneidman argues that Melville, himself a rejected child, in turn became a rejecting father, and "battered his own children psychologically." He coins the term "dementia domesticus" to describe Melville: a tortured individual "who shared his deepest self in his written works, who behaved within normal limits before most of the public world, but who at home was something of a tyrant."[47] Edwin Haviland Miller concludes from the available evidence that Melville was a heavy drinker, and that he was verbally abusive toward Elizabeth and the children with the intention to humiliate. He too mentions the family tale about Herman throwing Elizabeth down the stairs, but does not discuss the possibility of a pattern of physical abuse as well as verbal abuse. He does, however, see Malcolm's suicide as an act of hostility toward his father for a lack of attention and affection.[48] In Eleanor's correspondence with her mother in 1919, she asked, "Did he rail at things in general when he was angry, or were his attacks more personal?" Frances responded in the margin, "personal." In a subsequent letter Eleanor asked, "Then the milder manner of his last eight or ten years was not due to ill health, was it?" Frances wrote in the margin: "I should say, lack of energy."[49]

The Melvilles' second child and other son, Stanwix, suffered from a mysterious deafness after Malcolm's death, which Paul Metcalf and Miller read as a hysterical deafness in response to both Malcolm's gunshot and to arguments at home. In later years, Herman suffered from a "sudden & severe" illness during one of Stanwix's temporary visits, which disappeared when Stanwix left.[50] Indeed, the picture of the four Melville children is a tragic one: the eldest, Malcolm, dead by his own hand; Stanwix, "possessed with a demon of *restlessness*," according to his mother,[51] and dead at 35; Elizabeth, an invalid crippled with arthritis to the extent that a doctor once suggested that her fingers be straightened "*by force*";[52] and Frances, the only child to marry, who late in life would not hear the name of her father spoken.[53] After meeting Frances, Murray reported that it was a terrible experience for her even to recall her father; he diagnosed Herman's attitude in the home as one of "ritualized, emphasized, exaggerated aggression."[54]

Paul Metcalf, Braswell, Miller, Shneidman, and others who responded to the new letters in the ways I've been describing took them quite seriously. Joyce D. and Frederick J. Kennedy hailed them as an "unprecedented event in Melville scholarship" although "tantalizingly insufficient and inconclusive regarding the bizarre details that they hint at."[55] Braswell concluded that Elizabeth "must have suffered a very great deal for her brother to write to Dr. Bellows as he did."[56] Others, however, were more inclined to dismiss the discovery, in some cases by apologizing for Herman and blaming Elizabeth instead. Edward H. Rosenberry called the new letters an "unfortunate discovery" except in its indication that the Melvilles' marriage survived "a moment of truth"; other than that, Rosenberry says, they "tell us nothing we did not know about Herman's moodiness and emotional perversity ('insanity'), or about Lizzie's imperfect understanding of the tormented artist in her husband."[57] Tyrus Hillway reminds us that "on the whole she [Elizabeth] could not have been an easy person to live with," reporting the Gansevoorts' opinion that she was "disorganized" and "a poor housekeeper."[58] While family history presents Elizabeth this way—Eleanor reported that Elizabeth's "gifts as a practical housekeeper were never of the highest order" and that the daughter Frances was the "one practical household manager" in the family[59]—to invoke Elizabeth's alleged poor housekeeping as if it would have mitigated the seriousness of Herman's abuse is disturbing logic indeed. Gordon reports that men accused of wife beating "usually countered that their wives were poor housekeepers and neglectful mothers, making themselves the aggrieved parties."[60] That such charges should be made against Elizabeth in order to effect Herman's exoneration, whether by her own contemporaries or by Melville scholars, is thus all the more unsettling.

The scholar's desire to exonerate Melville is no doubt rooted in the perspective Shneidman describes in the introduction to his essay on Malcolm's suicide: "I wish to begin on solid ground, by making at least one statement with which everyone will agree: Herman Melville is the hero of the Melville Society." While Shneidman goes on to explain that such admiration should not preclude considerations of Melville's "all too-human characteristics," the apology with which he begins his essay indicates the immense power of this author's image as hero among Melville scholars.[61] This powerful image helps to explain why the terrible issue I here attempt to bring to wider attention has gone largely uninvestigated. Paul Metcalf's remark on Melville's "reputation" is pertinent: "By making him into a monument they tame him."[62]

This monumental image, as Metcalf himself suggests, is predicated upon blindness to or suppression of Melville's wife abuse. But this willful blindness in the service of reputation-making has not only tamed Herman Melville: it is also part of a greater blindness to the absolute priority of his domestic relations for understanding his writing. His wife abuse, as I will now demonstrate, is one crucial site in a network that also includes his agonized relation to writing and his dependence on the women in his household to produce those agonizing texts.

Melville's tortured relation to his writing is well known. People who knew him often commented on what Hawthorne called the "toilsome pen-labor" that kept him confined to his study day after day, with little rest and plagued by eye trouble, headaches, and sciatica, a regimen to which at least several people attributed what they believed to be his failing physical and mental health.[63] His account in *Pierre* (1852) of Pierre's excruciating process of composition has traditionally and correctly been read as an autobiographical sketch. Accounts written by Elizabeth Shaw Melville; her father, Lemuel Shaw; Herman's mother, Maria Gansevoort Melville; his sister, Augusta; Nathaniel Hawthorne; and others confirm the correspondences. Maria, for example, wrote to her brother Peter Gansevoort: "The constant In-door confinement with little intermission to which Herman's occupation as author compels him, does not agree with him. This constant working of the brain, & excitement of the imagination, is wearing Herman out."[64] Lemuel Shaw wrote to his son Samuel: "I suppose you have been informed by some of the family, how very ill Herman has been. It is manifest to me from Elizabeth's letters that she has felt great anxiety about him. When he is deeply engaged on one of his literary works, he confines himself to his study many hours in the day, with little or no exercise, & this especially in writing for a great many days together. He probably thus overworks himself & brings on severe nervous affections."[65] Augusta wrote: "We all feel that it is of the utmost importance that something should be done to prevent the necessity of Herman's writing as he has been obliged to for several years past. Were he to return to the sedentary life which that of an author writing for his support necessitates, he would risk the loss of all the benefit to his health which he has gained by his tour, & possibly become a confirmed invalid."[66] Robert Milder points out that family crises seem to have occurred for the Melvilles during or immediately after Herman's periods of intense writing: in 1852, when finishing *Pierre;* in 1856, when finishing *The Confidence-Man* and brooding about debts; and again in 1859–60, when reconciling himself to failure as a lecturer and writing his first volume of poems. By 1867, the time of the letters in question, Herman had become not only a failed novelist but also a failed poet.[67]

My introduction and previous chapters have discussed Melville's tortured relation to his writing, as well as his chronic association of writing with maddening forms of blockage. These frustrations with his writing illuminate a series of textual effects that associate women with blank pages and textual production. We can see this association in his first known published sketches, "Fragments from a Writing Desk," which appeared in the *Democratic Press, and Lansingburgh Advertiser* in May of 1839.[68] The title of these sketches itself emphasizes the material fact of the "fragments" as inscribed pieces of paper. Here I suspect too that the pseudonymous initials "L.A.V." under which he submitted and published the tale cryptically encode not the name of a person, but rather the name of the paper in which they appeared (*Lansingburgh Adver-tiser*). The first sketch sets out, in epistolary form, to describe to someone identified only as "M—" the types of female beauty found in Lansingburgh:

> I feel my powers of delineation inadequate to the task; but, nevertheless I will try my hand at the matter, although like an unskilful [*sic*] limner, I am fearful I shall but scandalize the charms I endeavor to copy.
>
> Come to my aid, ye guardian spirits of the Fair! Guide my awkward hand, and preserve from mutilation the features ye hover over and protect! Pour down whole floods of sparkling champaigne [*sic*], my dear M——, until your brain grows giddy with emotion.[69]

The narrator sets out to "delineate" the women's "loveliest faces" (193) and, at the same time, acknowledges that his "awkward" writing hand threatens them with mutilation. The activity of "delineation" refers to writing the lines that will attempt to represent those faces. "Delineation" and "mutilation" are oppositely valued activities of the writing hand.

Melville's conflicted writing activity is similarly imagined by way of the conjunction of "guardian spirits" with a writing hand. Elsewhere he poses a conjunction between an "angel" and his own writing, with sometimes bene-ficial and sometimes disastrous results. He invokes this image not only in his letter of response to Hawthorne's praise for *Moby-Dick,* but also in *The Confidence-Man,* in which an angel identified as "Bright Future" misleads China Aster into his disastrous acceptance of a loan, money he uses to buy "a good lot of spermaceti" (*CM* 212; see also introduction herein). I take this account to be an allegory, anticipating my argument in chapter 4 a bit, of Melville's "promising writing" turned to "poison writing" after *Moby-Dick.*[70] His changing invocations of wrestling with the angel speak to the fluctuations in his experience of writing as a process whose struggles and successes are beyond his control.

Melville's poem "Art" contrasts "placid hours" with the writing process. Here the writer necessarily relies upon and struggles with "the angel" in order to produce: "These must mate,/And fuse with Jacob's mystic heart,/To wrestle with the angel—Art."[71] The "Art" that the poem imagines in its last line does not reestablish the "placid hours" with which the poem opens. Rather, the achieve-ment the poem imagines is wrestling itself, the infinitive state aspired to in the last line. Conjoined with this struggle is a scenario of wrenched mating: the creation of art is "mating" between "unlike things" in order to "pulsed life create." As early as *Mardi*—during whose composition Elizabeth became pregnant—Herman's process of writing was so intimately predicated upon his domestic relations as to be inextricable. Howard notes, for example, that during the composition of *Redburn* and *White-Jacket* in the summer of 1849, both Malcolm and Stanwix were teething, and one of them was in the hot room next to Herman's study. "But Melville kept at his desk."[72] Here it is useful to remember, too, that Bartleby makes the office his home.[73]

Howard's biographical portrait imagines domestic conditions as what Melville's writing triumphs over, rather than what its terms are constituted by. Thus he consistently imagines Melville producing despite the "womenfolk" and "as he sat before his desk in the privacy of a locked room."[74] In this sense Howard's account recapitulates Melville's own desire to disembroil himself and his writing from domestic forces. By failing to see that Melville never could disembroil his production from the domestic, Howard also fails to see the marks that failure leaves on Melville's writing. Melville himself imagines that inextricable dependence in "Art," as "unlike things" that "must meet and mate" provide the necessary but confrontational matrix for wrestling with the angel.

Just as the "angel" and the writer are sometimes cooperating and sometimes at odds—a fluctuation that in itself points to struggle as the nature of Melville's relation to art—the two-faced writing hand in the invocation from "Fragments" both mutilates and preserves. Appropriately, the lovely faces that are the objects of the narrator's hand are embodiments of his writing paper. Thus the "fragment" represents the women's faces in terms it has already appropriated for itself as a material object. The narrator implores "M——": "Lay down I beseech you that odious black-lettered volume [in your lap] and let not its musty and withered leaves sully the virgin purity and whiteness of the sheet which is the vehicle of so much good sense, sterling thought, and chaste and elegant sentiment" ("Fragments," 191). The qualities of "the sheet" of paper—virgin purity, whiteness, chasteness, and elegance—are qualities then transferred to the women whom the written surface of the paper sets out to delineate: he describes them with terms including "purity," "fair," "chaste," and "elegant." The writing hand and the mutilating hand are the same hand, and this hand takes as its objects both pieces of paper and the faces of women.

In the second sketch, the association between the faces the narrator describes and his own written page continues. He receives a mysterious billet-doux from a romantic admirer and is led to a secretive house for a rendezvous with the unknown woman. He encounters her "habited in a flowing robe of the purest white." He gazes at her silent face, tormented by desire, then realizes, "Great God, she was dumb! DUMB AND DEAF!" ("Fragments," 203, 204; emphasis in original), and flees. The virgin whiteness thematized in these sketches under the sign of the female that is metonymically the whiteness of paper is ultimately figured as a blankness or dumbness that terrifies the narrator/writer. The "virgin purity and whiteness of the sheet" with which the narrator opens the first sketch becomes the woman in a white robe that he confronts in the second; a similar metonymy associates the woman he flings from him at the conclusion of sketch No. 2 ("I flung her from me, even though she clung to my vesture, and with a wild cry of agony I burst from the apartment!" ["Fragments," 204]) with the "ancient Lexicon" he flings from him in the first sentence of that sketch ("'Confusion seize the Greek!' exclaimed I, as wrathfully rising from my chair, I flung my ancient Lexicon across the room, and seizing my hat and cane, and throwing on my cloak, I sallied out" ["Fragments," 197]). The violence directed at a book with which the sketch opens is converted into the violence directed at a woman with which it closes, reinforcing the association between pages and women and presenting both as objects to be "flung" from him.

The nature of the particular threat investing the dumb face becomes clear when we consider that the "Fragments" present themselves, above all, as a debut. Thus the narrator announces to "M——," his mentor, that he is ready to enter society, having conquered his "hang-dog modesty" and at last developed "a good opinion" of himself ("Fragments," 191, 192). The thematized textuality of the sketches (the letter of announcement, the faces/pages, the lexicon, the billet-doux) contextualizes this debut in terms explicitly linked to writing. In such a context, the final confrontation with the blank face of the "dumb" woman assumes particularly threatening overtones for the new writer confronting the white page. As he gazes into the woman's dumb face, he "met the gaze of this glorious being with a look as ardent, as burning, as steadfast as her own" ("Fragments," 203), confronting a face like his own but incapable of speech. "I cried 'Speak! Tell me, thou cruel! Does thy heart send forth vital fluid like my own? Am I loved,—even wildly, madly, as I love?'" ("Fragments," 204). The "vital fluid" that Melville felt he and Hawthorne drank mutually (the "flagon of life" he refers to in his letter to Hawthorne)[75] here threatens to go unshared. Melville was to write later, in "Hawthorne and His Mosses," that fine authors are portrait painters whose texts "almost always" sketch their own portraits ("Mosses," 249); the narrator/writer's confrontation with the dumb face in "Fragments" is one that threatens to requite him only with its power of blankness. Indeed, even the woman's first appearance leaves him "mute" ("Fragments," 203).

In the confrontation with the dumb white face that concludes sketch 2, then, the writing debut of sketch 1 ultimately gives way to a terrifying scene of writing anxiety. The mutilating force in the "Fragments" is associated with the figure of "M——" ("Guide my awkward hand, and preserve from mutilation the features ye hover over and protect! Pour down whole floods of sparkling champaigne [*sic*], my dear M——"), the closest this early text comes to naming the unwritten name of the pseudonymous author. Melville family letters routinely abbreviate the name "Melville" with the letter *M*.[76] "Fragments" was presumably written in early 1839, when Melville was living at home with his mother, his four sisters, his elder brother, Gansevoort, who had become mysteriously bedridden, and his nine-year old brother;[77] later that year he would go to sea for the first time, leaving behind (temporarily) the home that Howard's biography persistently characterizes as "adjusted to an entirely feminine regime" and thus a chronic obstacle to his writing.[78]

Both the terrifying faces and the writing anxiety return in another form in Melville's next known publication, *Typee,* as the narrator encounters not a blank face but faces marked with "the hideous blemish of tattooing" (*T* 86). I argue in chapter 1 that the terrifying tattoos in his first novel are traces of his disfiguration of both the truth the author professes to represent and of the prior texts out of which he constructs it. The presence of paper, ink, and writing in the novel is also felt in the facial tattoo patterns in Typee, which span the countenance with broad black bands, a monstrously magnified form of the delineation also crucial in "Fragments." The movement I have traced from "Fragments" to *Typee* is the swing from the writer's blank of the former to the looming presence of printed text in the latter, and simultaneously from the "female" faces/pages in "Fragments" to the fearful facial tattoos specifically associated with male Typees. The femaleness of the former speaks to the domestic scene and its writing anxiety, while the maleness of the hideously inscribed faces of *Typee* is gender-specific to the male writers from whom Melville copied, and who thus effected the effacement of the "female" blank face/page.

Melville's metonymic chain associating writing with misery, women with misery, and women with writing is both most notable and most notably symptomatic of the effects I'm describing in "The Paradise of Bachelors and the Tartarus of Maids" (1855), in which the "Tartarus of Maids" is a paper mill staffed by pale girls who incarnate the blank paper the mill produces. As the narrator beholds Blood River, the menstrual flow that powers the mill, he remarks that it's "so strange that red waters should turn out pale chee—paper, I mean,"[79] substituting blank paper for the pale cheeks of the girls, a metonymy that drives the sketch. The production of paper is further linked to the female body in this tale in its oft-noted associations with copulation, gestation, and birth.[80] Thus a "nurse formerly," presumably a midwife, who has left her profession because "business is poor in these parts," handles instead "piles of moist, warm sheets, which continually were being delivered into the woman's waiting hands" ("Tartarus," 333). By 1853–54, when the tale was composed, Herman was the only man in a household composed of women and children: his wife, Elizabeth; their three children; his mother, Maria; and his three unmarried sisters, Helen Maria, Augusta, and Frances Priscilla.[81] Thus, as several critics have pointed out, the Melville household itself seemed both to be generating children and to be staffed by virginal operatives.[82]

Criticism of the tale is largely divided over whether it is a biological allegory or an indictment of the machine age.[83] The distance that critics—and perhaps Melville as well, in writing allegorically—want to sustain between the biological and industrial elements of the story, and also between the character of the narrator and Melville himself, is a distance that needs to be collapsed. Q. D. Leavis, for example, correctly points out a link by noting that woman's toil produces Melville's children as well as his writing paper, thus drawing the biological and industrial elements of the story into relation.[84] What has not to date been grasped is that the biological and the industrial "levels" of the story are inextricably parts of *a single scenario,* by which I mean that the women who labored over Melville's children were *the same* women who produced his writing paper.

Thus the two "dimensions" of the tale that have been most compelling to critics converge in the Melvilles' domestic sphere, where Herman struggled to produce writing while the women of the household acted as laborers in the tormenting processes of both textual production and domestic economy, including child-bearing and rearing. The Melvilles' domestic sphere populated by women and children is the site of the writer's textual production, and its "girls" are his factory operatives. The fact that Melville's model for the sketch was his visit to a local paper mill in the Berkshires[85] to buy paper for his own writing merely reinforces the association between the factory girls and the women who assisted him with his writing at home. Judith A. McGaw's historical study of nineteenth-century papermaking in the Berkshires points out that the tale is a "deliberate alteration of what he [Melville] must have observed," since the mill he visited was not staffed exclusively by female workers, and they did not operate the heavy machinery. McGaw points out that, while his description of the mill and the machines is "essentially accurate," he excluded all the male workers and their jobs.[86] It is of course crucial that he eliminate the male factory operatives—but not the male boss—from his vision of production, since both the biological subtext and the operations of production in the Melville home called for female laborers.[87]

In confronting the miserable blankness of the paper the mill endlessly produces, the narrator imagines what will become of the sheets. "All sorts of writings would be writ on those now vacant things—sermons, lawyers' briefs, physicians' prescriptions, love-letters, marriage certificates, bills of divorce, registers of births, death-warrants, and so on, without end" ("Tartarus," 333). The endless production of paper simultaneously raises the specter of writing "without end"; thus the relentless production of blank paper associated with the girls challenges the narrator's own ability to produce. The endless papers he catalogs are not literary texts, but domestic matters: births, illnesses, marriages, deaths. The narrator is, of course, a "seedsman" whose seeds are disseminated in paper envelopes, but these seeds—while "intentionally" no doubt part of the sexual allegory—are more crucially a figure for Melville's own writing. Melville also figures writing as seed in "Hawthorne and His Mosses," in which Hawthorne's writing is metaphorically seminal: "But already I feel that this Hawthorne has dropped germinous seeds into my soul. He expands and deepens down, the more I contemplate him; and further, and further, shoots his strong New-England roots into the hot soil of my Southern soul" ("Mosses," 250).

As he stands watching the machinery, the narrator reflects, "A fascination fastened on me. I stood spell-bound and wandering in my soul. Before my eyes—there, passing in slow procession along the wheeling cylinders, I seemed to see, glued to the pallid incipience of the pulp, the yet more pallid faces of all the pallid girls I had eyed that heavy day. Slowly, mournfully, beseechingly, yet unresistingly, they gleamed along, their agony dimly outlined on the imperfect paper, like the print of the tormented face on the handkerchief of Saint Veronica" ("Tartarus," 333–34). The paper pulp passing before the narrator is first associated in its "pallor" with the faces of the pallid girls, reinforcing the dominant association in the tale between girls and paper. Yet the girls' "agony dimly outlined" on the paper unwittingly changes gender in the final clause, as the "pallid faces" of the girls are replaced by "the print of the tormented face on the handkerchief of Saint Veronica," a now explicitly male face, Christ's, in which the narrator's own face begins to emerge. Now the "agony" and "torment" that the tale is concerned to attribute to the girls begins to participate in an intimately related story, the story of Melville's tormented confrontation with his own writing.

The configurations of this activity were for him deeply associated with the circumstances of production in what Evert A. Duyckinck called "the daughter-full house."[88] By the time of the composition of *Mardi* (1849), Melville's third novel, his wife and his sisters had become his copyists and were necessary to his process of production. Elizabeth and at least one of Herman's sisters copied

Mardi; Elizabeth copied "Hawthorne and His Mosses" and was instrumental to the production of the poetry; Helen copied *White-Jacket* and perhaps *Pierre;* Augusta copied "The Two Temples," *The Confidence-Man,* and, apparently, "Bartleby, the Scrivener." Parker reports that Helen and Augusta were taking turns as copyist by 1850 and 1851.[89] Elizabeth had writing duties to fulfill, and her letters describe making plans for the rest of her day around her "copying." Augusta in particular was exhaustless in copying manuscript.[90] These writing duties were stressful for the Melville women. On 3 August 1851, Elizabeth wrote to her stepmother, "I cannot write any more—it makes me terribly nervous—I don't know as you can read this I have scribbled it so."[91] By the time Herman turned to poetry, his daughters Frances (Fanny) and Elizabeth (Bessie) were also put to work in the service of his writing. Eleanor recounted that Frances recalled with derision "the rhythm with which her father would recite, while pacing the floor, certain verses he had written, looking for approbation, she thought, from his wife and daughters." Herman also awakened one of his daughters at two in the morning to read proof of *Clarel.*[92] In 1879, Elizabeth complained that she was sick and "hardly able to guide my pencil"; in the same letter, she described Bessie's "poor hands," crippled with arthritis and consequently bound up in splints.[93] Assessed in their broader context, it's hard not to see the particularities of these illnesses as responses to enforced literary duties. Eleanor reports that Herman's sisters " 'were all a little afraid of him,' " that his daughters "developed resentments against him," and that Elizabeth was "emotionally unequal" to life with Herman.[94]

We also know that, at least on occasion, Elizabeth was sworn to secrecy about Herman's writing projects and about his health, and was in fact afraid to speak or write about either of these subjects. Miller notes that Herman forced Elizabeth to be secretive, and that in order to live with him she "had to accept his abuse, the anger which he projected on her, and to lie and to apologize in order to salve the feelings of relatives."[95] In 1860, she says of his poetry, "It has been such a profound secret between Herman and myself for so long." In a letter of 1869, two years after the domestic crisis with which I opened this essay, she begged, "If you see Herman, please do not tell him that I said he was *not well*" (emphasis in original). In a letter of 1875, she writes, "—pray do not mention to any one that he is writing poetry—you know how such things spread and he would be very angry if he knew I had spoken of it—."[96] The link between Elizabeth's misery and enforced silence and Herman's writing emerges starkly in a letter of 1876, declining a visit from Herman's cousin, Catherine Lansing. Enclosed inside Elizabeth's letter explaining that she and Herman were too busy reading proof to entertain a visitor was a second letter that reads as follows:

> Dear Kate, I have written you a note that Herman could see, as he wished, but want you to know how painful it is for me to write it, and also to have to give the real cause—The fact is, that Herman, poor fellow, is in such a frightfully nervous state, & particularly now with such an added strain on his mind, that I am actually *afraid* to have any one here for fear that he will be upset entirely, & not be able to go on with the printing . . . If ever this dreadful *incubus* of a *book* (I call it so because it has undermined all our happiness) gets off Herman's shoulders I do hope he may be in better mental health—but at present I have reason to feel the gravest concern & anxiety about it—to put it in mild phrase—please do not speak of it—you know how such things are exaggerated—& I will tell you more when I see you—which I hope will be before long—you know how I enjoy your visits— And I count on your affection for us, not to say your good sense, to take this as you should & in no wise feel hurt at it—Rather pity & pray for yr ever affectionate Cousin Lizzie.[97]

Elizabeth was clearly afraid of her husband, who apparently scrutinized her correspondence and commanded her secrecy. Since, as I have argued, Herman's simultaneous dependence on and resentment of Elizabeth and the other Melville women constitutes the secret "madness & anguish" of his writing, it is not at all coincidental that Herman's only "domestic" fiction, *Pierre*, is also the only one of his texts that explicitly presents the production of writing in excruciating and destructive terms.

As I note in my introduction, the women produced fair copies from which they omitted punctuation, at Herman's direction, so he could add it himself.[98] In a letter to her stepmother of 5 May 1848, Elizabeth wrote:

> I should write you a longer letter but I am very busy today copying and cannot spare the time so you must excuse it and all mistakes. I tore my sheet in two by mistake thinking it was my copying (for we only write on one side of the page) and if there is no punctuation marks you must make them yourself for when I copy I do not punctuate at all but leave it for a final revision for Herman. I have got so used to write without I cannot always think of it.[99]

If we imagine Herman scrutinizing the copies produced by his copyists, and running down his sheets of paper with quick, pointed gestures of the hand and arm—called "punctuation" because marking points resembles puncturing—we can also see that the physical act of punctuation marking that he reserved for himself speaks to an aggressive relation to his paper. Herman often invokes images of "striking," as I've already shown in chapter 2, in contexts that powerfully suggest his relation to his writing. When returning proofs of *The Piazza Tales* to Dix & Edwards, he wrote, "There seems to have been a surprising profusion of commas in these proofs. I have struck them out pretty much; but hope that some one who understands punctuation better than I do, will give the final hand to it."[100] In the manuscript for *The Marquis de Grandvin,* in which Melville meditates upon "the old philosopher penally branded with a horrible name—misogonist [*sic*], I think," he later writes: "The inordinate aim, and the inadequate achievement! The soaring ambition, and the drop at the fatal puncture of the pen."[101] This remark figures writing failure through a violent pen puncture. It also recalls the lament in *Mardi,* "Oh! that an eagle should be stabbed by a goose-quill!" (599); that stabbed eagle is also associated with Pierre's failed authorship through his eagle-shaped title-page, as I discuss in chapter 2.

Herman's metaphoric association between writing and violence emerges in a letter of 1849, after the disappointing reception of *Mardi:* "Hereafter I shall no more stab at a book (in print, I mean) than I would stab at a man.— . . . Had I not written & printed 'Mardi,' in all likelihood, I would not be as wise as I am now, or may be. For that thing was stabbed *at* (I do not say *through*)—& therefore, I am the wiser for it.—But a bit of note paper is not large enough for this sort of writing—so no more of it."[102] Here Melville analogizes "stabbing" at a book with "stabbing" at a man, suggesting that the acts are (at least) metaphorically equivalent. To Melville's particular association between different kinds of arm motion, we can add broader conceptions of handwriting in the period during which he learned to write. Writing masters of the day, among them the influential B. F. Foster, who taught at the Albany Academy, stressed that the arm was the primary force in writing. Foster's work and the Carstairian system upon which it was based taught writing first "simply by the movement of *the arm,* without any sustaining point; and to secure this, the fingers are tied, so as to be incapable of motion, and the arm is not allowed to touch the table. As soon as the perfect command of the arm is acquired in this manner, the learner is allowed to rest the part near the elbow on the table, and taught to use his fore arm."[103] Nash points out that the new word in penmanship in the forties was "muscular," and that through the forties, fifties, and beyond, "muscular means forearm movement."[104]

When Melville parenthetically qualifies his eschewal of stabbing at books—"I shall no more stab at a book (in print, I mean)"—he presumably means he will continue to criticize books outside of print (in discussion, for example). His qualification here also suggests he will continue to "stab" at books that are not yet printed, which, as I have already argued, was his relation to his own manuscript. Furthermore, while at one level his figuration of *Mardi* as a text that can be stabbed *at* but not *through* suggests that it was philosophically too thick to be demolished by its critics, at another level his language suggests a constitutive

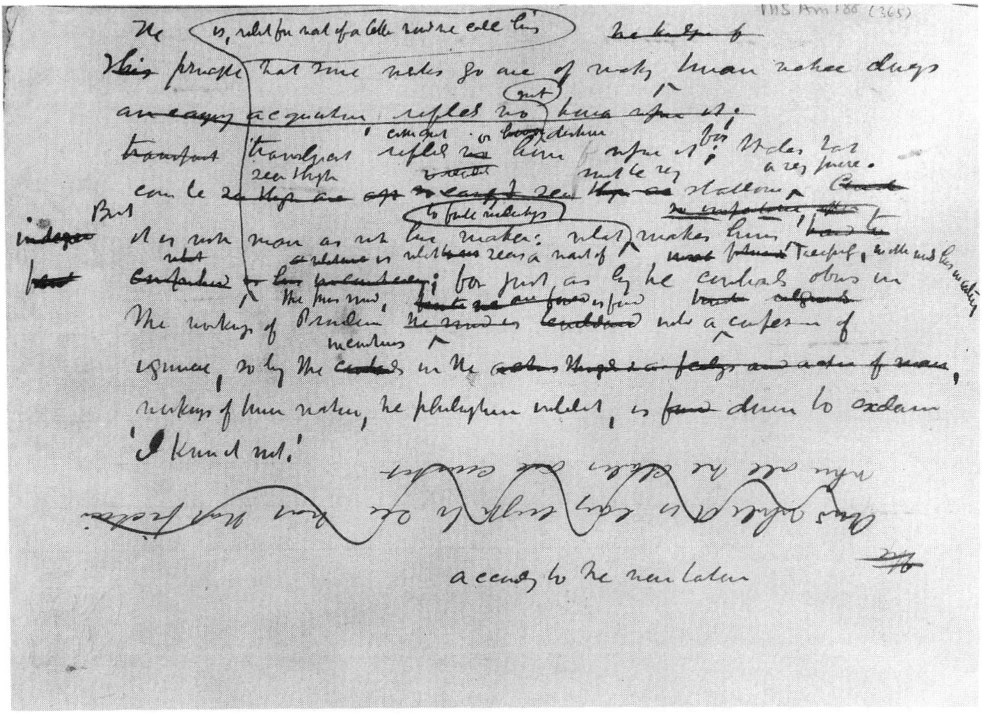

Illustration 4. Manuscript fragment from chapter 14 of *The Confidence-Man,* in Herman Melville's hand, with revisions and upside-down passage. By permission of the Houghton Library, Harvard University [bMS Am188 (365)].

inability to penetrate the surface of the text, for himself as well as for other aggressors: a blocked "striking through" that returns in Ahab's frenzied cry to "strike through the mask!" of the dead, blind wall of the white whale.

The mask that Ahab wants to strike through is specifically made of "pasteboard," the binder's board made of pasted layers of paper[105] whose resonance for the author is starkly literal. "Striking through" the pasteboard mask carries a profoundly material connotation for Melville's own relentless striking through and crossing out and rewriting in an effort to find a satisfactory relation to his own white page (see, for example, illustration 4). The pasteboard mask that can't be struck through, the text that can't be stabbed through, and the copies that he must himself punctuate are dramas of composition in which paper acts as a material site of blockage, frustrating the author's desire to penetrate and so to transcend material conditions. Thus in the letter cited above, "a bit of note paper is not large enough for this sort of writing": its material dimensions are figured as that which frustrates the author's aspirations to write beyond them, a spatial metaphor for a meta/physical problem.

The material dimensions of his writing frustrations are, I have been arguing, *constitutive of* the terms of Melville's fiction. The network of relations I've described allows us to see that "striking through" is a materially loaded gesture for Melville, in terms of his violent frustration with the pages over which he labored and with the laboring women in his household. In *Mardi*, the only woman on board the *Parki* is the pilfering Annatoo, whose presence threatens the world of her male shipmates: she takes apart the ship's instruments and drops its log overboard. But Annatoo meets an early death. During a terrible storm, "the two shrouds flew madly into the air, and one of the great blocks at their ends, striking Annatoo upon the forehead," pitches her out of the ship and into the whirlpool (*M* 117). At the end of *Pierre*, as the domestic fiction at last goes to sea, Isabel turns into Annatoo as it becomes clear that she too should be struck out of the boat. She cries, "Unhand me! Let me plunge!" Although Pierre and Lucy "mechanically . . . dragged her back," the language of the passage barely represses its desire to let her drown (355). Isabel is, of course, Pierre's copyist (282).[106] "Striking" Annatoo out of the ship, and striking women out of the fiction whose relative womanlessness has been oft remarked, would thus constitute another attempt to remove the sites of blockage—although they were not the only ones—that Herman Melville struggled with throughout his writing life.

Chapter Four

"Those mere phantoms which flit along a page" in *The Confidence-Man*

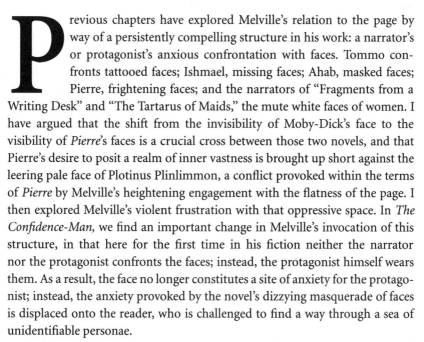

P revious chapters have explored Melville's relation to the page by way of a persistently compelling structure in his work: a narrator's or protagonist's anxious confrontation with faces. Tommo confronts tattooed faces; Ishmael, missing faces; Ahab, masked faces; Pierre, frightening faces; and the narrators of "Fragments from a Writing Desk" and "The Tartarus of Maids," the mute white faces of women. I have argued that the shift from the invisibility of Moby-Dick's face to the visibility of *Pierre*'s faces is a crucial cross between those two novels, and that Pierre's desire to posit a realm of inner vastness is brought up short against the leering pale face of Plotinus Plinlimmon, a conflict provoked within the terms of *Pierre* by Melville's heightening engagement with the flatness of the page. I then explored Melville's violent frustration with that oppressive space. In *The Confidence-Man*, we find an important change in Melville's invocation of this structure, in that here for the first time in his fiction neither the narrator nor the protagonist confronts the faces; instead, the protagonist himself wears them. As a result, the face no longer constitutes a site of anxiety for the protagonist; instead, the anxiety provoked by the novel's dizzying masquerade of faces is displaced onto the reader, who is challenged to find a way through a sea of unidentifiable personae.

The problem of writer's block has by now become chronic for Melville, not in the sense that he is unable to produce writing, but, rather, that he relates to his page as an obscuring, frustrating, resistant force against which he battles as he writes. This chronic problem that he figures in the dead, blind wall of Moby-Dick, in Ahab's desire to strike through that mask, and in Pierre's self-destructive desk habits, becomes *The Confidence-Man*'s oft-lamented "unreadability," as Melville displaces his anxiety about impenetrable faces/pages, turning that frustration onto the reader. The shift to third-person narration in *Pierre* represents for Melville a newly configured position for the observation of text itself; those features of *The Confidence-Man* often considered "unreadable" take the space Melville had begun to negotiate in *Pierre* a step further: differently configuring text as a thing to look at.

Within the plot of *The Confidence-Man,* the title character wears constantly changing faces that disable penetration. In addition to dramatic changes in costume and physical shape, his countenance changes completely with each of his manifestations. At least three of his dupes (the good merchant, the collegian, and the miser) encounter successive personae back to back, without discerning any continuity between them. When the Confidence-Man emerges as John Ringman (the man with the weed) at the start of chapter 4, having just departed the scene as the Black Guinea at the end of chapter 3, he familiarly accosts the baffled Henry Roberts (the good merchant) and asks, "Is it possible, my dear sir . . . that you do not recall my countenance? why yours I recall distinctly as if but half an hour, instead of half an age, had passed since I saw you. Don't you recall me, now? Look harder" (18). The Confidence-Man's challenge is effective precisely because he has no real face that could be recognizable. The man with the traveling-cap, another persona of the Confidence-Man, proclaims in the dimly lit emigrants' quarters, "Honesty's best voucher is honesty's face," to which his dupe, the miser, responds, "Can't see yours, though" (75).

After the man with the traveling-cap scams the miser, the miser goes in search of him and encounters the Confidence-Man's next persona, the herb doctor, and cries, " 'Why, why, why . . . why you, yes you—you, you—ugh, ugh, ugh!' " (101). His cough creates a space in which the reader is encouraged in a momentary belief that the miser has seen through the Confidence-Man's disguise. But one of the Confidence-Man's tricks is to prepare the ground for later personae by describing their appearances and recommending them highly. In this instance, the miser recognizes not the Confidence-Man's face but the clothes that the herb doctor wears, which the man with the traveling-cap has already described to him. At this moment of textual hesitation, the miser verges not on recognizing the Confidence-Man but on being further duped by him. The double edge of the chapter's title, "Reappearance of one who may be remembered," refers both, within the plot, to the Confidence-Man, who may be remembered by the miser in the space of his cough—but who is not—and, within the reading experience, to the miser, who may be remembered by the reader after the passage of several vertiginous chapters from which the miser was absent.

In this way, the Confidence-Man's face within the nominal plot and the pages of *The Confidence-Man* itself are explicitly analogized texts that both produce effects of resistance and difficulty. While within the plot of the novel the Confidence-Man wears constantly changing faces that disable the penetration of other characters, the proliferation of ambiguously and multiply identified characters (including but not limited to the title character) disables the reader. Thus the role the Confidence-Man plays within the plot is restaged at the level of the novel as a text to be read. In other words, the Confidence-Man functions within the nominal plot as a figure for the novel itself, all of whose characters in fact face the reader with resistance.

The narrator's first digression about inconsistency of character, for example, takes as its subject not the Confidence-Man, as one might expect, but the good merchant. The characters generally lack names and are identified instead by epithets like "the hook-nosed man," "the other," and "the stranger." A single epithet can apply to more than one character: "the stranger" refers to incarnations of the Confidence-Man as well as to other characters. While a single epithet might apply to different characters, at the same time each nominal character also goes by multiple epithets. Thus "the man with the weed" is also called "the unfortunate man" and "John Ringman." "The man with the big book" is also "the Man with the traveling-cap," and is further identified as the president and transfer-agent of the Black Rapids Coal Company. These epithets are the verbal "faces" of characters, the labels by which we identify them in the absence of faces to look at; for us these proliferate bewilderingly, corresponding to the proliferation of faces within the plot.

Thus the impenetrable face of *The Confidence-Man* is no longer a blind wall confronting the narrator and/or protagonist, but rather the impenetrable, "unreadable" face of the text Melville now turns on the reader. The particular terms of the well-known hostility and bafflement that characterize the reception of *The Confidence-Man* from the time of its publication on April 1, 1857, until well into the twentieth century are products of this displaced frustration. The complaint that the book cannot be read was in fact one of the characteristic features of criticism for a century after its publication. One review reported, "After reading the work forwards for twelve chapters and backwards for five, we attacked it in the middle, gnawing at it like Rabelais' dog at the bone, in the hope of extracting something from it at last." Another called *The Confidence-Man* Melville's "hardest nut to crack," and speculated, "We are not quite sure whether we have cracked it ourselves—whether there is not another meaning hidden in the depths of the subject other than that which lies near the surface." Van Wyck Brooks complained in 1947 of the book's "clutter of faceless characters and its dubious meaning." In 1954, Elizabeth S. Foster's pioneering introduction to the novel commented that its "obscurity was perhaps intentional" and reported, "Obviously, *The Confidence-Man* still keeps many, or most, of its secrets."[1]

I have argued that this notorious "unreadability" is the result of the specific changing terms of Melville's relation to his own pages. It is my contention that he achieved a greater control in *The Confidence-Man* than he had in any of his prior novels, and that that control was a product of his explicit and particular engagement with the obstructing page that was at the core of his own writing anxiety. That he turns the obstructing face outward, as I have maintained, does not necessarily function at the level of a deliberate "strategy" on Melville's part to repel readers. The fundamental aggression in his personality noted by Shneidman and others suggests more accurately that aggressive attitudes and behaviors toward his readers (among others) paradoxically coexist with his publishing ambitions,[2] a paradox that in itself constitutes another blocking configuration in Melville's troubled encounter with his own pages.

The terms in which Melville now embraces the impenetrability against which both Ahab and Pierre "strike" are worked out most strategically through the notion of "character" central to the novel. *The Confidence-Man*'s insistent meditations on the word *character* include chapter titles ("In which a variety of characters appear," "Inquest into the true character of the Herb-Doctor"), discourses among characters (which take as their subjects "character" references, confidence in or suspicion of someone's "character," the "character" of the landscape, the consistency of "character," a "character" seen in the theater, engraved Greek "characters," and so on), and the three chapters that are the narrator's asides on character (chapters 14, 33, and 44). These persistent invocations of the word *character* serve to locate it as a constant but inconsistent signifier (and indeed the fundamental inconsistency of character is the subject of chapter 14), suspending its reference and placing it in the realm of variability occupied by the Confidence-Man himself, who appears constantly but has no enduring substance beneath his changing surfaces. The link between the title figure and the signifying problem of "character" is suggested by Mark Winsome, who pronounces "a Mississippi operator" to be, finally, "an equivocal character" (196). Meanwhile, Winsome himself, who has long and correctly been identified as Emerson,[3] invokes in this very allusion writing known for its inconsistency.[4] I should add that Mark Winsome's own name alludes to the idea of a written character's (pleasant) appearance—a winsome mark—at odds with what the novel construes as a brutal philosophy.

In his examination of the *OED*'s entry for *character*, J. Hillis Miller argues that the parsing out of definitions "makes it sound as if any given use of the word *character* could be pigeon-holed neatly in one or another of the multitudinous meanings and submeanings, literal, figurative, and transferred, which it has distinguished. But any given use of the word will involve a complicated interplay among various meanings, literal and figurative, all more or less but not quite determined by the context."[5] Melville motivates the word *character* in this novel as just such a multitudinous signifier that cannot be "pigeon-holed," in Miller's phrase. Melville's presentation of "character" as an inconsistent signifier that he renders resistant to reading also places it at odds with cultural investments in the period in the "transparency" of character. Karen Halttunen's work on American advice manuals of the mid-nineteenth century demonstrates a cultural preoccupation with "character" which, according to the prevailing Lockean psychology of the time, was imagined to be like a lump of soft wax.[6] During a period in which hypocrisy was widely believed to be poisoning American social relations, the type of the confidence man emerged (although the term "confidence man" was probably not coined until 1849)[7] as a conniver whose bad influence threatened to destroy the young man's too-malleable character. The advice manuals urged young men to defend themselves against his wiles through character formation, an enterprise of self-creation and self-defense that is the moral valence of the term "*self*-made man."[8] The predominant concern with character in these manuals is part of a powerful cultural impulse that Halttunen describes as the desire to shape all social forms into sincere expressions of inner feeling. Proper conduct, according to sentimental ideology, was above all a perfect "transparency" of character, a sincerity that was readable through face-to-face encounters.[9] This rage for transparency was also expressed by way of the cultural fascination with systems of correspondence between outer shape and inner meaning, among them physiognomy and phrenology. The narrator rejects the allure of such transparency, remarking that all systems "having for their end the revelation of human nature on fixed principles, have, by the best judges, been excluded with contempt from the ranks of the sciences," including among them palmistry, physiognomy, phrenology, and psychology (71).

The novel's extended reflection on the word *character* in fact insistently critiques presumptions of epistemological transparency, a transparency Melville first presents as impossible and then replaces with various forces of opacity and obstruction. Primary among these antitransparent forces is the text's own material surface. "Transparency" is a word chapter 14 specifically invokes as the opposite of the "inconsistency" the novel embraces as its own realm: "Always, they [authors] should represent human nature not in obscurity, but transparency" (70), Melville writes, and in his draft of the chapter we can see a lingering focus on the word "transparent."[10] In the same chapter, the narrator notes that readers dislike inconsistent characters "from perplexity as to understanding them," and asks: "If the acutest sage be often at his wits' end to understand living character, shall those who are not sages expect to run and read character in those mere phantoms which flit along a page, like shadows along a wall?" (69). The opacity of personal character that refutes all systems of correspondence between inner and outer is transformed here into a corollary opacity located specifically on the page: Melville aligns the unreadable opacity of character with the unreadable marks on the page, which have now become "phantoms." Crucially, these phantoms take precedence over "living character": the "if . . . then" logic of the passage as presented indicates the chapter's greater investment in the characters that "flit along a page."[11] Melville's model of writing in the novel, as I will show, distills issues of "content" onto the surface of the page and ultimately to the level of the written character as such as an opaque and obstructing site.

These "phantoms" that are now explicitly marks on a page recall the phantoms that emerge in *Moby-Dick* and *Pierre,* the furtive, "looming," and vaguely threatening forms I read as responses to Melville's scene of writing. Moby-Dick is the "grand hooded phantom" that Ishmael first sees at the end of "Loomings" as he contemplates the chapters to follow, and it is through this whale-wall "shoved near" that Ahab would strike; and the destructive phantoms Pierre sees disembarking in his soul ultimately become the looming pale face of Plinlimmon at which Pierre looks up from his desk. In *The Confidence-Man* those phantoms materialize as written characters on a page. When the narrator critiques as facile those novels whose characters can "be comprehended at a glance" (70), the implicit alternative—the novel that meets the "glance" of the beholder with resistance—is precisely the alternative visual scenario with which *The Confidence-Man* identifies itself. Its pages and the "phantoms" upon them are the blocking forces that obstruct the "glance" that Melville now attributes to a reader ("those who are not sages [who] expect to run and read character").

The page as a site of blockage resisting attempts to strike through is figured

in terms not only of inconsistency and opacity, but also of a flatness or emptiness that renders attempts to penetrate futile. In Melville's revealing revisions to
chapter 14, he repeatedly worked over the phrase "in those mere phantoms
which flit along a page, like shadows along a wall." "Phantoms" was "ghosts" in
an earlier draft; "mere" was "empty"; the "shadows" were described as "equally
empty"; and "a page" was originally "the novelist's page."[12] We can see from
these revisions that Melville's notion of "mere" phantoms grew out of a notion
of emptiness attributed to his own ("the novelist's") written page as a site of flat
resistance to penetration. This scenario reconfigures Ishmael's metaphor of the
subterranean miner who cannot "pick" through the surface of the page. The
flattening out of depth within "the novelist's page" also fully materializes (as a
page) the outcome of *Pierre*'s anxiety about whether what Pierre fails to see is
receding at a great distance or pushed up right beneath his face.

The novel's insistent meditations on the word *character* are thus fundamentally tied to its thematization of its own materiality and of its "characters"
(in the sense of its personages) as "mere" written "characters" scrawled across a
page. The word *character* derives from a Greek word that signifies an instru-
ment for marking or graving, and its denotations derive from its etymological
association with writing.[13] Melville was of course deeply conversant with and
interested in definitions and etymologies. *The Confidence-Man*'s exploitation of
literary character as a graphic realm is deeply rooted in the signifying history of
the term as well as in prevailing cultural notions of personal character as
inscription on a malleable surface.[14] Miller's exploration of the signifying do-
main of the word *character* points to its many meanings as "an intimate chain
or network of correspondences. To interpret someone's character (handwriting) is to interpret his character (physiognomy) is to interpret his character
(personality) is to interpret his character (some characteristic text he has written), in a perpetual round of figure for figure. To read character is to read
character is to read character is to read character."[15] While Miller's study does
not take Melville as its subject, his analysis sheds important light on Melville's
etymologically motivated exuberance with the word. But the particularities of
Melville's engagement with character also depart from Miller's assessment,
because Melville's confrontation with the specifically material presence of character ultimately inflects *The Confidence-Man* in a different direction than Miller's perpetual round of figuration, as I will show.

The graphic qualities of the title character—I use the word *graphic* to
denote that which is drawn with a pencil or pen, pertaining to drawing, painting, or writing—are particularly striking in his first two embodiments, the
starkly white "man in cream-colors" with his fair cheek, flaxen hair, and white

fur hat (3), and the starkly black Black Guinea, a "grotesque negro cripple" with "black fleece," "black face," and "an old coal-sifter of a tambourine" (10). This opening black-and-white contrast sets the scene for a confidence game of black writing on a white page. The speculation about the Black Guinea is that his blackness is literally "put on" white: "He's some white operator, betwisted and painted up for a decoy" (14). A number of the Confidence-Man's subsequent manifestations are also associated with shades of black and white, including the agent of the Black Rapids Coal Company, the man with the weed in mourning dress, the man in a gray coat and white tie, and the herb-doctor in a snuff-colored surtout (74). "Snuff-colored," the brownish color of pulverized tobacco, here also carries the denotation of "snuff" as the black charred portion of a wick, a proleptic figure for the extinguished light that concludes the novel. Other characters, too, are identified by shades of black and white, among them the gentleman with gold sleeve-buttons with his strikingly white accoutrements and negro body-servant (36), the woman in a mourning "twilight" dress (43), and the man named Pitch.[16] Later, Frank points out that Shakespeare's character Autolycus "in that paper-and-ink investiture of his, . . . acts more effectively upon mankind than he would in a flesh-and-blood one" (172), both conflating clothing with paper and ink (thus strengthening the paper-and-ink connotations of white and black clothing) and, in turn, associating literary "character" with marks on a page.

The confidence game of writing on a page motivates the novel's thematized preoccupation with the production of "papers" for authentication, as well as the Confidence-Man's fondness for books and papers as props. Chapter 1 opens with a placard offering a reward for the capture of a "mysterious imposter" (3) who is thus from the outset conceived in printed terms. The crowd surrounding the Black Guinea request "documentary proof . . . any plain paper . . . attesting that his case was not a spurious one" (13), and although he cannot provide such papers, he offers instead his oft-discussed catalog of "ge'mmen" who can speak for him. The Black Guinea's catalog metonymically associates the "papers" he lacks with the "ge'mmen" whose descriptions he provides as substitutes. These "ge'mmen" in turn carry, or claim to carry, the "papers" for which they stand. When the agent of the Seminole Widow and Orphan Asylum is asked, "Of course you have papers?" he responds, "Of course," and produces the memorandum book and pencil in which he promises to record contributions for publication (33–34). The "president and transfer-agent" of the Black Rapids Coal Company carries a large book with a gilt inscription, and a "small, printed pamphlet" (48) stating the condition of the company. The herb-doctor produces "a printed voucher . . . duly signed" testifying to the effectiveness of his products (88). The cosmopolitan substitutes the barber's notice with a written agreement of his own design: " 'Now, then, for the writing,' said the cosmopolitan . . . ' . . . Strange, barber,' taking up the blank paper, 'that such flimsy stuff as this should make such strong hawsers' " (234–35). F. O. Matthiessen thus did not realize in what way he was right when he rejected *The Confidence-Man* as "two-dimensional."[17]

As the previous discussion indicates, I mean to register my claim that *The Confidence-Man* insists that we see its characters as "mere" written characters scrawled across a page, at least in this primary formulation, at the level of Melville's "intentions" for the project. Several studies have pointed out the novel's prevalent motifs of writing, such as the early description of the Fidele's design as one "like secret drawers in an escritoire" (8). I want both to accept the centrality of this theme and to differ from existing assessments of how we are to understand its implications by stressing its material relation to the configurations of Melville's own scene of writing.[18] Seen in these terms, the theme of writing specifically speaks to Melville's relation to his own pages as one he imagines in terms of resistance, and the novel's implementation of graphic characters and their papers are not invocations of writing in a vaguely thematic sense, but rather consequences of Melville's specific relations to the pieces of paper, either blank or in the process of inscription, that he looks at as he sits at his desk.

That *The Confidence-Man*'s characters scrawled across a page constitute a site of blockage is figured within the terms of the plot during a discussion between Mark Winsome and the cosmopolitan:

> "I conjecture him to be what, among the ancient Egyptians, was called a ——" using some unknown word.
> "A ——! And what is that?"
> "A —— is what Proclus, in a little note to his third book on the theology of Plato, defines as —— ——" coming out with a sentence of Greek. (193)

The literally unreadable and insistent dashes that appear in this exchange constitute Winsome's definition of "an operator, a Mississippi operator" (196). The uninterpretable words for which the unreadable dashes stand are thus the name of both the title character and the title of the novel: "Confidence-Man." This exchange presents the novel's signature in a series of dashes, a signature whose effect is one in which the graphic crosses from signification to impenetrability, from characters that can be read to mere marks on the page that obstruct such attempts.

The crossover in *Pierre* from invisible depths to visible marks whose sight is "tragic" is reconfigured in *The Confidence-Man* as a crossing from legible to impenetrable marks. In some cases, as in the previous instance, these impenetrable marks are illegible ("———"); in other cases, they are legible words but impenetrable signifiers (for example, the "Indian," a word we can read but whose meaning is impenetrable, as I will discuss later). The rhetorical and logical mark of the crucial crossing from signification to impenetrability in *The Confidence-Man* is tautology, precisely that threat from which the narrator of *Pierre* shrinks.[19] In *The Confidence-Man*, Melville explores rather than defers the blocking force of tautology that he associates with the material presence of writing.[20] As the written pages of *The Confidence-Man* insist upon the opacity of their own writtenness, rather than conceiving of that writtenness as transparent, they become the note from Pierre to Glen that the narrator of *Pierre* could not bear to reproduce. By this I mean that one of the constitutive tautologies in *The Confidence-Man* is precisely that which threatens in Pierre's note: a character is a character. In *Pierre*, reproducing the material characters of Pierre's letter to Glen threatens to block the transmission of "ideas themselves" through precisely the tautology that the latter novel now embraces as its subject and method.

The *Confidence-Man*'s extended reflection upon character as a realm of antitransparent written marks accompanies an implementation of tautological constructions through which we can see some of the consequences of character as a "theme." The narrator's three chapters on character in fact fall under the three tautological chapter titles: "Worth the consideration of those to whom it may prove worth considering," "Which may pass for whatever it may prove to be worth," and "In which the last three words of the last chapter are made the text of the discourse, which will be sure of receiving more or less attention from those readers who do not skip it."[21] Tautology, as a matter of style, repeats a phrase or word; as a matter of logic, it takes a statement as its own cause. Tautological constructions act as mirrors, reflecting one proposition with another version of itself. This mirror effect suspends language at the level of its own materiality, refusing to penetrate its surface in order to "mean" something.[22] Thus tautology violates the proposition that the surface of language has an "inside" or space of meaning, instead offering itself *as* language, twice. As Charlie says to Frank—both of them confidence men, an embodiment of the tautological structure essential to the novel—"Agreeable, how we always agree" (160).

One tautological plot device appears when the good merchant tells the agent of the Black Rapids Coal Company the story of the unfortunate man (chapter 12), thus repeating to one incarnation of the Confidence-Man a story told to him by another. The Confidence-Man's technique of authenticating his own specious forms of circulation by recommending one of his incarnations under the guise of another one is a tautological method for establishing credit. Foster points out that the structure of the novel is one in which the final scenes of the book "suggest incidents and ideas of the beginning but in reverse order mostly, as though the novel were being unrolled towards the beginning at the same time as towards the end." For example, in the first scene the lamblike man's message is juxtaposed with the barber's sign, and the barber and his philosophy return at the end; the Confidence-Man's second incarnation, the Black Guinea, mirrors the next-to-last one, the man with the brass plate.[23] The rhetorical corollary to these structural mirrors opens chapter 14: "As the last chapter was begun with a reminder looking forwards, so the present must consist of one glancing backwards" (69).

In chapter 14, the narrator's first aside on character, he tells us that human nature cannot be systematically understood because, although the "grand points of human nature are the same to-day as they were a thousand years ago," their "expression" is variable (71). He writes: "But as, in spite of seeming discouragement, some mathematicians are yet in hopes of hitting upon an exact method of determining the longitude, the more earnest psychologists may, in the face of previous failures, still cherish expectations with regard to some mode of infallibly discovering the heart of man" (71). The "face" that asserts itself here in rhetorical terms ("in the face of previous failures") is motivated by an implicit opposition to the metaphorical heart that concludes the sentence ("the heart of man").[24] The face here is the emblem of "failures" to penetrate, a failure under whose auspices the chapter is introduced by way of its tautological title.

In the other two asides on character, chapters 33 and 44, Melville implicates character in similarly tautological operations. Chapter 33 discusses critical readers who desire characters from "real life" (182) and refers them to chapter 14 ("all such readers . . . are now referred to that chapter where some similar apparent inconsistency in another character is, on general principles, modestly endeavored to be apologized for" [183]). Here the narrator's strategy is not to hand over "real life," but instead merely another chapter already embedded in the novel's tautological operations. Hence his parting shot to such readers: "One word more." Chapter 44 takes the concluding words of the previous chapter, "Quite an Original," as its text, thus implicating characters themselves—in this case, the letters "Quite an Original"—in the discussion of "original characters in fiction" that the chapter takes as its ostensible subject.

The tautological suspension of the novel's "characters" at the material surface of the text is one Melville plays with as the Confidence-Man subtly and wittily flattens out the illusions of depth upon which he and novels as such capitalize, insisting upon the page itself as the site of the novel's tautological operations. The exchange with the good merchant warrants requoting: "Is it possible, my dear sir . . . that you do not recall my countenance? why yours I recall distinctly as if but half an hour, instead of half an age, had passed since I saw you. Don't you recall me, now? Look harder" (18). The distinction between "half an hour" and "half an age" is the difference between kinds of plot-time: the time of the scam with its illusions of "half an age" and the secret time of the Confidence-Man's change of disguise in half an hour.[25] The subtext to both of these kinds of plot-time is the time of the reader's experience of the text in general and of the Confidence-Man's time-scam in particular. The Confidence-Man's claim that "half an age" has passed since the last encounter between the two men proffers a ruse of depth not only to the dupe he scams here but also to his equivalent, the reader who enters into fiction ready to believe that "half an age" can pass in "half an hour" with a few turns of the page. The narrative similarly empties itself out in the title of chapter 11, "Only a page or so," and in another title Melville drafted but did not use: "Less than a page."[26]

The tautological suspension of characters at the surface of the page is further invoked by the use of number in chapters 11, 33, and 44. As these double numbers repeat written marks—11, 33, 44—they extend the chapters' interest in tautology, working out a further materialization of marks as such like that worrying *Pierre*. There, notes written by Wonder & Wen, Peter Pence, and Donald Dundonald threaten, in their alliterative use of character (*WW, PP, DD*), the "tautology" (*P* 227) of marks that finally overtakes the narrator when he refuses to reproduce Pierre's letter to Glen. Such tautology is reconfigured here in *The Confidence-Man* as Melville not only duplicates written marks but abstracts such marks even further from a realm of content than did *Pierre*: both by using numbers rather than letters and by placing them in what, in the context of a novel, is usually a signifying space unrelated to the content of the novel itself: the number in the chapter heading.

The rhetorical corollary to the materialization of text that I've been describing (by which I mean the obtrusion of physical text itself as inscribed paper) is a phenomenon characteristic of the Confidence-Man's rhetoric in which words *as words* become the subject of his discourse. It is this feature of his rhetoric that motivates the charges that the Missourian, Pitch, makes against the Philosophical Intelligence Officer, whom he accuses of being a "punster": "Yes, you pun with ideas as another man may with words" (124), he remarks. The substance of Pitch's mind-bendingly abstruse accusation is that, as a punster, the Confidence-Man plays with ideas, creating seeming analogies whose terms have a superficial connection—a connection established merely through the juxtaposition of words—but not a substantive one. By proposing an analogy *as such,* the Philosophical Intelligence Officer asserts a connection between ideas; but, as Pitch discerns, the analogies are wordplay with no "deeper" (signifying) foundation: they are merely verbal assertions of connection. Thus the form of the P.I.O. Officer's language makes claims for its content that are in fact empty.[27]

That the novel takes characters and words as subjects as it insists on the tautological opacity of the page becomes clear in chapter 29. Frank and Charlie sit down together over a bottle of wine:

> A common quart bottle, but for the occasion fitted at bottom into a little bark basket, braided with porcupine quills, gayly tinted in the Indian fashion. This being set before the entertainer, he regarded it with affectionate interest, but seemed not to understand, or else to pretend not to, a handsome red label pasted on the bottle, bearing the capital letters, P.W.
>
> "P.W.," said he at last, perplexedly eyeing the pleasing poser, "now what does P.W. mean?"
>
> "Shouldn't wonder," said the cosmopolitan gravely, "if it stood for port wine. You called for port wine, didn't you?" (160–61)

The summary solution to the mystery of the characters *P* and *W,* after which the cosmopolitan comments, "I find some little mysteries not very hard to clear up," is subtly derailed throughout the chapter, which takes this label-text for its unstated subject. Irwin nicely points out that " 'P.W.' could stand for any number of two-word combinations with these initials."[28] The subsequent discourses upon "pure wine," poison wine ("He who could mistrust poison in this wine would mistrust consumption in Hebe's cheek"), and promising wine ("this wine with its bright promise") stand as other candidates for the "meaning" of the characters in question.[29] Melville begins the chapter with a subtle anticipation of the graphic manipulations to follow. The opening words, "THE WINE, PORT, being called for," call attention through reversal (wine port/port wine) to the material malleability of the words and letters as such that will be the subject of the chapter.[30]

The permutations of the constant *P* in chapter 29 spin well beyond port, pure, poison, and promising wine. In fact, the letter *p* dominates the extensively alliterative chapter throughout. When Charlie reports, "I saw a good thing the other day; capital thing; a panegyric on the press" (165), the forceful alliteration of the particular "capital thing" he cites, the panegyric on the press—here presumably meaning "capital" as "first-rate"—also calls attention to the letter *p* that dominates the group of words as such. Thus the alliterative "capital thing" recalls "the capital letters, P.W.," subordinating the content of the "capital thing" to the material presence of a thing made out of capitals. The panegyric is, of course, itself a text—"I got it by heart at two readings" (165)—thus literally a thing made of letters.

It is the logic of the character as such that motivates the bizarre production of seemingly arbitrary topics of conversation in chapters 29 and 30, from Charlie's pledge, Aristotle's "Politics," the panegyric on the press, and the apostle Paul to Polonius, the Puritans, Pizarro, and Peru. The character p also motivates the terms of the dialogue ("Pardon, pardon," "practical punning," "panacea"), the phenomena peripheral to the conversation (Charlie laughs, "pointing to the figure of a pale pauper-boy" [163]), and the narrator's descriptive language ("placidly pleased," "princely kindness," "perplexedly eying the pleasing poser"). The effect of the insistence on the p flattens the dimensions of the scene that conventionally create a novel's illusion of depth—narration, dialogue, plot, and setting (on a steamer on the Mississippi, with emphasis, for my purposes, on the sound of the last syllable)—onto the written surface of the paper.

The chapter's attention to graphic characters and the implications of their status as writing converge with the "characters" of Frank and Charlie. They are "characters" in the conventional sense that they are among the novel's cast of personalities and also in the sense that both, as con men, are also actors, performing "in character." When Frank recollects the story of Phalaris, the capricious tyrant of Sicily, he and Charlie simultaneously exclaim opposite sentiments:

"Funny Phalaris!"
"Cruel Phalaris!"

This exchange presents another word-subject—by which I mean a word that, *as word*, is the subject of discussion—in the name "Phalaris" that falls under the capital p. In setting up the contrast here between the boon companions who profess to share identical sentiments, Melville also juxtaposes the graphic characters that, as the capital letters of their names, are synecdochically associated with them (f and c, "Funny" and "Cruel," "Frank" and "Charlie"). The letters c and f are also associated with the constant (although variable) p ("Cruel Phalaris!" "Funny Phalaris!"), the floating character that presides over the verbal legerdemain that constitutes the chapter. Although neither line of dialogue is attributed to a speaker, Charlie's laughter at the "pale pauper-boy" at least suggests that it is he who finds humor in suffering and thus is the one who says

Phalaris is "Funny" while Frank says he's "Cruel," a chiastic shift that associates Frank with *C* and Charlie with *F*, a graphic version of their identic shifts and exchanges. But of course the lines are specifically not attributed to speakers; the two letters and the two men are equivalent tokens in a confidence game of characters. Frank, after all, is also the cosmopolitan, and so remarks to Charlie (known at this point as "the stranger"), "Our sentiments agree so, that were they written in a book, whose was whose, few but the nicest critics might determine" (158).

Melville's graphic effects with other letters extend the confidence game of characters and their changing manifestations out of which the "plot" of the chapter is generated. *W*, for example, motivated by the label in question, appears in formulations like "western pottery" (168), spun out of W.P./P.W. The *w* that potentially designates wine thus also represents the presence of writing as such in a chapter self-consciously obsessed with graphic effects. The notions of "pure writing," "poison writing," "promising writing," and "port writing"— substituting "writing" for "wine" in all cases—are signatures for Melville's writing career. His agonized relation to writing (pure/poison) and his early success (promising) are written into the first three formulations, while "port" suggests his career as a writer of sea stories, including this one in which the Fidele makes port stops throughout. That writing can fall under the rubric of "poison" is clear elsewhere in the novel, when the man with the weed dismisses the book the collegian is reading as "poison, moral poison"—a book also significantly described as "shallow" (26). The connotations this *w* carries as a sign for "writing" concomitantly suggest a materialized *p* that is print on a page of paper in a world in which characters are made of black print on a white page. Earlier in the novel, when the Black Guinea is asked to produce the "papers" to prove that his case is not spurious, he bemoans that he "haint none o' dem waloable papers" (13), transposing the letters "P.W." and this time designating the *p* as "papers." But the characters "P.W." importantly remain ultimately inconsistent as signifiers, within which inconsistency they conjure the material presence of writing itself: for Melville, a tautological force that disables penetration to a realm of truth.

The space opened within *The Confidence-Man* for Melville's own history of authorship starts to complicate the *p* that I have read so far as motivated at an "intentional" level for graphic effects. The obsessive inscription of *p*-effects begins to exhibit more uncanny ties to other moments in Melville's writing life. For example, just as *The Confidence-Man* graphicizes the terms of *Pierre*, so that Plotinus Plinlimmon's preternaturally white face becomes in *The Confidence-Man* the face of the text, the *p*-effects in the later novel constitute a graphic distillation of the face of *Plotinus Plinlimmon* and the character *Pierre*. According to the *OED*, the letter *p* is an abbreviation for proper names beginning with *p*, and "p." and "pp." are also abbreviations for "page" and "pages," respectively. The pronunciation of "Pierre" in particular emphasizes the name of the initial letter.

The graphic connotations of the letter *p* resonate in the phrase "p's and q's," which meant, in nineteenth-century usage, one's words or one's letters. The *OED* suggests that this construction might have sprung from the difficulty with which a child discriminates the letter *p* from the letter *q*, its mirror image, in learning to read and write. *P* is thus a particular letter, the child's written letter *p* as well as the prototype of the letter, standing, as in "p's and q's," for any letter. Given the prevalence of terms and metaphors in the English language springing from print culture,[31] a more persuasive origin for the need to mind one's "p's and q's" would be the compositor's imperative to return types for particular letters to the section of the case in which they belonged—the letters *p*, *q*, *b*, and *d* being especially tricky because they could be mistaken for one another if the types were turned the wrong way.[32] The letters *p* and *q* also follow one another in the alphabet, and thus face each other like a mirror in the chain of alphabetic characters, looking forward and backward like the image with which Melville opens chapter 14.

The *OED* tells us that *p* "presents probably a greater number of unsolved etymological problems than any other letter." One need only think of Melville's extensive and scrupulous use of the word *character* in *The Confidence-Man*, his etymological implementation of the name Pierre in that novel (which means "stone" and resonates in the novel's extended imagery of brick and stone, as critics have noted),[33] and the Etymology and Extracts sections of *Moby-Dick* to realize the practical and theoretical interest that etymology, word relationships, and, as the present discussion contends, letters as such held for him. In this regard, Melville's association of the deaf-mute with the Confidence-Man also resonates in the letter *p*, which, phonetically, can be a "mute" letter.[34] At the end of the narrator's reflection upon character in chapter 14, in a passage I cited earlier for other reasons, we learn that all systems "having for their end the revelation of human nature on fixed principles, have, by the best judges, been excluded with contempt from the ranks of the sciences." The narrator's list of such systems is "palmistry, physiognomy, phrenology, and psychology" (71), all of which, need I stress, begin with the letter *p*. The *p* that functions as Melville's obstruction on the surface of the page is thus also the metaphorical obstruction—a character flaw, as it were—that graphically derails the systems the narrator here rebukes.

One scrap of paper among the manuscripts of *The Confidence-Man*, with a draft for the title of chapter 40 (the story of China Aster) in Melville's customary hurried and illegible script on one side, presents, on the other side, in uncharacteristically careful and even ornamental print, the large centered words "First Part." Centered beneath them appears a precisely formed capital letter "P" (see illustration 5). This sole "P" is inscribed differently than is the "P" in "Part," as if constituting a different character, and its central and lone placement on the page suggests that it was written not as the first letter of a word or paragraph, but rather as the character "P" as such. The editors of the Northwestern-Newberry edition conclude from this scrap only that Melville was contemplating dividing the work into labeled parts during a late stage of composition. In the Historical Note, Branch et al. describe the scrap "with only the centered words 'First Part' " (309). The single "P" goes unremarked, as does the fact that these handwritten letters are formed and laid out with a care unlike any of the other manuscript fragments,[35] a discovery of particular interest in terms of the argument at hand because it illustrates not only Melville's graphic awareness of characters, of white space, and of laying characters onto white space, but also his predilection for the letter *p*.

Of three manuscript scraps among the extant manuscript pages from *The Confidence-Man*, each written on both sides of the paper, five of the six are inscribed horizontally across the width of the page. Only in the case of the "First Part/P" is the paper turned in a vertical direction, more notably so in that the writing on the other side is inscribed horizontally.[36] This "P" enacts with a sheet of paper within the horizontal plane of writing on a desk the projection of the face of Plinlimmon into the vertical plane in *Pierre*, a projection that I argued is a verticalization of the horizontal space of the written page before him.

Melville often pinned or pasted revisions into his text on horizontal scraps.[37] Since he usually cut his horizontal scraps out of the full-size pages on which he was composing, these scraps are often of the same width as his full pages, but only a fraction of their length. The vertical scrap is additionally anomalous in this regard, since its vertical direction indicates that it is clearly not intended to be pinned or pasted horizontally across a full-size sheet as an insert. Furthermore, the fact that the writing on it is centered within the space of the scrap suggests that it was itself visualized as a "whole" sheet. For these reasons, I believe that Melville saw this scrap as an image of a full page, which further supports my claims about its relation to verticalization in *Pierre*.

The image of a "whole" sheet of writing paper that informs Melville's use of the "P" scrap also supports my claim that the spectral presence of the page,

First Part

P

which "loomed" and "lurked" in *Moby-Dick* and *Pierre*, lies "behind" the terms of *The Confidence-Man*. That a spectral presence of "the novelist's page" as a looming white phantom resonates within Melville's writing life as a persistently haunting image is one I read into the figuration of pages in *The Confidence-Man* as white forms, despite the fact that the surviving manuscript leaves of the novel are in fact light blue. Pierre's writing paper, too, is "significantly stamped, 'Ruled; Blue'" (270), the punning significance of which is both his oppression by his writing paper ("ruled") and the affect produced by his relation to it. According to the 1847 Webster, "blue" indicates "lowness of spirits; melancholy" as well as "to be confounded or terrified."

The shift from one kind of verticality to another—that is, from positing a face in a vertical space wherein Pierre looks up at it from his desk, to changing the direction of a horizontal sheet of paper on a desk—enacts the full materialization of the page in two dimensions that the narrative trajectory from *Pierre* to *The Confidence-Man* also works out in the ways I have been describing. To these verticalizations we can add the opening scene in chapter 1, in which the deaf-mute, whom I have already described as a writer figure, confronts a "placard" that describes the "mysterious imposter" who is presumably himself in a more explicitly textualized form. This specular scene recasts Melville's claim in "Hawthorne and His Mosses" that authors write their own portraits into their work: in this case, Melville presents an author looking at his text in the figure of the deaf-mute looking at a verbal description of himself. The confrontation with the placard again verticalizes the text, turning it into a mirror of the author's textual face. The connection is strengthened by the fact that the deaf-mute holds the slate on which he writes "up before him on a level with the placard, so that they who read the one might read the other" (4). Here the deaf-mute enacts a metonymy in which the printed poster describing the Confidence-Man stands next to the handwritten manuscript, conjoining the printed text with the author's act of writing and simultaneously displaying the difference between the two.

This cream-colored deaf-mute figure recalls the white deaf-mute woman in "Fragments from a Writing Desk" (1839), whose face threatens the emerging author in ways I delineate at length in chapter 3. But the Confidence-Man/author figure himself now occupies the position of deaf-mute whiteness that is threatening in "Fragments" and that the earlier narrator confronts and flees. Furthermore, the author/deaf-mute is not terrified as was the narrator of

Illustration 5. Manuscript fragment from *The Confidence-Man:* "First Part/P." By permission of the Houghton Library, Harvard University [bMS Am188 (365)].

the earlier sketch; instead, he is placid, and the anxiety has been displaced onto the crowd. These displacements of threat and anxiety enact the structural adjustment in facial confrontations with which I began this chapter.

The deaf-mute and his inscriptions on his slate in fact present the master trope of writing in the novel. He traces a series of phrases combining the constant initial word "Charity" with changing complements: "Charity thinketh no evil"; "Charity suffereth long, and is kind"; "Charity endureth all things"; "Charity believeth all things"; "Charity never faileth" (4–5). "The word charity, as originally traced, remained throughout uneffaced, not unlike the left-hand numeral of a printed date, otherwise left for convenience in blank" (5). Melville invokes the same structure when "a charitable lady" begins "twenty different sentences, and left off at the first syllable of each. At last, in desperation, she hurried out, 'Tell me, sir, for what do you want the twenty dollars?' " (45). Twenty sentences become twenty syllables and then twenty dollars in the space of a paragraph. The character *p* operates according to the same model, appearing as a constant initial letter attached to endlessly shifting companion characters (*port, pure, poison, promise*). The text's graphic effects based on this structure also manipulate and vary the constant syllable *char*, from which spring the words *charity, Charlie, Charlemont, charming, charlatan*, and *character*, all of which appear frequently.[38] *Char* also means a charred substance, like the snuff discussed earlier, and the extinguished light that concludes the novel.

The textual preoccupation with the syllable *char* and its expanded forms also provides one subtle motivation for Melville's choice of the eccentric name "China Aster," a near-acrostic for *character*:

CH*INA* ASTER
CH   ARACTER[39]

In Melville's often nearly illegible hand, the words *character* and *characters* are so compressed that their graphic presence suggests other words. In writing *characters*, for example, Melville's hand typically leaves out the middle syllable (*ac*), so that the word looks more like *charters*. The graphic presence of the word thus shades into other signifiers, which reinforces my hunch that *character* shades into *China Aster* through a repetition and displacement of characters.[40] Robert Sattelmeyer and James Barbour have persuasively argued that Melville borrowed this name from a contemporary popular religious annual for young people, *The China Aster*.[41] If they are correct and I am also correct, then this name was one Melville used both to parody the homiletic and, at the same time, to opacify a signifier for it. Melville again strategically invokes the aster in a similarly opacified form in the poem "Field Asters," in which asters are figures for his own explicitly unreadable poems. There, Melville designates the asters "wild ones," which recall the "wildings" in Melville's title for the unpublished volume in which the poem was included—*Weeds and Wildings, with a Rose or Two.* This echo is one sign that the asters figure his poems. The drama of the poem is one of thwarted interpretation: "But who their cheer/Interpret may, or what they mean/When so inscrutably their eyes/Us star-gazers scrutinize" (ll. 5–8).[42] The asters remain inscrutable objects of vision.[43]

That Melville's practices of inscription sometimes emptied out the difference between nominally distinct signifiers is suggested in miniature by one of his drafts of chapter titles. One item reads, "The Philanthropist & Misanthrope," followed by something the editors of the Northwestern-Newberry edition interpret as "The Rifle & Pipe."[44] That reading may in fact be correct; but the handwriting looks very much like "The Pipe & Pipe." Even if these are two different words, and I am willing to accept that they may be, their graphic presence is nearly identical. The suggestion of tautology here operates both at the level of logic (in the repetitive formulation) and at the graphic level (in the near-identical graphic forms themselves). My suggestion is thus that the long-noted problems of reading Melville's hand—problems that he was also aware of, and that had informed his writing history in important ways—are problems of illegibility that inform his thematization of resistant pages in this novel. The word *character*, as I've already noted, also means handwriting.

Melville's compositional practices also generate the terms of *The Confidence-Man* in other ways. The endless variations Melville plays against what I have designated as constants at the level of word (for example, *character*), syllable (for example, *char*), and character (for example, *p*) are thematized versions of his characteristic compositional practices, including heavy revisions, cross-outs, and substitutions. Only an unfortunately thin group of Melville's manuscript leaves is known to exist, and the manuscript pages for *The Confidence-Man* constitute the only batch of manuscript material known to survive from any of his published books of the 1850s.[45] The evidence we do have of Melville's processes of composition indicates that his writing was characterized by frequent false starts, word and phrase substitutions, revisions, and transpositions,[46] aspects of the labor of writing as such that *The Confidence-Man* thematizes in structurally analogous ways.

The model of variations played against a constant germ is a version of one of the seed techniques of Melville's writing. He often began to write with a packed sentence which he then expanded, revised, and broke up into an extended passage. Chapter 14 emerged from one of these seed-sentences (see illustration 6).[47] The deaf-mute's acts of writing and revision on his slate present

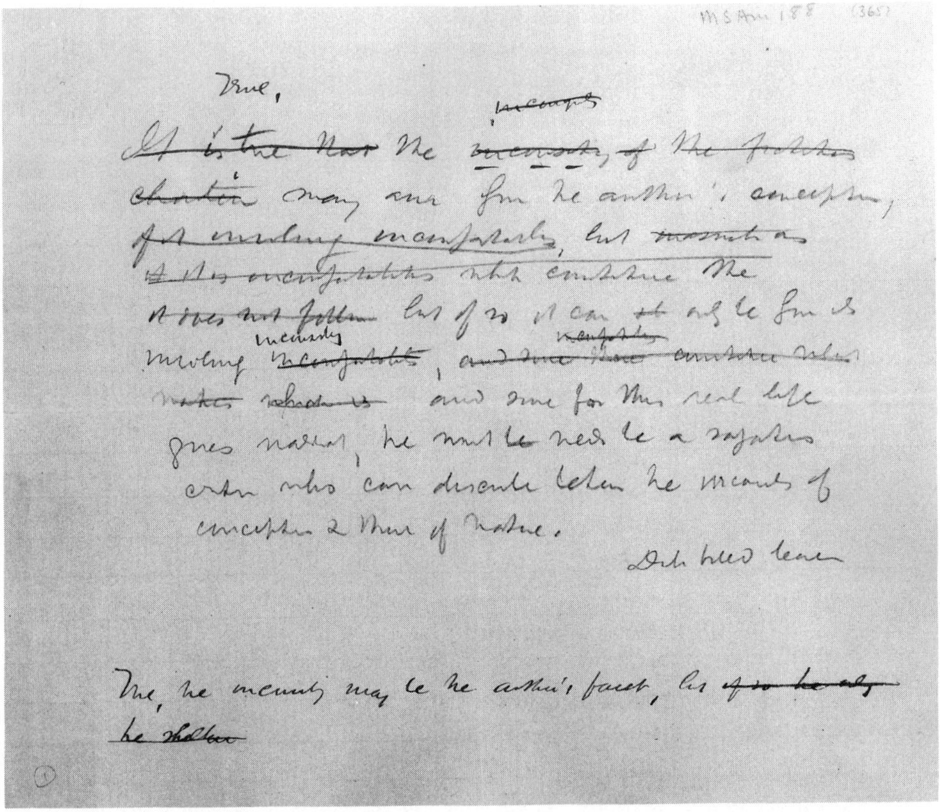

Illustration 6. Manuscript fragment from chapter 14 of *The Confidence-Man,* in Herman Melville's hand. By permission of the Houghton Library, Harvard University [bMS Am188 (365)].

a version of the false start. He amends "Charity thinketh no evil" to "Charity suffereth long, and is kind," to "Charity endureth all things," and so on. Rebecca J. Kruger Guadino points out that this scene figures the author who edits his text in response to audience reaction, and that the novel's frequent difficulties with definitions, analogies, and logic all speak to processes of writing and reading.[48] Similarly, Melville's effects with the letter *p* (and others) in chapter 29 thematize with gusto the customarily laborious processes of word and phrase substitution, revision, and transposition that lie behind Melville's published pages. For example, the endless substitution of one *p* word and phrase for another; port wine for pure wine then poison wine; "The wine, port" for "port wine," and so on, leave on and incorporate into the written page versions of the writing process.

The scenario at the end of chapter 30, in which the cosmopolitan who has identified himself as Frank says to Charlie, "I am in want, urgent want, of money" (178), is rewritten in chapter 39, as Egbert plays Charlie, and the cosmopolitan, now playing a character named Frank, says, "Charlie, I am in want—urgent want of money" (202). In the story-within-a-story of China Aster, the epitaph China Aster writes for himself is edited by a character named "Old Plain Talk," who has the "retrenched inscription" chiseled upon the stone. Old Plain Talk's friend Old Prudence reviews the stone-text, "spelling out the epitaph word by word," and decides "one short sentence is wanting." Plain Talk reports that the arrangement of chiseled words will not allow for interlining, so the addendum is "chiseled at the left-hand corner of the stone, and pretty low down" (220). This tale of writing, editing, and publication by personae whose names include an acrostic for *character* and two allegorical names that feature a capital *p* includes the difficulty of making changes to plates in the stones that cannot be interlined. Melville's perhaps best-known frustration with plates arose during composition of *Moby-Dick*. G. Thomas Tanselle reports that, since Melville arranged to have the book typeset and plated before he was finished writing it, "he undoubtedly felt restricted in the kinds of revisions that were feasible."[49]

The textual exchanges between Melville and his sister Augusta, who copied this manuscript, provide additional practical instances of his heavy manipulation of characters during the writing and revision process. For example, he crossed out Augusta's "squall" and corrected it with "squirrel," and doctored the letters of her "rare one" to read "rara avis" instead of crossing it out (see illustration 7).[50] His manuscript page, which is heavily marked with lines, arrows, circles, and carets, upside-down passages, and sections cut off one sheet and pinned to another, points to the extensive labor with which he manipulated his written words (see illustrations 7, 8, 4). The surviving manuscript leaves evince conspicuous differences in his practices of inscription. Wide divergences in the degree of care and fullness with which he formed letters and words indicate differing degrees of attention to his handwriting, implying that, on at least some occasions, penmanship was a conscious activity intended to produce marks of particular style and shape. For example, he apparently inscribed one draft very carefully (it is uncharacteristically legible) so that a typesetter could read it.[51]

Melville's relation to the materiality of writing as constitutive of *The Confidence-Man*'s terms includes not only manuscript production, under which rubric I mean to include his own handwriting activity and also the labor of copy and fair-copy production with his wife and sisters, but also the stages of

He seemed *did not at least unsee unseeable* *him thus seemed.*

Surely he who demands consistency *is denied in an author, should at least do so in consistent terms.*

will

must wholly consist of

As the last chapter was begun with a reminder looking forwards, *so opens* the present one looking backwards.

To some it may raise a degree of surprise that one so full of confidence as the *good* merchant has throughout shown himself up to the moment of his late sudden *outburst*, should in that instance have betrayed such a depth of distrust.

upon the whole It may be thought that *the discordancy is such as to* it makes him *seem an* inconsistent *character.* Inconsistent he is. *Yet why be too severe upon the author for it?* But it *may be* urged, *as the author urges,* there is *nothing* a sensible reader *or them* more carefully looks for *or a sensible* *one of fiction is* author *will be more careful to see to* than consistency in *the* characters of fiction. *which when strictly seems* *this seems* Reasonable enough. But is it, or is it not, in conflict with *that equally important* principle *laid* down, *for the author,* that invent as *an author of fiction* may, he must still be faithful *at bottom* to the *known* facts of real life. For this last being required, *of him,* is it not *over* taxing his powers *rather too hard,* also to require of him *none but truly* consistent characters, seeing that it is the universal *admission* that in real life *such a* character is a *rara avis?* [One reason of that *repugnance* of readers to *inconsistent* characters *in fiction,* no doubt arises from *the perplexity as to understanding them.* But if the acutest philosopher be perplexed to understand *the many* character *of people he is in contact with; shall* *those who are not philosophers* ex- pect to run *& read characters* in those *ghosts of them* which flit *through a fiction,* like shadows along a wall? That fiction where *all the* characters can by reason of *their* consistency be comprehended at a glance, *by every one,* either exhibits but *sections* of character making *them* appear for wholes, or else is wholly untrue to reality. While, on the other hand, that author who draws a character, even though to common view *discordant* *inconsistent* contradictory in its parts as the flying squirrel, *equally,* production that finally result in printed and published text. I ascribe the inextricability of these scenarios in the novel to Melville's powerful sense here of his own writing as material configured differently at multiple sites. Thus his exploration of the tautological realm of the graphic at the level of manuscript production opens into a simultaneous invocation of books as printed objects emerging from a network of author-publisher-reader relations. Both kinds of production of text invoke sets of practices within Melville's history of authorship that are constitutive of *The Confidence-Man*'s terms.

By setting up the panegyric on the press in chapter 29 with "press" understood as the printing press, "that great invention" (165), and then unexpectedly turning the panegyric in the next chapter into a discourse on a winepress (165–67), *The Confidence-Man* opens a space for permutations within the identity of the "press" within which printed books, including Melville's own, emerge. Chapter 30 contrasts the "black press" and the "red press," and here too we can hear the print quality of the Black Guinea's blackness. Critics have pointed out that the "red press of Noah" figured in this chapter refers to the biblical story of Noah's drunkenness,[52] and thus to the winepress; however, the implicit subtext here is an allusion to another Noah, Noah Webster, whose *An American Dictionary of the English Language; Exhibiting the Origin, Orthography, Pronunciation, and Definitions of Words,* published by Harper in a revised edition in 1847, was a text Melville struggled to abide by as he wrote, a particularly burdensome charge given the frustrations with spelling I discuss in chapter 1. It is this material context for the production of writing, for an author who also suffered from chronic eye problems, that resonates in Charlie's question, "Who giveth redness of eyes by making men long to tarry at the fine print?" (167).

The discussion of Mark Winsome's "doctrine of labels" in chapter 36 recalls the graphics of the wine "label," both of which suggest the printed paper labels that often appeared on book covers and spines of the period.[53] Here in chapter 36, another surge of the character *p* motivates the terms of the chapter, including descriptive language ("plain propriety of the Puritan sort," "for a man to pity where nature is pitiless, is a little presuming"), topics of conversation (the Pitti Palace, Proclus, and Pharoah), and even the appearance of the (albeit unnamed) Poe, peddling a text. Poe is in fact a forerunner of Melville's in his concern with the physical presence of text, and, in the conclusion to *The Narrative of Arthur Gordon Pym,* with the appearance of marks that might or might not be "alphabetical characters," including a figure resembling a *p* that is

Illustration 7. Manuscript fragment from *The Confidence-Man.* Augusta Melville's copy of chapter 14, with corrections and revisions in Herman Melville's hand. By permission of the Houghton Library, Harvard University [bMS Am188 (365)].

Chap. 14

Worth the consideration of those
to whom it may be worth considering.

As the last chapter was
begun with a reminder looking forwards, the
present must consist of one glancing backwards.
To some, it may raise a
~~degree of~~ surprise, that one so full of easy confidence
as the merchant has throughout shown himself
up to the moment of his late sudden ~~outbreak~~ impulsiveness
should in that instance have betrayed such a
~~depth~~ of distrust. He may be thought inconsistent.
Inconsistent he is. ~~But why~~
~~too severe upon the author for it~~ But, it may be
~~urged~~ said, there is nothing that an author a discreet writer of fiction
~~will~~ should rule more carefully see to, as there is nothing a ~~discreet~~ sensible
~~discreet~~ reader of ~~it~~ will more carefully look for,
in the depicting of character to prove its verity in the depicting of character
than ~~consistency~~ that sort of keeping
in character called consistency. Which indeed seems
reasonable enough. But is it or is it not, in conflict with
another requirement of another, perhaps
~~the principle~~ equally ~~important~~, that ~~in~~ works of
of a certain class
fiction should at bottom be faithful to ~~fact~~? For
this last being ~~required~~, is it not somewhat overtaxing
the novelist's
~~an author's~~ power, also to require of him none
but consistent characters; seeing that it is ~~the~~
every one knows   Why are men enough?
~~universal admission~~ that in real life ~~such a~~
~~character~~ is a rara avis? Which being so, the
repugnance of reader to meeting with such ones
in books ~~of invention~~ can hardly arise from any sense
with the contrary kind

a signature effect for Poe.[54] The Philosophical Intelligence Officer, who, as noted previously, carries a book and a pamphlet and promises "publication" to contributors, also wears a label, "a small brass plate, inscribed P.I.O." (114). This brass "plate" metaphorizes the metal plates from which impressions of books were made—Melville was extensively involved with the plates of his own books[55]—and once again associates the letter *p* with the production of printed text. An "Intelligence Office," according to Webster (1847), was "an office or place where information may be obtained, especially respecting servants and places of employment."[56] The brass plate stamped with a *p* and with the mark of employment, specifically inflected in the direction of domestic employment ("servants"), figures Melville's own employment as an author, whose domestic bearings I explore at length in chapter 3. In what is apparently a draft of the title of the chapter in which the P.I.O. man appears (chapter 22), Melville stresses the idea of "housekeepers" and "those who keep house,"[57] additionally suggesting Melville's conflation of writing employment and domestic servitude.

The man with the brass plate appears in the same chapter in which the character Pitch extols the coming of machines, "these thousand new inventions," to displace "the human animal" (117). Although Pitch's list of machines does not include a printing press, the printing press appears in the subsequent panegyric as "that great invention" (165), as I noted above. There its image is conjured up by Frank as a "great invention," and then displaced by the wine-press; a similar emergence and displacement occurs in the novel's last chapter, as the old man praises a newfangled gadget, the traveler's patent lock, with the words, "This beats printing" (246). The subtle presence and deflection of the printing press in other discussions of great inventions makes its absence from Pitch's list a conspicuous one in the novel's own terms. But its deflected presence in the other instances I've cited resonates here too, since, although absent from Pitch's list, it emerges instead in the P.I.O. officer's "plate" and even in Pitch's name: a contemporary of Melville's who wrote an account of the Harper establishment pointed out that printer's ink was "not liquid, like writing-ink, but is thick and viscid, like pitch."[58]

The author's relation to publishers is one under whose sign the novel opens, with the image of "chevaliers" hawking goods. One hawks "the lives of Meason, the bandit of Ohio, Murrel, the pirate of the Mississippi, and the brothers Harpe, the Thugs of the Green River country, in Kentucky" (4). Samuel Mason or Meason, John A. Murrell, and the Harpe brothers were all noto-

Illustration 8. Manuscript fragment from chapter 14 of *The Confidence-Man*, in Herman Melville's hand, with revisions. By permission of the Houghton Library, Harvard University [bMS Am188 (365)].

rious outlaws.[59] Both "Meason" and "Murrel," by capital letter and by metrical cadence, are also signature effects for Melville's name, fleshed-out versions of the solitary "M——" that appears in "Fragments from a Writing Desk" as a mark of the author. The "brothers Harpe" figure Harper & Brothers, who published *Typee, Omoo, Mardi, Redburn, White-Jacket, Moby-Dick,* and *Pierre* as well as a number of Melville's magazine pieces. (Wiley & Putnam published *Typee* in their Library of American Books, but in 1849 Melville closed out his account with Wiley & Putnam, purchased the plates, and transferred them to the house of Harper.)[60] Ezra Greenspan notes that "by 1840 the Harpers were notorious even in the trade for their piracy of foreign writers."[61] Mason Brothers was also a New York publishing house, and in 1855 Mason defended publishers' routine bribery of critics for soliciting good reviews.[62] That Melville alludes to the economy of authorship and publication by way of thugs, bandits, and pirates in a book about confidence men is not surprising, since credit transactions in the antebellum American economy in general, and in the publishing industry in particular, were by necessity based on "confidence" in the absence of a reliable form of paper money.[63]

These loaded author and publisher figures are "creatures, with others of the sort, one and all exterminated at the time" (4). This tale of extermination told by the chevalier's proffered text is also the tale told by Melville's text, one of many instances of the tale-within-a-tale structure that, as I will argue presently, ultimately reflects upon Melville's history of authorship. The Harper establishment in New York was destroyed by fire in 1853,[64] a fire that destroyed, among other things, the inventory of all of Melville's books at roughly the same time that his career as a novelist was essentially exterminated in the aftermath of *Pierre.* Arthur Stedman, Melville's literary executor, saw the Harper fire in these disastrous terms; he noted that it kept Melville's books out of print "at a most important time. The plates were not injured, but in the case of all the works the printing and binding of new editions had to be done over again."[65]

The important presence of Melville's own publishing history in this novel allows us to explore further the model for writing that I've been mapping as one operative at the level of the character, the syllable, and the word. This model also operates structurally in narrative terms, motivating the production of stories-within-stories. As one story spins off a series of other tales and other narrators, Melville insists upon the ultimate impenetrability of the layers of textuality and simultaneously renders the reliance of one printed source upon another an additional instance of tautology, since the surface of print as such is never penetrated, but only recirculated. The chapters on Indian hating, for example, take as their subject the textuality of both the Indian and the Indian-hater, a textuality allegorized in the Judge's tale "of the little colony of Wrights and Weavers" (147) butchered by a treacherous tribe. Here the homonym "Wrights" (writes) and its counterpart "Weavers," emblematize the production of texts in a dense weave of speakers and tales. (Melville's poem "The Weaver," published in *Timoleon* [1891], also figures the Melvillean scene of writing, with its lonely and reclusive weaver enclosed in a room, laboring at "a lonely loom,/His busy shadow on the wall" [ll. 3–4]. What "looms" on the wall here is the shadow of the weaver himself; his busy relation to his "loom" becomes the substance of the looming in whose shadow he produces.) In fact, the wine label that I have already explored as an emblem of writing enters the text at the conclusion of the Indian-hating chapters (chapters 26–28). Its basket of "Indian fashion" and its red label (noting the "Indian" connotations of the color) associate this emblem of writing (noting the pun red/read, also operative in *Pierre*) with the "Indian" and "Indian-hater" whose story has just concluded.[66]

The Indian-hater is a type of character that derives its substance from written accounts. The "acquaintance" tells the story of Colonel John Moredock as told by Judge James Hall, a chain of mediation further complicated by the suggestion that the acquaintance, who later identifies himself as Charlie, is himself a confidence man. It is he who wears a violet vest and thus seems to represent one of the "ge'mmen" on Black Guinea's list that otherwise never appears. It is thus with great irony that the cosmopolitan, awaiting the tale of Colonel John Moredock, inclines his ear "so disposed towards the speaker that each word came through as little atmospheric intervention as possible" (143), a parodic allusion to the layers of narrative and interwoven speakers that constitute the story.

Hall was well known for his habit of using the same material repeatedly in his writings; he told the story of the Indian-hater in at least three publications.[67] Hall's role in this chain of layers of storytelling thus also has print connotations. His text describes Indian hating as an animosity that springs from stories about the Indian's nature rather than from the Indian's nature itself. He writes of the Indian-hating backwoodsmen, "They know the story only as it was told to them. They have only heard one side, and that with all the exaggerations of fear, sorrow, indignation and resentment."[68] Melville follows Hall: " 'Still, all this is less advanced as truths of the Indians than as examples of the backwoodsman's impression of them' " (146), an "impression"—itself a printing term—that produces the Indian as a text written by the backwoodsman from a text written by Hall. The backwoodsman himself was a notorious masquerader and teller of tall tales in nineteenth-century American culture.[69] The Indian known to the white man is thus a wholly textual phenomenon, and the face written onto him obscures his "true" face in the same way that, behind the roles constructed for him in "Benito Cereno," the face of Babo, "the black," remains impenetrable.[70]

The Indian-hater, too, is a textually constituted phenomenon, primarily one for whom "a special word has been coined" (141). As Marc Shell has noted, the Greek word *charaktēr* meant the "upper die used by the coinmaker or impressed mark on the coin." According to Shell, the coin "preceded by two millennia the printing press and the printed page,"[71] an observation that helps us to see how coin falls within the novel's signifying economy of character. Jean-Christophe Agnew correctly argues that words are the coin of Melville's relation to his reader in this novel, and like coin they are so frequently exchanged as to lose any stable connection with an operative order of signification. Agnew also points out that money and speech in *The Confidence-Man* are figures for one another. Agnew situates these observations about words in a larger "cultural history of market relations" and argues that the novel is Melville's response to market culture.[72] I want to differ from Agnew's useful point by emphasizing the written rather than spoken nature of the language at issue, which, for example, fosters the certainly operative pun on *capital* as money and as written character. In antebellum America, "capitals" were a type of handwriting whose production required special instruction.[73] This alteration of focus also allows us to see the specific material basis of Melville's relation to Agnew's "market," that is, the production of both handwritten and printed text.

Like the *p* that finally remains an opaque mark, the character of the Indian-hater—and thus presumably of the Indian he hates—remains fundamentally impenetrable. "The career of the Indian-hater *par excellence* has the impenetrability of the fate of a lost steamer" (150), says the acquaintance quoting the judge. All known examples of the Indian-hater necessarily "impair the keeping of the character" because they dilute its pure, impenetrable form, like the characters "P.W." whose pure wine was also poison.

Melville's other stories-within-stories are also predicated upon chains of tales or texts. Thus the story of the unfortunate man (chapter 12) is told by the unfortunate man himself, and again by the man in a gray coat, both personae of the Confidence-Man, to the good merchant, who then tells the story to another Confidence-Man, the transfer-agent of the Black Rapids Coal Company, making the circulation of this story a tautological exchange. The story of China Aster is told by Egbert, playing Charlie; he says he will tell it in the style of the unnamed "original story-teller," whose style has "tyrannized" over him (207).

Taken as a group, these stories invoke relations not only to one another but also to other printed sources as a chain of tales. For example, the protagonist of the story-within-a-story of Charlemont, the gentleman-madman, alludes to

William Gilmore Simms' novel *Charlemont; or, The Pride of the Village* (1856). Simms' *Charlemont* is dedicated to James Hall, who is at the center of the chapters on Indian hating. Texts by Hall and Simms were also printed sources for Melville on the lives of the outlaws Meason, Murrell, and the brothers Harpe.[74] The network of associations Melville weaves here ultimately points to a particular chain of author-publisher relations: Simms, Hall, and Melville were among the authors included in Duyckinck's Library of American Books (as was Poe, who appears in chapter 36); Egbert has been widely interpreted as Henry David Thoreau, who had pressed Duyckinck to publish *A Week on the Concord and Merrimack Rivers* in the series; and Mark Winsome has been widely interpreted as Ralph Waldo Emerson, whom Duyckinck went to great lengths to entice into contributing to the Library, unsuccessfully.[75] That Duyckinck promoted the Library in part by enlisting its authors to puff one another's books[76] is another instance, located at the level of publishing history, of the tautological method of establishing credit discussed earlier as the Confidence-Man's primary technique. Chapters 11 and 33, two of the novel's three tautologically numbered chapters, set up stories-within-stories: chapter 11 introduces the story of the unfortunate man, and chapter 33 sets up the story of Charlemont.

Since Melville adapted his chapters on Indian hating from James Hall's *Sketches of History, Life, and Manners, in the West* (Philadelphia, 1835), often borrowing directly from Hall's wording,[77] it is important to note the elided presence of printed text in Melville's process of composition as a context for this chain of "oral" tales. If I am correct in arguing that one of the things Melville meditates upon in *The Confidence-Man* is the Library of American Books, and of his own contribution to that Library—*Typee*—then I believe I am also correct in arguing that Melville's use of sources in *The Confidence-Man*, a career-long practice that he now folds into a reflection on his own publishing history, is also a meditation upon his writing practice in *Typee* in particular. In retrospect, he renders his construction in *Typee* of an "authentic" world of "beautiful vocal sounds" out of printed text an example of the tautological method of writing stories-within-stories that he embraces in *The Confidence-Man*, in which the text points not to nature itself but only to another printed source.[78] It is in this same reassessing light that I place Melville's well-known response to Titus Munson Coan, the author's young fan who yearned to discuss Polynesia with him. Coan himself was from Hawaii, the child of missionaries, and whenever he tried to elicit Polynesian reminiscences, Melville invariably replied, "That reminds me of the eighth book of Plato's *Republic*."[79] This hilarious rebuff is also one that situates Melville's memories of *Typee* with respect to printed text rather than experience. These shifts in his relation to his first novel accompany

The Confidence-Man's heightening engagement with the page as Melville distills issues of "content"—whether of wine, or charity, or character—to the written character and the "novelist's page" as such.

It remains to be said that in its distillation of prose fiction to the level of the character as such, and in its focus on letters and words as things, *The Confidence-Man* is a particularly appropriate last novel before Melville's full-scale change in genre, to poetry.[80] In *Weeds and Wildings with a Rose or Two,* for example, Melville engages in extensive alliterative wordplay sprung from the title of the volume, with the words *rose, rosary, Rosamond,* and *Rosicrucians,* for example. Conversely, effects of perfect rhyme hinge upon changing initial characters and preserving those at the ends of words. These effects, which evince Melville's interest in graphic manipulations as a subject of primary importance to the poems, both recall Melville's investigations of character in *The Confidence-Man;* such manipulations eventually take form in Billy Budd's "stutter," in which a repetition of characters as such ultimately produces words: " 'd-d-driving,' " " 'g-g-go,' " " 't-t-toss' " are three such examples (*BB* 332). In the *Billy Budd* manuscript, we can see Melville adding and deleting characters that create the effect of Billy's stutter. In the passage that reads in manuscript " 'If you d-d-dont start, I'll t-t-toss you back over the rail!' " Melville strikes through a *d* preceding "dont" and carets in a single *r* preceding "rail!"[81] In this sense we can see that *Billy Budd* did indeed spring from Melville's poetry, not only in its order of composition[82] but also in its relation to words on the page, which also helps to explain the tale's repeated references to the poetic.

After publication of *The Confidence-Man,* Melville wrote poetry almost exclusively for the rest of his life. Poet James Galvin recently commented on writing his own first book of prose: "As a poet, I—I spend probably an unhealthy amount of time staring at blank pieces of paper and not touching them. And so then doing this prose book was almost like being someone else for a while in relation to the page, which is part of its attraction."[83] Melville's change in genre—the reverse of Galvin's—also signals a new relation to the page, particularly from the standpoint of white space, to which I now turn.

Chapter Five

Battle "Pieces"

~

I n Melville's first published volume of poetry, *Battle-Pieces and Aspects of the War* (1866), the scene of battle the poems most fundamentally record is the scene of their own composition. Melville depicts that scene of conflict and struggle in terms of war, and in this sense the Civil War is of only secondary importance to his volume.[1] These embattled poems are also battle pieces in that they are "pieces" of writing with whose material dimensions Melville is forcefully engaged. By *dimensions* I mean both the word's figurative sense of magnitude with respect to an abstract thing (for example, when we speak of the "dimensions of a problem") and the literal extent or size of a particular thing (as in the "dimensions of the room"). The material presence of writing had become a conceptual problem for Melville that had specific and particular consequences in his engagements with individual, physical pages. That material field itself, by my account, is his crucial field of battle.

The word *piece* designated a work of painting, sculpture, or literature by the sixteenth century, a work of drama by the seventeenth century, and a musical composition by the nineteenth century; Hennig Cohen stresses that Melville chose the title of his collection with a particular awareness of battle pieces as a genre of painting.[2] Cohen points out that Melville attended the National Academy of Design's annual exhibition in New York in April of 1865, the same month in which Richmond fell; it was to the fall of Richmond that Melville's preface attributed the "impulse" behind *Battle-Pieces*. Cohen stresses what he calls Melville's "pictorial intention" in the volume. Because Melville saw himself presenting "a series of pictures," Cohen points out, the "visual connotation" of the title was important to him.[3] The volume's painterly quality is also palpable in such poems as " 'Formerly a Slave.' An idealized Portrait, by E. Vedder, in the Spring Exhibition of the National Academy, 1865," " 'The Coming Storm': A Picture by S. R. Gifford, and owned by E.B. Included in the N.A. Exhibition, April, 1865," and "The Temeraire," inspired by J. M. W.

Turner's "The Fighting Temeraire," which Melville saw in 1857. Melville's note to the poem refers to the "well-known painting by Turner."[4] To the volume's interest in painting, we can add Timothy Sweet's observations that *Battle-Pieces* also explores photography, for example, in "On the Photograph of a Corps Commander." Sweet calls photography "another visual model for representation" in a volume framing the question of representation through a number of devices.[5] Cohen's incisive remarks about Melville's "battle-pieces" as a genre indebted to painting and Sweet's attention to photography help us to see the extent to which the poems are visually thematic in their allusion to painting and photography. But it's also crucial to extend this point, and to see that for Melville the poems are not only visually thematic, but are also themselves visual objects.

The word "Pieces" appears frequently in Melville's poetry: for example, the prefatory note to *Battle-Pieces* refers to "the Pieces in this volume";[6] "The House-Top" carries the subtitle "A Night Piece"; *John Marr and Other Sailors* features the section titles "Sea-Pieces" and "Minor Sea-Pieces"; and the title of "John Marr" was originally followed by the subtitle "(a sketch introductory to the Piece next following)." The word also appears frequently in his manuscript notes to the printer: "a page should precede this Piece—a page bearing the Sea-Pieces title"; "A liberal space, or, perhaps, a page should be left between these two Pieces"; "These two Pieces might occupy, if it is manageable, a page by themselves"; and "To the Printer: where the line has a red cross in margin—*indent*. And so in other Pieces similarly marked."[7] Robert C. Ryan points out that Melville characteristically wrote each poem on a separate piece of paper, often cutting his paper in different sizes to suit individual poems. This compositional practice speaks to Melville's awareness of his poems as both materially discrete and materially variable entities (separate pieces, different sizes) whose physical form he consistently engaged as part of his process of production. In this sense, I stress, Melville was engaged with his poems as material, visual objects, and so to call them "battle-pieces" was not merely to allude to painting (although it was in part that) but also to denominate the nature of the poems themselves as he conceived it.

Melville characteristically spelled *pieces* with an initial capital when referring to his own work,[8] as the above examples illustrate. In this sense the *p* that signifies the materialization of characters as writing on a page in *The Confidence-Man* informs the status of the poetry—designated "Pieces"—toward which that novel's effects point. Melville made a major shift as a writer after *The Confidence-Man*. Although he had long written poems and had incorporated them into his fiction (in *Mardi*, for example), it is important to recognize that

Melville did not write poetry primarily or conceive of himself as primarily a poet until after this last full-scale novel was published.[9] In that writing poetry usually involves a greater control on the part of the writer over the ultimate look of the words on the page than does writing prose, this aspect of the change in genre was especially powerful for him. To say that Melville as poet was fundamentally concerned with manifestations and fluctuations of white space, and with his own changing relation to that space, is one way of understanding his pioneering experimentation with mixed prose and poetry within the same nominal "Piece" ("John Marr," "Rip Van Winkle's Lilac," "At the Hostelry," and "Naples in the Time of Bomba" are among the poems that I would consider such experiments), an interest that eventually produced *Billy Budd*, whose germ was the poem "Billy in the Darbies."[10]

In addition to his embattled involvement with the page while writing his poems, he was also extensively involved with the printing of those poems that were published.[11] His notes to the printer on the manuscripts and proofs indicate his deep interest in such issues as spacing, typography, and layout. Thus in both scenes of poetic production—the generation of manuscript and of printed text—Melville's relation to his poems is fundamentally characterized by his interest in controlling the white page, a space that is both inherently more present to the poet than to the novelist and also more fundamentally visible within the nominal product itself. Thus his battle with pieces of writing that are now poems represents a change in the terms of his contest with the page.

Battle-Pieces opens with "The Portent. (1859)." Not listed in the table of contents, and set off from the rest of the poems by a blank page and by its italic type, this poem occupies a special position in the volume. While within the nominal plot of the collection—a roughly chronological survey of events and incidents of the Civil War—the hanged body of John Brown portends the impending catastrophe, this new subject is figured in terms already deeply resonant in Melville's writing:

The Portent.

(1859.)

Hanging from the beam,
 Slowly swaying (such the law),
Gaunt the shadow on your green,
 Shenandoah!
The cut is on the crown
(Lo, John Brown),
And the stabs shall heal no more.

> Hidden in the cap
> . Is the anguish none can draw;
> So your future veils its face,
> Shenandoah!
> But the streaming beard is shown
> (Weird John Brown),
> The meteor of the war.

The "portent" is one whose face of anguish is hidden by the hangman's cap so that only the beard is visible. William Bysshe Stein calls Melville's choice of the word "cap" here "incongruous," since what he is describing is the hangman's "hood."[12] This ominous figure with a face hidden by a cap/hood recalls the white whale that Ishmael envisions in "Loomings" as a "grand hooded phantom," and whose hidden or absent face quietly drives him to a point near frenzy. In *Moby-Dick*, the indistinctly seen portentous or threatening form implicit in the word *loomings* either hides its face or has no face; that form is refigured at the entrance to *Battle-Pieces*, hanging with a covered face and suspended by a blank page. "The Portent" thus introduces *Battle-Pieces* by way of terms analogous to those that introduce *Moby-Dick*.

The power of these explicitly introductory terms for Melville is, I suggest, their power to invoke his relation to a writing project. The figure with a veiled face is associated with "anguish"; it is a "shadow"; and it is a shadow that provokes an image of "stabs" ("And the stabs shall heal no more"), an image through which Melville elsewhere metaphorizes his relation to the page. The "anguish none can draw" (l. 9) thus structurally recalls the "depths of anguish" in Isabel's note to Pierre. Both are imagined as spaces of deep meaning in contest with the space of the page. In *Pierre*, the anguished narrator's desire to posit endless depths within the page flattens out against the aggressive force that "draws to itself," just as the portent's anguish here is what "none can draw"; both thwart capture on the two-dimensional space of the page. This portent anticipates conflict, but the conflict the volume manifestly designates as the Civil War is more fundamentally Melville's own scene of writing.

It is in these terms that I understand the discrepancy, often noted in the criticism of *Battle-Pieces*, between the dates of the historical events to which the poems refer (dates often recorded in the poems' titles) and the time of composition, which, as Melville says in his preface, was primarily after the war ended. The war began in April of 1861, but, as Stanton Garner points out, in the spring and summer of 1861 Melville seems to have been writing nothing at all.[13] Several critics have handled this problem by arguing that, in "The Portent," for example, Melville powerfully recollects, from a distance of some years, the feeling of anxious anticipation in 1859, when John Brown was hanged. If that's true, I maintain, it's true only because Melville's feeling of anxious anticipation as he sets out to produce a volume of poems in 1865 can be analogized to the temperament of a prior historical moment, not because that earlier moment is the source of the anxiety. Richard Harter Fogle notes correctly that the poems are "decidedly more retrospective than they appear." Cohen comments that the poems "were not often the product of white heat generated by immediacy, but rather of the cool calculation which the passage of time makes possible." I concur with both critics in their sense of Melville's mediated relation to the historical events of the war while composing the poems.[14]

The tone of anxiety, ominousness, and conflict aroused in "The Portent" persists in the titles that follow it: "Misgivings. (1860.)," "The Conflict of Convictions. (1860–1.)," and "Apathy and Enthusiasm. (1860–1.)."[15] Motivated within Melville's stated occasion for the collection by a conflict that is specifically the war—"With few exceptions, the Pieces in this volume originated in an impulse imparted by the fall of Richmond" [v]—the feeling of conflict presides over the collection in a much less specified sense. Melville remarks in his prefatory note: "The aspects which the strife as a memory assumes are as manifold as are the moods of involuntary meditation—moods variable, and at times widely at variance. Yielding instinctively, one after another, to feelings not inspired from any one source exclusively, and unmindful, without purposing to be, of consistency, I seem, in most of these verses, to have but placed a harp in a window, and noted the contrasted airs which wayward winds have played upon the strings" [v]. The aeolian harp to which Melville alludes here is of course a common Romantic trope for poetic inspiration. Coleridge's "The Eolian Harp" (1796) figures the mind as a harp:

> Full many a thought uncall'd and undetain'd,
> And many idle flitting phantasies,
> Traverse my indolent and passive brain,
> As wild and various as the random gales
> That swell and flutter on this subject Lute![16]

Melville's invocation of an aeolian harp, and of the "yielding" and variability of the mind inspired to produce poetry, situates his own collection with respect to a poetic tradition concerned with the process by which, to borrow from Coleridge again, the mind "tremble[s] into thought."[17] Melville later published a poem entitled "The Aeolian Harp/At the *Surf Inn*" in *John Marr and Other Sailors with Some Sea-Pieces*. The poem presents a wailing tale of shipwreck, another persistent site for Melville in the conjunction between inspiration/

writing and violence/destruction, and insists that such "Shrieking up in mad crescendo" (l. 3) is the stuff of "Real" poetry (l. 6). His prefatory note to *Battle-Pieces*, then, underwrites his poems about an external, "geographical" conflict ("The events and incidents of the conflict—making up a whole, in varied amplitude, corresponding with the geographical area covered by the war" [v]) with a "conflict" and "strife" associated with the "moods" of poetic production.

I thus thoroughly disagree with Joyce Sparer Adler, who argues that Melville was torn by his unconditional support for the war waged by the North, given his general pacifism, and that this conflict is the source of the tension in the poems. According to Adler, this "inner stress" kept him from writing until the fall of Richmond eased his feelings enough to allow him to relive his experience of the war.[18] Garner's argument is similar in nature: he maintains that Melville was deeply disturbed by the impending crisis of civil war and kept trying to flee "the role he may already have foreseen for himself" as its poet.[19] Even Melville's chronic health problems, according to Garner, are not really issues of physical and mental well-being but rather of "spiritual infirmity" provoked by the evil of fratricide.[20] Garner consistently argues that the historical events of the war determine Melville's actions, moods, and poetic images. Garner's commitment to establishing these historical connections as those of primary relevance leads him to assessments like the following conclusion about "Presentation to the Authorities, by Privates, of Colors captured in Battles ending in the Surrender of Lee": "It is mystifying because it is difficult to discover a historical event on which the poem might be based."[21]

Again in this volume, as he had in his novels, Melville relied extensively on sources, including newspaper reports, paintings, and *The Rebellion Record*, a periodical digest of the war,[22] another indication that "events" as such were not his primary engagement. William Dean Howells' review of the volume is more apt than has been recognized:

> Mr. Melville's work possesses the negative virtues of originality in such a degree that it not only reminds you of no poetry you have read, but of no life you have known. Is it possible—you ask yourself, after running over all these celebrative, inscriptive, and memorial verses—that there has really been a great war, with battles fought by men and bewailed by women? Or is it only that Mr. Melville's inner consciousness has been perturbed, and filled with the phantasms of enlistments, marches, fights in the air, parenthetic bulletin boards, and tortured humanity shedding, not words and blood, but words alone?[23]

Howells points here to Melville's distance from the events of the war, a distance he sensed in the poems themselves. The "tortured humanity shedding . . .

words alone" that Howells reads in Melville's "inner consciousness" points to the strife that I have identified as Melville's agony of production.

The moods of poetic production are forcefully evoked in "Apathy and Enthusiasm," which presents a powerful instance of the double-edged "conflict" in *Battle-Pieces:*

Apathy and Enthusiasm.
(1860–1.)

I.

O THE clammy cold November,
    And the winter white and dead,
And the terror dumb with stupor,
    And the sky a sheet of lead;
And events that came resounding
    With the cry that *All was lost,*
Like the thunder-cracks of massy ice
    In intensity of frost—
Bursting one upon another
    Through the horror of the calm.
    The paralysis of arm
In the anguish of the heart;
And the hollowness and dearth.
    The appealings of the mother
    To brother and to brother
Not in hatred so to part—
And the fissure in the hearth
    Growing momently more wide.
Then the glances 'tween the Fates,
    And the doubt on every side,
And the patience under gloom
In the stoniness that waits
The finality of doom.

II.

So the winter died despairing,
    And the weary weeks of Lent;
And the ice-bound rivers melted,
    And the tomb of Faith was rent.
O, the rising of the People
    Came with springing of the grass,
They rebounded from dejection
    After Easter came to pass.
And the young were all elation
    Hearing Sumter's cannon roar,

And they thought how tame the Nation
    In the age that went before.
And Michael seemed gigantical,
    The Arch-fiend but a dwarf;
And at the towers of Erebus
    Our striplings flung the scoff.
But the elders with foreboding
    Mourned the days forever o'er,
And recalled the forest proverb,
    The Iroquois' old saw:
Grief to every graybeard
    When young Indians lead the war.

The opening scene of "cold November" is another refiguration of "Loomings," whose "damp, drizzly November in my soul" (*MD* 3) and hooded phantom "like a snow hill in the air" (*MD* 7) resonate in the poem's opening images of cold winter whiteness. The nature of the parallel here is one of mood with respect to the writing project at hand. Indeed, the occasion for "Loomings" is Ishmael's description of the mood that leads him to go to sea—"Whenever I find myself growing grim about the mouth" (3)—while the title "Apathy and Enthusiasm" itself stresses moods in conflict.

The language of the poem—its "gloom" (l. 21), "stoniness" (l. 22), and "foreboding" (l. 40), for example—powerfully invokes Melville's scene of writing. The "sheet of lead" in line 4 is associated with the "winter white and dead" of line 2 and the "terror dumb with stupor" of line 3; the "sheet" that is the sky is also the "sheet" that is the white page before him, either white with dumb blankness or "leaded" with pencil. Melville in fact often composed poetry and made provisional fair copies in pencil, and he used colored pencils for editing.[24] His manuscript pages are often so covered with writing as to obliterate their own white space. The experience of looking at these pages thus makes dramatically and visually present Melville's own written pages as "sheets of lead."[25]

The metaphor comparing the sky to a sheet of lead thus reverses its components here. While initially "the sky" appears to be the tenor of the metaphor and "a sheet of lead" the vehicle (that is, it is to the sky that features of the sheet of lead are attributed), Melville is not so much generating an effective "image" for the appearance of the sky as he is positing a tenor that will effectively bear the vision of a threatening leaded sheet. Thus the sky becomes the vehicle of the underlying metaphor whose tenor is Melville's page. Newton Arvin correctly noted in 1949 that in all of Melville's poems, "and especially in *Battle-Pieces,* one has to make a simple distinction between the pictorial imagery, the imagery 'given' by the themes themselves, and the true metaphors." While Arvin remarks that of course the pictorial imagery of *Battle-Pieces* is that of war, he is less specific about what he takes "the intense force of the elemental imagery" to be derived from.[26] Melville's provisional relation to his nominal subject, which I illustrate by way of this example, is a provisionality that underwrites much of the volume. It is this effect, I believe, that has produced the ineffectiveness of *Battle-Pieces* both in its own time and in ours as a poetic record of the war. Most criticism of *Battle-Pieces* acknowledges the volume's ineffectiveness, even if, like Garner's recent study, it seeks to change that status.

Within the plot of "Apathy and Enthusiasm," the conflicting moods denoted in the title are attributable to separate parties, youth against elders and brother against brother. The poem recounts the growing fissure between brother and brother and the naive elation with which the young greet the onset of war. The "enthusiasm" of youth is implicitly contrasted with the "apathy" of others whose identity is not immediately clear. Although an initial reading suggests that these others are presumably the "elders" (l. 40), this conclusion is incorrect in ways I will demonstrate. But the conflict nominally occurring between parties is attributable at the level of the production of the poem to the poet himself. Such an assessment sheds light on the otherwise curious choice of the word "apathy" to describe the mood contrasted with "enthusiasm." Webster's 1847 *American Dictionary*, the dictionary Melville himself used, defines *enthusiasm* as "1. A belief or conceit of private revelation; the vain confidence or opinion of a person that he has special divine communications from the Supreme Being, or familiar intercourse with him. 2. Heat of imagination; violent passion or excitement of the mind, in pursuit of some object, inspiring extravagant hope and confidence of success."[27] It defines *apathy* as "want of feeling; an utter privation of passion, or insensibility to pain.—SYN. Insensibility; unfeelingness; indifference; unconcern." For a writer with as fine-tuned a sense of language as Melville, *apathy* seems an oblique choice at best to describe the feeling of the elders about the coming conflict. The specific terms we get within the poem for the affect of the elders, "foreboding," "mourned," and "grief," for example, hardly seem synonymous with "apathy." Their affect is not a "want of feeling" but the presence of a powerful feeling opposed to that of "enthusiasm."

The poem that precedes "Apathy and Enthusiasm" in *Battle-Pieces*, "The Conflict of Convictions," represents the "conflict" within the poem by marking competing voices stanzaically and typographically: a voice in roman type set along the left margin alternates with an italic, indented, parenthetical voice, and a concluding voice appears in the final stanza, also indented and entirely in upper case. The ostensibly contrasted states of apathy and enthusiasm in the next poem are not so distinctly or visually marked. Within the plot, it is clearly the youths who are associated with "enthusiasm" ("the young were all elation," l. 32), but, as I have already indicated, the elders with whom the young are most clearly contrasted—a contrast at the heart of the poem's concluding couplet— are not plausible candidates for "apathy." The word closest to apathetic affect in the poem (but still not synonymous) is in fact "dejection," a quality attributed to "the People" in part 2. It is from the state of dejection that they "rebounded," presumably "rising" from a prior state. It is after this "rising of the People" (l. 28) that we hear of the "elation" of the young.

I parse out these terms with such specificity because only by attending to these intricate movements can we see that the states of apathy and enthusiasm are not associated primarily with two parties—not the young and the elders, although the stress at the end of the poem might initially encourage such a reading, and certainly not brother and brother in part 1, both of whom are enthusiasts—but rather with the two parts *of the poem itself* as representatives of two moods. The first locates itself in a moment before the "rising," "spring- ing," and "rebounding" into the "elation" of part 2. Cohen notes that the source of this poem, including the Easter imagery, is probably an editorial from the *New York Times* of April 16, 1861, entitled "The Resurrection of Patriotism," which was reprinted in *The Rebellion Record*, upon which Melville drew for at least twenty of the war poems.[28] The title of the editorial itself focuses on a shift in moment and in mood rather than a conflict between parties.

The strands of imagery and implication I have been exploring suggest that the states of "apathy" and "enthusiasm" are represented within the poem for- mally, that is to say, in the contrast between parts 1 and 2. So the emotional blankness of apathy—"Want of feeling; an utter privation of passion," in Web- ster's description—is associated with the blank stupefying landscape Melville associates at the opening of the poem with the scene of writing ("clammy cold November," "winter white and dead," "terror dumb with stupor," "sheet of lead"). The emotional blankness of apathy associated with a blank scene of writing is not devoid of affect for the poet; its "calm" is filled with "horror" ("Through the horror of the calm" [l. 10]).

A formal analysis of the poem supports my contention that the emotional blankness of apathy that the poem stresses in its title is associated with the blankness of the scene of writing. Part 2 is composed of twenty-two lines, and its careful and patterned use of period end-stops indicates that Melville con- ceives of these lines in four groups of four and one group of six, that is, four quatrains and a sestet. The rhyme scheme of *abcb defe ghgh ijkj lmnmom* also observes this pattern. With minor variations, the meter is trochaic tetrameter, alternating an eight-syllable line of four trochees with a line of trochaic tetrameter catalectic, that is, a seven-syllable trochaic line with a masculine ending. Fifteen of the twenty-two lines are end-stopped.

Comparing these regularities in part 1 with part 2 is illuminating. Part 1 is composed of twenty-three lines, one line more than part 2. Although the first ten lines follow the same pattern we find in part 2—end-stopped alternating lines of trochaic tetrameter and trochaic tetrameter catalectic with a rhyme scheme of *abcb defe gh*—at this point irregularity sets in. The rhyme scheme thenceforth follows a *hijggijklkmlm* pattern, and the catalectic line takes over completely, with the important exception of line 14, "The appealings of the mother," which appropriately retains the feminine ending.

Unlike part 2, part 1 resists arrangement into internal stanzas, one effect of Melville's differing uses of punctuation in the two sections. In part 2, periods appear as end-stops in lines 4, 8, 12, 16, and 22—reinforcing the feeling of quatrains and sestet—and line 20 ends with a colon to introduce the final couplet. But in part 1, periods appear as end-stops in lines 10, 13, 18, and 23, resisting the invitation to arrange lines into stanzas that we find in part 2. The period at the end of line 10, the first period end-stop in part 1, is crucial: it concludes the group of lines whose pattern is repeated in part 2, and thus signals the interruption of the patterns of meter and rhyme that will be restored later as the people rise from dejection. Furthermore, part 1 breaks from this formal ease at a moment when something bursts through the "horror of the calm." What "burst" here are, secondly, the "events that came resounding" (l. 5) and, primarily, the ice-cracks to which those events are compared. As in the poem's opening image of the leaden sky, the ostensible metaphor here too takes precedence over its "literal" referent. In this simile, it is to resounding "events" that features of the "thunder-cracks of massy ice" are attributed, but these "events" are of secondary importance to the movement of the poem. It is the image of ice, like the "leaden sheet" in the earlier metaphor, that is rendered primary, invoking the landscape of the scene of writing.

What "bursts" through the formal calm of the poem, a "calm" to this point rendered metrically and rhythmically, is in fact the next line: "The paralysis of arm" that, within the nominal "plot" of the Civil War, prevents the arm from lifting itself in violence against its enemy. But as I have argued, that arm is not "apathetic," so this line too works against its nominal subject. What is apathetic, I have claimed, is the blank, horrifying calm at the scene of writing. Here, it is the paralysis specifically of the writing arm that breaks through, and in considering that paralysis we find both the apathy in which the poem makes its greatest investment and the generative site of its formal difficulties. It is this line, line 11, that constitutes the "extra" line in part 1, which, as I have already pointed out, is composed of twenty-three lines to part 2's twenty-two lines. I am additionally led to identify line 11 as the "extra" line by the rhyme scheme: while prior to this point the rhyme follows the pattern of part 2 (*abcbdefegh*), after this point the section establishes a new pattern (*ij gg ij klk mlm*). The *h* rhyme in line 11 stands outside the pattern to follow but does not advance the pattern previously established. It is either a near-rhyme with the preceding line (calm/arm), or a full rhyme in Melville's Northeastern accent, in which both the *l* in "calm" and the *r* in "arm" may have been silent (pronounced cawm/ awm). In either case, it represents a rhythmic moment of paralysis, in which the poem becomes stuck. Whereas in part 2 the rhyme scheme works in concert with internal end-stopped groupings of lines, this is not the case in part 1, in which, for example, what is the rhythmic sestina of lines 18–23 does not correspond to a syntactical unit, since line 18 concludes with a period end-stop and a new syntactical unit begins in line 19. The rhyme patterns and syntactical patterns of part 1 conflict with one another, and with those of part 2, formal clashes that speak to the poem's nominal interest in conflict and, more primarily, to its constitutive interest in conflicts of writing.

"The paralysis of arm" in part 1 is further linked to the production of writing, in that part 1 never produces a complete grammatical sentence. Part 2 produces one complete grammatical utterance after another (the winter and weary weeks died; the rivers melted; the tomb was rent; the rising of the People came; they rebounded; the young were all elation; they thought; and so on); but in part 1, the serial nouns constituting either a compound subject or individual subjects (November and winter and terror and the sky and events, and so on) never take verbs, a grammatical failure to produce action further associated with paralysis. Arvin's perceptive analysis of Melville's "passion of linguistic creativeness" points out that Melville invents nouns "rather forcibly and even violently from verbs" and "had a love of rare adjectives derived from nouns" but that he is "uninventive of verbs."[29] This, taken with my analysis here and in preceding chapters, suggests a stylistic relation to verbs on Melville's part related to his chronic anxiety about paralysis and blockage.

Had the word "bursting" (l. 9) appeared as "burst" (which could function either as a present or a past tense), the first ten lines of the poem would have become a complete sentence (of the form "x and y and z burst"). But the participle "bursting" thwarts grammatical completion of the sentence. The dash in line 8 sustains a double reference: "bursting" is a participial modifier for either the "events that came resounding" or "the thunder-cracks of massy ice" to which those events are compared. Thus lines 9–10 qualify but do not complete the preceding propositions, despite the period in line 10 that suggests a sentence has been completed. Melville's punctuation here thus works against his syntax. The grammatical incompletion of part 1 continues after the first period, despite periods in lines 13, 18, and 23; the idea of the series that opened the poem also continues (and the hollowness; and the fissure; then the glances; and the doubt; and the patience). Thus his syntax works against his punctuation.

Although logically speaking "The paralysis of arm" could be accommodated as an item in this stanza-long series of nouns (and the paralysis; and the hollowness; and so on), the absence of the conjunction *and* before "The paralysis" instead marks its difference from the series in process. This leads me to argue that lines 9 through 12 need also to be read against their punctuation and as the ghost of a third quatrain, that is, *within* the form *against which* this stanza is working, as follows:

> Bursting one upon another
>> Through the horror of the calm. [,]
>> The paralysis of arm
> In the anguish of the heart; [.]
> (*punctuation in brackets is mine*)

The syntactical multiplicity of "bursting" effected through its preceding dash is worthy of Emily Dickinson. In the ghost stanza I've proposed, the participle "bursting" becomes an introductory modifier modifying "paralysis" and suggesting that the paralysis of arm in the anguish of the heart bursts "one upon another" through the horror of the calm. Not only does the line itself "burst" through the formal surface in the ways I discussed above, which also suggests that line 11 is in fact the "extra" line in the stanza (and by "extra" in this context I mean one that both interrupts and that fails to be accommodated to broader formal patterns), but its association stanzaically and rhythmically with the preceding two lines suggests that its content, "paralysis of arm," is what bursts through the horror of the calm to which the poem's "apathy" speaks.

It is initially curious that paralysis in the face of the dead, the dumb, the stupefying, the leaden, should be associated with the action of "bursting," which suggests sudden violent breaking in response to pressure and strain; affectively speaking, it suggests emotion breaking forth and is thus the opposite of apathy. The emotion breaking forth, I suggest, is Melville's overwhelming, terrible awareness of that blank scene. Through the horror of the calm frozen landscape bursts the ice; through the horror of the "clammy cold November" bursts the writer's block in confrontation with the dead white landscape of the blank page (and here "calm" and "clammy" graphically echo one another, reinforcing the relation between these states of cold blankness). Writing anxiety is thus associated both with apathy (a "privation of passion" that accompanies block and inability to produce) and with the terrible frustration that accompanies that apathy, which crashes in upon him. What my account suggests is that the moments of blank dumbness are moments in which the apathy or privation of the "violent passion or excitement of the mind" that we find in the state of enthusiasm are themselves the moments of horror.

The poem thus considers in relation to one another the apathetic state of writer's block characterized by a "privation of passion" and the state of enthusiasm in which writing flows with "heat of imagination." Robert Penn Warren has commented repeatedly on what he calls the "violences" of Melville's versification, a term he uses to get at the harshness, atonality, and lyrical deficiencies critics have long noted as characteristic of the poetry.[30] In this poem, the violent prosody of part 1 emerges from the apathetic state of writer's block, while the heat of imagination in the state of enthusiasm produces the conventionally finished product (syntactically, rhythmically, and formally) of part 2. The arm paralyzed by a state of writer's block is the same arm that in the torment of getting the fiction on paper stabs and strikes in frustration. In *Battle-Pieces* the paralyzed/violent arm of writing underwrites the violent arm of war.[31] In "Apathy and Enthusiasm," the employments of the writing arm underwrite the "moods" that the prefatory note describes as the source of the collection, without necessarily predicating them upon war. (Cohen calls the poem "relatively lacking in topical allusion.")[32] Earlier, I argued that Melville's provisional relation to his nominal subject produces the volume's ineffectiveness as a record of the war. "Apathy and Enthusiasm" presents another such disjunction that illuminates the effect of the volume as a whole: one in which historically specific and even dated events feel disconcertingly out of step with whatever the poems are really about.

The mood of "enthusiasm" is again Melville's particular subject in "A Canticle: Significant of the national exaltation of enthusiasm at the close of the War." The fourth and fifth stanzas of this seven-stanza poem oppose the figures of the "Iris" and the "Giant of the Pool." The Iris is a figure of delicate beauty rescued from the threat of siege:

> Stable in its baselessness
>   When calm is in the air,
> The Iris half in tracelessness
>   Hovers faintly fair.
> Fitfully assailing it
>   A wind from heaven blows,

> Shivering and paling it
>   To blankness of the snows;
> While, incessant in renewal,
>   The Arch rekindled grows,
> Till again the gem and jewel
>   Whirl in blinding overthrows—
> Till, prevailing and transcending,
>   Lo, the Glory perfect there,
> And the contest finds an ending,
>   For repose is in the air. (ll. 24–39)

The iris, paled to blankness, is thus besieged by familiar Melvillean forces. The "repose" achieved at the end of stanza 4 is soon newly threatened in stanza 5:

> But the foamy Deep unsounded,
>   And the dim and dizzy ledge,
> And the booming roar rebounded,
>   And the gull that skims the edge!
>   The Giant of the Pool
>   Heaves his forehead white as wool—
> Toward the Iris ever climbing
>   From the Cataracts that call—
> Irremovable vast arras
>   Draping all the Wall. (ll. 40–49)

The besieging blankness in stanza 4, apparently defeated, reasserts itself here in the form of the huge figure of the "Giant of the Pool" who is "ever climbing" toward the threatened iris. The iris, presumably a flower but never in the poem identified as such, carries the deep visual resonance of a part of the eye, a resonance reinforced by the "Cataracts" out of which the Giant of the Pool climbs. These cataracts signify not only the watery depths of the Giant's "Pool," but also a disease of the eye that constitutes an additional threat to the iris. The threatening white Giant is like an "Irremovable vast arras/Draping all the Wall," a permanent force of obscured vision.

Melville's chronic eye problems that affected both his reading and his writing are conflated here with his persistent problems of writer's block as an inability to see through the obscuring force of the page. In 1872, Melville's daughter Elizabeth (Bessie) noted that he couldn't "use his eyes at all." In a letter to his cousin Catherine Gansevoort a few days later, he writes, "And now so far as this is an acknowledgment of your valued gift, it is the earliest I could make with my own hand and eyes."[33] The handwriting of this letter is thick and uncontrolled, and gets progressively thicker with increasing space between the words, a roughly contemporary example of how Melville's problems of vision affected the production and visual configuration of his writing on the page.[34]

The topos of blockage in "A Canticle" alternates with visions of "passage" in stanzas 3 and 7, both addressed to the "Lord of hosts." Each stanza includes the refrain:

> By a wondrous way and glorious
> A passage Thou dost find—
> A passage Thou dost find:
> Hosanna to the Lord of hosts,
> The hosts of human kind. (ll. 19–23 and 58–62)

These moments of imagined "passage" are presented as moments of relief; at the level of the plot, the "passage" is presumably the path out of the war whose "contest" (l. 38) underlies the poem's images of siege and threat. But while the poem is a "canticle" about the "exaltation of enthusiasm at the close of the war," the blockage experienced by the speaker is never relieved. He does not share the "passage" found in the second person by the Lord ("A passage Thou dost find"). Instead, the iris remains "half in tracelessness" (l. 26), confronting the white wall and unable to strike a passage through it, a characteristic blockage here figured as writing difficulty: "half in tracelessness" suggests that marks and blankness are phenomena actively opposing one another. In this sense the poem imagines two states like those of "Apathy and Enthusiasm," but while it nominally focuses only on the latter (in the title and the refrain), that state is precisely the state the speaker never achieves. I thus disagree with Garner's assessment of this poem as a victorious vision of successful passage. Garner writes that the Lord of hosts "is victorious, not because He led the armies into Satan's depths but because He found a 'passage' to the outcome implicit in His divine plan."[35] This reading misses the fact that the speaker does not share the victory, but is instead stuck in the state without passage, the "traceless" paralysis of arm that accompanies opaque vision. In this sense the force of Melville's poem (frustration, blockage) works against its nominal subject (exaltation, enthusiasm, passage).

The oppressiveness of the paralysis associated with the apathetic scene of writer's block is figured by the imprisoning claustrophobia of "In the Prison Pen. (1864.)":

In the Prison Pen.
(1864.)

> LISTLESS he eyes the palisades
> And sentries in the glare;

'Tis barren as a pelican-beach—
　　But his world is ended there.

Nothing to do; and vacant hands
　　Bring on the idiot-pain;
He tries to think—to recollect,
　　But the blur is on his brain.

Around him swarm the plaining ghosts
　　Like those on Virgil's shore—
A wilderness of faces dim,
　　And pale ones gashed and hoar.

A smiting sun. No shed, no tree;
　　He totters to his lair—
A den that sick hands dug in earth
　　Ere famine wasted there,

Or, dropping in his place, he swoons,
　　Walled in by throngs that press,
Till forth from the throngs they bear him dead—
　　Dead in his meagreness.

Unlike "Apathy and Enthusiasm," which takes as its nominal subject conflicting states, and "A Canticle," which takes as its nominal subject only "exaltation" but figures it as a state that the speaker himself does not achieve, "In the Prison Pen" figures oppressiveness without imagining its opposite. The uncharacteristic metrical perfection of the poem thus becomes particularly interesting, as the poem associates its own unbroken formal regularity with the unbroken forces oppressing the prisoner. The formal regularity of the poem thus functions on the side of what prohibits the prisoner from "bursting through," to borrow the term from "Apathy and Enthusiasm" for its own formal rupture. But I make this point with the full realization that what bursts through the formal regularity in "Apathy and Enthusiasm" is a state of paralysis, while enthusiasm is imagined on the side of unimpeded regular verse. Alternatively, then, in "In the Prison Pen" we find that unimpeded regular verse becomes itself an oppressive force of blockage, not an "enthusiastic" one that offers passage.

Here we can sense what was for Melville a paralyzing poetic bind: the rejection of conventional technical perfection as inadequate to his poetic desires, and his simultaneous sense that what bursts through his resistance to writing that way—if bursting through is achieved at all—is the state of writer's block itself. It is in these terms that I locate the force of Warren's insight that Melville did not learn his craft, but that the craft he did not learn was not the same craft his more highly regarded contemporaries did learn.[36] Reconsidered with particular respect to Melville's poetry, my claim here also resituates Melville's comment early in his career that he felt hopelessly stuck between two kinds of writing (his oft-noted "botches") and consequently produced neither to his own satisfaction.

At the level of the plot, the word "pen" in the title of "In the Prison Pen" denotes an enclosure prohibiting escape. Although the phrase "Prison Pen" might suggest a redundancy,[37] since presumably "prison" also denotes an enclosure prohibiting escape, the figuration of one enclosure within another effectively speaks to conditions in the prison camps like Andersonville that Melville surely has in mind here; his note to "On a natural Monument in a field of Georgia" refers to Andersonville (*BP* 253). Built in southwest Georgia in early 1864, Andersonville was notorious among Northerners for its overcrowding and shocking conditions. Each prisoner there occupied an average of thirty-four square feet of space, "without shade in a Deep South summer and with no shelter except what they could rig from sticks, tent flies, blankets, and odd bits of cloth."[38] The scene created by such a camp, recorded in photographs of the period,[39] explains Melville's metaphor of a "pelican-beach": pelicans live in enormous colonies in which each nest is spaced one bird-length apart, and the coastal areas in which they establish these colonies are barren, brutal landscapes, devoid of vegetation under a smiting sun.[40] Line 3 thus gets at both the barrenness of the landscape and the self-enclosure amidst overcrowding that characterize both pelican-beaches and camps like Andersonville.

But Melville's "pen" is also associated with the speaker's unemployment in stanza 2. His "vacant hands" suggest the "pen" as writing implement, and the suffering associated with his "vacant hands" seems to be a particular consequence of his imprisonment by the "pen." The hands themselves recall the "paralysis of arm" in "Apathy and Enthusiasm"; as in the former poem, the inability to use the arm/hands appears in conjunction with a blank landscape. There, it was wintry, dumb, and white; here, it is "barren as a pelican-beach" (l. 3), a barrenness that produces listlessness (l. 1), a state of indifference importantly akin to "apathy." Although presumably, at the level of the plot, the prisoner genuinely has "nothing to do" (l. 5), the presence of the "pen" in this scene of confinement and suffering suggests that the "vacant hands" on another level are not vacant in the sense that they are physically empty, that is, holding nothing, but rather that their "vacancy" expresses an empty state of mind, despite the fact that they are holding a "pen." The "vacant hands" are the emblems of this state of mind in which he can only "tr[y] to think" through the "blur . . . on his brain." For this prisoner of the pen, "nothing to do" signifies nothing to write, a scene of writer's block figured as imprisonment that recalls

Pierre's self-imprisonment and suffering at his writing desk. At the same time, the prisoner's isolation amidst populousness combined with the "plaining" faces swarming about him suggest Melville's self-enclosure in his study within a house overpopulated by family members all living in close quarters. Indeed, in the prose "Supplement," Melville discusses relations between North and South by noting both that "in private life true reconciliation seldom follows a violent quarrel" and that current resentments are "so close as to be almost domestic in their bitterness" (270, 272).

Furthermore, the "blur" and the "glare" in which the prisoner struggles suggest visual difficulties in which we can sense Melville's chronic eye troubles. The "smiting sun" beats down on a landscape without shed or tree; its flatness is broken only by a "den . . . dug in earth" by "sick hands" (l. 15). This scenario invokes inscription on the flat surface of the page by the "sick hands" of a prisoner who feels beaten and battered ("smiting") by his activity. Melville's note to "On a natural Monument" compares the experience of looking through the seventy-four "large double-columned pages in fine print" of the published pamphlet listing those buried at Andersonville to getting lost among head-stones, aligning the visual experience of looking at printed text with the imag-ined experience of looking at prison camp graves (253–54), a visual analogy that reinforces my claims about the poem in question.

Read in terms of the Melvillean scenarios of depth and surface as I have presented them, headstones register as the importantly superficial mark of a space "dug" in a flat field. We still have the galley proofs of *John Marr*, edited in Melville's hand; the proofs are long single columns of small print.[41] *John Marr* was of course published later than *Battle-Pieces*, but I invoke the evidence we do have—Melville's experience of textual production in 1888—to exemplify the levels of his involvement with his own printed text that obtained earlier as well, and to point out that his relation to printed text was visual in a way not always predicated upon the specific act of reading. As his analogy about looking through "large double-columned pages in fine print" suggests, he also saw text as a visual object covered with marks that are not necessarily or immediately read (which is to say, as marks rather than as words).

A palisade is a fence made of "pales" or stakes, sharpened on top and set in the ground as fortification. The "palisades/And sentries" thus both function as forces of enclosure. The "wilderness of faces dim,/And pale ones gashed and hoar" (ll. 11–12) that exert a claustrophobic and thus additionally imprisoning force echo the "pales" of which the "palisades" are made. The denotation of that word meaning a kind of fence would correctly be singular, *palisade;* the plural form, *palisades,* denotes a kind of high cliff found along the Hudson

River and elsewhere. In "The Blanket," Ishmael recalls "the old Indian characters chiselled on the famous hieroglyphic palisades on the banks of the Upper Mississippi" (*MD* 306), a recollection that equates *palisades* with a writing surface. The plural manifestation of "palisades" in line 1 thus conjoins the imprisoning palisade fence with the geological palisades Melville elsewhere associates with writing, and simultaneously participates in the poem's multiplication of pales like the "wilderness of faces dim."

The prisoner is finally "walled in by throngs that press" (l. 18), the "throngs" of faces that begin to wall up before him. These pale white faces that emerge during the scene of writing recall the faces tormenting Pierre, and in particular the face of Plotinus Plinlimmon that leers as he struggles to write. This facial topos reenacts Pierre's projection of his relation to the sheet of paper on his desk into the vertical plane of his window, where Plinlimmon's "tower face" inescapably walls up before him. The poem also reenacts the fates of both Pierre and Bartleby literally walled in at the Tombs, where they die. "In the Prison Pen" is in this sense the poetic version of *Pierre,* and here, too, the "prison" and the "pen" in the title of the poem also signify in their alliterative recollection of Plotinus Plinlimmon's name and of the letters—*pp*—that Melville distills in *The Confidence-Man* to the level of the character.

Thus we can see Melville's poems as "battle pieces" for whose form and terms the conflicts and moods of the scene of writing are constitutive. The site of resistance in these poems of conflict and writer's block is the white sheet associated with the "paralysis of arm," like the blank page suspended at the opening of *Battle-Pieces* after the suspension of John Brown's body, a conjunction that renders the blank page a metonymic portent.[42] The suspension at the end of *Billy Budd* of both Billy's body and of "Billy in the Darbies" speaks to a related problem of poetic production. *Billy Budd* distinguishes its own form from the "symmetry of form attainable in pure fiction" (*BB* 380), I maintain, because the " 'forms, measured forms' " (380) of poetry lie at its heart: *Billy Budd* too is one of Melville's experiments in mixed prose and verse. Vere's obsession with the "disruption of forms" (380) thus resonates with Melville's relation to genre in general, and to poetry in particular.

Vere's attempt to reinstitute "measured forms" by hanging Billy is a gesture of authoritarian measurement associated with the force of poetic convention. It is in this way that I understand the importance of the tale's use of the language of poetry.[43] Billy's sacrifice at the hand of "measured forms," recounted in the concluding poem by a foretopman "gifted, as some sailors are, with an artless *poetic* temperament" (*BB* 384; emphasis in original), recalls the oppressive regular verse of "In the Prison Pen" that triumphs with Vere over Melville's irregular poetry. It is in these terms that we can see why the darbies are central to the poem, and why the poem ends with a plea to ease constrained hands: "Just ease these darbies at the wrist." In this sense, *Billy Budd*—composed at the end of Melville's life, as he was simultaneously working on his last two volumes of poetry—is Melville's reflection upon his own career as a poet.

The battle-pieces I have discussed posit two conflicting states generated by the scene of writing: apathy and enthusiasm. The first state is identified with the scene of writing and is clearly achieved. The other is posited only by imagining a "passage" from the state of apathy that consistently remains blocked or unsatisfying. My assessment here is one way of understanding why Melville constantly changes poetic form in this volume. William Shurr comments that Melville does not use a single poetic form twice in *Battle-Pieces,* and Fogle argues that in Melville's verses "some preexisting and still-undissolved model can almost always be perceived,"[44] another sign of Melville's battle with form. Darrel Abel points out that Melville thought the dulcet rhythms of traditional English verse were inappropriate to his subjects and thought process.[45] In *Battle-Pieces* considered as a collection, Melville's unyielding formal experiments sustain a poetic battle against regularity.

The quite explicit analogy between poetic form and war in "A Utilitarian View of the Monitor's Fight" aligns Melville's own "ponderous" (l. 2) verse with "plain mechanic power/Plied cogently in War" (ll. 9–10). This poem is above all about war poetry rather than about war itself: the word "view" in the title speaks to how the poet sees the problem of writing about war. The opening formal proposition—"Plain be the phrase, yet apt the verse,/More ponderous than nimble" (ll. 1–2)—helps to gloss the third stanza:

> Yet this was battle, and intense—
> Beyond the strife of fleets heroic;
> Deadlier, closer, calm 'mid storm;
> No passion; all went on by crank,
> Pivot, and screw,
> And calculations of caloric. (ll. 13–18)

The affect here—dead, close, calm amid storm, void of passion—invokes Melville's scene of writing as the "battle" in question. By constantly changing how he engages the page from poem to poem (and sometimes within poems), Melville refuses to let the oppressive white space rest.

P.S.: Marks in "John Marr"

~

"J ohn Marr," the title poem of Melville's 1888 volume *John Marr and Other Sailors with Some Sea-Pieces,* privately printed in an edition of twenty-five copies,[1] is composed of a prose piece followed by a poem. The prose section tells the story of a landlocked ex-sailor, "disabled . . . by a crippling wound received at close quarters," who suffers silently in the face of thoroughgoing unresponsiveness from man and nature. The "blank stillness" of the prairie that reminds him of ocean gives geographic form to Moby-Dick, whose blank physiognomy Ishmael discusses in a chapter entitled "The Prairie." The blank stillness that reigns unbroken on this prairie—"the bed of a dried-up sea," in John Marr's words—is occasionally broken by "the prairie-hen, sometimes startled from its lurking-place."[2]

John Marr's life—geographically isolated, among people with "no art at all"—is one in which "something was lacking." He likens the "unresponsiveness" of the people around him to "the apathy of Nature herself." In his attempts to fill his "void" at heart, "he is obstructed" (phrasing that Melville rewrote from past into the present tense as he worked on the manuscript).[3] In this state of isolated enclosure, John Marr confronts the "phantoms" that are the faces of his past—chums, wife, child—phantoms that are first "absent to sight," then "losing something of their first indistinctness and putting on at last a dim semblance of mute life." The phantoms shift from invisibility to equivocal vision ("dim"), but even as his visual relation to them changes, they remain silent. In the text of the poem that follows, John Marr is "striving . . . to get into verbal Communion with them; or, under yet stronger illusion, reproaching them for their silence," as he sees them "Swimming out from seas of faces" (l. 22).[4]

123

The chronic unresponsiveness John Marr confronts is "of a piece with the apathy of Nature herself as envisaged to him here on a prairie where none but the perished Mound-Builders had as yet left a durable mark." The "envisaged" apathetic blankness of the prairie is nature's face; that apathetic blank face is "of a piece"—invoking Melville's own poetry—with an apathy that I have elsewhere linked to writer's block. The apathy of the terrain thwarts "durable marks," and the problem that faces John Marr is whether he can produce durable marks in the face of such resistance. We know that he has left one such mark, in the shape of the "mound, though a small one, in the wide prairie" in which he commits his wife and son to the earth; the status of his "mound," given that only the perished Mound-Builders have "as yet" left a durable one, is rendered uncertain. His name, "Marr," comes not only from the verb "mar," whose denotations include "to injure," and "to hamper, hinder, interfere with"—John Marr is not only wounded but, in his isolation, "cut off, quite cut off"—but also from "John Marr"'s extended reflection upon marking marks. The word *Marr* echoes in the word *mark,* whose importance the text itself stresses. "Marr" also carries the initial capital *M* that is a signature for "Melville."[5]

The phrase "none but the perished Mound-Builders had as yet left a durable mark," which ends a sentence in the printed text, continues in the manuscript: "and that not distinguishable at a glance," which is then struck through.[6] The page is written in black ink, in Melville's hand; a page number and bracket appear in blue pencil at top left; at the bottom right corner, in red pencil, appears a large backward *p* (see illustration 9).[7] I call this a backward *p* rather than a *q,* bearing in mind my discussion about "p's and q's" in chapter 4, because I take this reversed *p* to be the symbol for "paragraph," which was so represented at the time (and still is).[8] The end of this sentence does mark a paragraph break in the printed text, and the manuscript features numerous other notes to the printer in Melville's hand. He writes, for example, "To the Printer: where the line has a red cross in margin—*indent.* And so in other Pieces similarly marked."[9]

But the interest of this mark extends beyond its utility as a paragraph marker. This is an unusual mark in the *John Marr* manuscript, unlike the *Typee* manuscript, in which the entire text is peppered with paragraph marks. In the *Typee* manuscript, Melville used a *p* facing forward, as shown in illustration 3. As illustration 9 shows, the mark in *John Marr* is comparatively large, and appears in the white space beneath the paragraph, rather than adjacent to or even overinscribing the first word of the new paragraph, as is the case in *Typee.*

The text above this large red mark is a meditation about durable marks; the canceled phrase "and that not distinguishable at a glance" recalls chapter 14

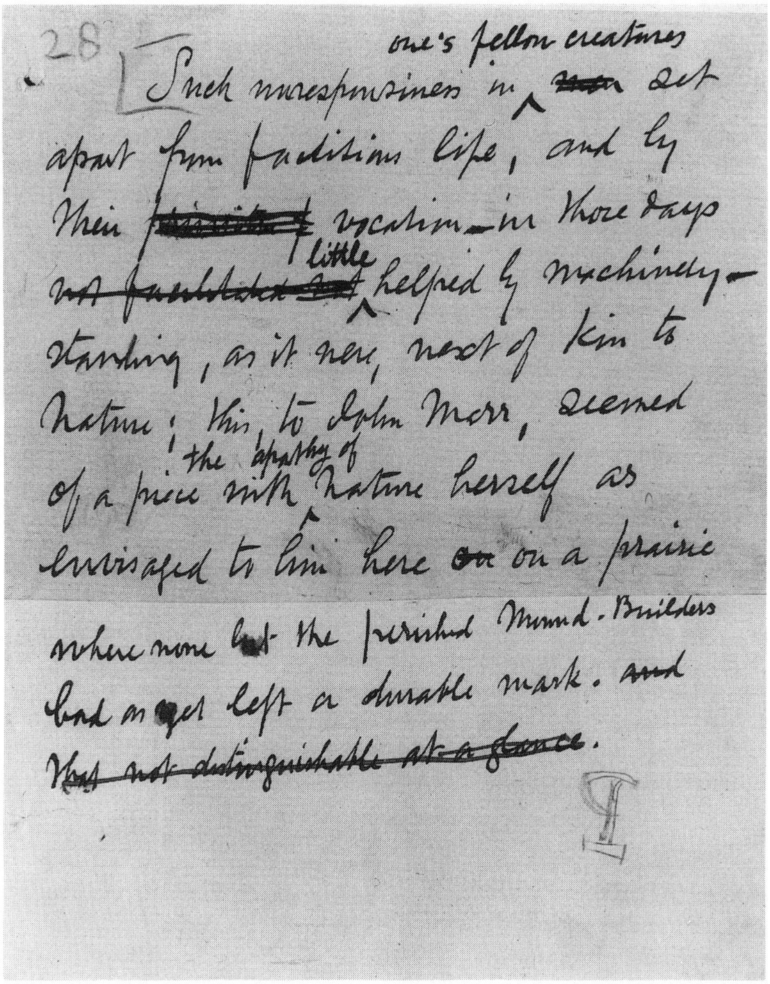

Illustration 9. Manuscript page from *John Marr and Other Sailors with Some Sea-Pieces*, showing large backward *p* in red pencil. By permission of the Houghton Library, Harvard University [MsAm188 (370)].

of *The Confidence-Man* and its extended meditation upon characters as "those mere phantoms which flit along a page, like shadows along a wall" (*CM* 69). The durable mark that is "not distinguishable at a glance" in "John Marr" echoes with the "fiction, where every character can, by reason of its consistency, be comprehended at a glance" in *The Confidence-Man* (69–70). *The Confidence-Man* presents the latter proposition as the opposite of Melville's own text, which is thus placed under the sign of characters that *cannot* "be comprehended at a glance," mere phantoms flitting along the novelist's page. In this sense the meditation in "John Marr" upon a mark "not distinguishable at a glance" redeploys *The Confidence-Man*'s terms for its own operations.

The Confidence-Man's extended meditation upon the letter *p* as a graphic mark returns here in "John Marr." The character *p* is written backwards, graphically embodying the tautological mirror structure that opens chapter 14: "As the last chapter was begun with a reminder looking forwards, so the present must consist of one glancing backwards." At the same time, that backward-glancing *p* is a typographical and editing symbol, one Melville uses to shape the final appearance of the material text but that will not itself appear *as* a mark. This "durable mark" is thus one whose very durability exists under erasure; it configures the layout of the visible text but its effect will finally be apparent in its own invisibility, its absence as a mark from the final printed page. By its nature as a paragraph mark, the mark of its durability on the printed page is white space.

Melville's mark appears in the ample white space at the bottom of a page. The *John Marr* manuscript shows that he often leaves the bottom quarter of these pages blank, a space sometimes filled in by what appear to be later insertions of text, squeezed in in a cramped hand or patched in. Melville thus wrote this white space into his manuscript *as* white space, and simultaneously envisioned it as a field—an apathetic terrain—in which text might or might not later emerge. His rich engagement in "John Marr" with the durability of marks, emblematized in what is, perhaps, finally a scribble, constitutes a drama of in/visibility upon the surface of the page by whose blank visage "he is obstructed."

Notes

~

Introduction

1. "Hawthorne and His Mosses," *PT* 249. Subsequent page references are included in the text.

2. In the pages that follow, I use the words *material* and *materiality* in my assessments of the scene of writing to get at two primary sets of significations, which, I argue, bear upon one another in Melville's case. First, I mean to get at a thorny philosophical issue for Melville: the opposition between the material and the ideal. For purposes of this study I usually use the term *transcendental* to designate idealist strains of thought, for historical reasons. (Emerson's definition of transcendentalism was "idealism as it appears in 1842." See "The Transcendentalist" in *Ralph Waldo Emerson: Selected Essays*, ed. Larzer Ziff [1982; New York: Viking Penguin, 1985], 239.) Second, I mean the matter of writing, its physical forms and components. I include here both the physical aspects of writing as an activity (for example, where and how Melville writes, and what his compositional habits are) as well as the physical features of the written page itself (for example, ink, paper, handwriting, spelling, typeface, and so on). I bring all these material conditions to bear on Melville's texts, in fact arguing that the material frequently gives rise to both their "figurative" and their "literal" aspects.

It is crucial to understanding the argument that follows that the term *material* be distinguished from both the figurative and the literal. While the terms *figurative* and *literal* are concerned with a word's inflections of meaning, the meaning of a word, whether figurative or literal, differs from the status of a word as itself a thing: produced in a particular manner with particular tools, shaped a particular way, composed of particular letters, inscribed in a particular space on the page. To consider a word as a material thing is not to consider its "content" (denotation, connotation, or figuration) at all. My analyses often combine attention to material issues with attention to issues of figuration, but these must be understood as fundamentally different properties of words.

My invocation of the "materiality of writing" calls upon such recent work as that by Michael Fried and Jonathan Goldberg, both of whom invoke similar terminology. On the complex significations of the word *materialism*, see Raymond Williams, *Keywords: A Vocabulary of Culture and Society (New York: Oxford UP, 1976)*. The phrase "scene of writing" as I use it carries the trace of Jacques Derrida's essay "Freud and the Scene of Writing," with its investigation of "a historical repression and suppression of writing since Plato" (*Writing and Difference*, trans. Alan Bass [Chicago: U of Chicago P, 1978], 196–231).

3. Merton M. Sealts Jr., Historical Note to *PT*, 459.

4. To Evert A. Duyckinck, 3 Mar. 1849 and 2 and 14 Dec. 1849, L 122, 149.

5. To Nathaniel Hawthorne, [1 June?] 1851, L 191.

6. To Evert A. Duyckinck, 3 Mar. 1849, L 122.

7. In his analysis of the magazine culture of Melville's day, Perry Miller notes that anonymous publication was a kind of game with readers, who were challenged to recognize styles. Editors would often later reveal the author's identity. Pseudonymous publication, according to Miller, was a practice that sustained the aristocratic pretense that one wrote not for pay but for amusement (*The Raven and the Whale: The War of Words and Wits in the Era of Poe and Melville* [1956; Westport, Conn.: Greenwood, 1973], 36). I have suggested ways in which these conventional practices were inflected in the case of Melville in particular.

8. To Richard Bentley, 16 Apr. 1852, L 228; also see Leon Howard and Hershel Parker, Historical Note to *P*, 367.

9. Edgar A. Dryden argues that Melville's commitment to truth-telling in fiction threatened madness because such truths were destructive. Melville's anxieties about discovering these destructive truths led to his adoption of narrative masks that provided him with psychological impunity. He also takes Melville's remarks in "Hawthorne and His Mosses" that "all fine authors are fictitious ones" and that fiction is the "great Art of Telling the Truth" to indicate that "all of Melville's narrators are, in some way, portraits of the artist at work." See Dryden's first chapter, "Metaphysics and the Art of the Novel," *Melville's Thematics of Form: The Great Art of Telling the Truth* (1968; Baltimore: Johns Hopkins UP, 1981), 3–29, 29; also Thomas C. Carlson, "Fictive Voices in Melville's Reviews, Letters, and Prefaces," *Interpretations* 6 (1974): 39–46.

10. "What I feel most moved to write, that is banned,—it will not pay. Yet, altogether write the *other* way I cannot. So the product is a final hash, and all my books are botches" (to Nathaniel Hawthorne, [1 June?] 1851, L 191; emphasis in original).

11. "I love all men who *dive*. Any fish can swim near the surface, but it takes a great whale to go down stairs five miles or more," he wrote to Duyckinck in a discussion of Emerson (to Evert A. Duyckinck, 3 Mar. 1849, L 121).

12. To Lemuel Shaw, 6 Oct. 1849, L 139.

13. "It seems to me now that Solomon was the truest man who ever spoke, and yet that he a little *managed* the truth with a view to popular conservatism; or else there have been many corruptions and interpolations of the text" (to Nathaniel Hawthorne, [1 June?] 1851, L 193; emphasis in original).

14. To Nathaniel Hawthorne, [1 June?] 1851, L 191. John Bryant's thesis that an "aesthetics of repose" that is "mild, silent, calm" is a constant in Melville's writing is, I believe, out of touch with Melville's relation to his writing and with his experience of the writing process (*Melville and Repose: The Rhetoric of Humor in the American Renaissance* [New York: Oxford UP, 1993], 9).

15. The term *thematic* needn't be defined only in this way, but I define it as such to specify simultaneous and sometimes competing effects in Melville's case. Werner Sollors

puts warranted pressure on the notion of the "thematic" and its implementation in literary studies in *The Return of Thematic Criticism,* pointing out both contemporary disparagement of thematic studies and the ways in which such disparagement is often a polemical position blind to its own practice. Sollors points out that what he calls "the antithematic affect" is "so deeply ingrained that one might think of it as an episteme of contemporary criticism," although critics continue to engage in "widespread, yet undeclared 'thematic' practice" under other names while openly disclaiming "thematology" as such (Introduction, *The Return of Thematic Criticism,* Harvard English Studies 18 [Cambridge, Mass.: Harvard UP, 1993], xiii). Sollors and the critics whose work he collects in his volume usefully examine the theoretical, historical, and practical dimensions of thematology. I place my own work within this critical realm both in its designation of a "theme" in Melville's work, and in its interest in thinking through the implications of such a designation in adequately complex terms.

16. The quoted phrase is from Melville's poem "Art," *Collected Poems of Herman Melville,* ed. Howard P. Vincent (Chicago: Hendricks House, 1947), 231, l. 11. My vision of the page here is indebted to Michael Fried's compelling assessment of the specifically facial quality of the page and its invocation of the materiality of writing in the work of Stephen Crane, Joseph Conrad, and Frank Norris. See "Almayer's Face: On 'Impressionism' in Conrad, Crane, and Norris," *Critical Inquiry* 17.1 (1990): 193–236, and *Realism, Writing, Disfiguration: On Thomas Eakins and Stephen Crane* (Chicago: U of Chicago P, 1986).

17. Based on my assessment of the manuscript at the Houghton Library, Harvard University [MSAm 188 (387)]. For a genetic transcript of "Art," see *Collected Poems,* 506–7.

18. To Evert A. Duyckinck, 24 Feb. 1849, L 119, and to Evert A. Duyckinck, 26 Mar. 1851, L 183.

19. To Allan Melville, 10, 13, 14 Nov. 1856, L 303; also see Davis and Gilman, *Letters* 181, n. 9.

20. His uncle, Peter Gansevoort, provided the funds to publish *Clarel* in August of 1875. After Gansevoort's death, his daughter, Catherine Gansevoort Lansing, gave Melville another $100 to cover additional publication expenses that the original $1,200 gift had not covered. Apparently Melville agonized over this additional gift, alternately accepting it and returning it and then accepting it again over the course of almost a year. Melville accepted the $100 in August 1876; thought better of it in September and donated it to the organization mentioned; accepted another $100 from Catherine in January 1877; revoked it by letter in March; and finally returned the money in June, apparently ending the exchange. (To Peter Gansevoort, 26 Aug. 1875, L 431–32; and to Catherine Gansevoort Lansing, 25 July 1876 and 2 Aug. 1876, L 437–41, 13 Sept. 1876 and 26 Sept. 1876, L 443–45, 4 Jan. 1877, L 449, and 7 Mar. 1877, L 449–51.) On his attempts to sell Arrowhead, see Jay Leyda, *The Melville Log: A Documentary Life of Herman Melville, 1819–1891,* 2 vols. (New York: Harcourt Brace, 1951), 2:506.

21. He characteristically omitted certain letters of the alphabet singly or in groups, and abbreviated certain words ("recvd" for "received" and "Mondy Eveng" for "Monday Evening," for example). These "condensed words" are not always consistent, and Davis and Gilman speculate that they are in some cases deliberate abbreviations, but in others are more likely irregularities produced by Melville's "haste or carelessness" in the formation of letters. See Merrell R. Davis and William H. Gilman's introduction to *Letters,* esp.

"Melville's Hand," xxi–xxv (also rpt. in L 847–51), and Lynn Horth, Note on the Text, L 824–37. On the difficulties of reading Melville's handwriting in general, see John Bryant, "Melville's L-Word: First Intentions and Final Readings in *Typee*," *New England Quarterly* 63.1 (1990): 120–31, and the Textual Notes to Davis and Gilman's *Letters*. Of course not all of Melville's habits of hand were unique to him; for example, abbreviating words was common in nineteenth-century epistles. But I situate Melville's habits of hand, both those that are unique and those that are conventions, in terms of his particular relations to the page. Even practices that were conventions did not signify the same way for all writers. On writing practices within the Melville family more generally, see note 89 to chapter 3.

22. My study thus lends a particular material content to Milton R. Stern's important argument about Melville and idealism: "The totality of the books presents man's search for an informing ideal that is more than physical causation. . . . And Melville always presents the quest as futile" (see chap. 1, "The Absolute and the Natural," *The Fine Hammered Steel of Herman Melville* [1957; Urbana: U of Illinois P, 1968], 11, 1–28).

While my argument is predicated upon a recognition of the historically specific cultural depth of many of Melville's central terms—antebellum investments in notions of "transparency," for example, appear in everything from advice manuals and physiognomical tracts to Emerson's essays, so Melville's figuration of scenarios of transparency and its impossibility lends culturally specific inflection to his particular engagements—the cultural work of those terms themselves, construed from that standpoint of inquiry, is finally of secondary consequence to my study. And while I engage at greater and lesser length particular cultural effects (for example, conceptions of penmanship and of character in the antebellum North), I read Melville's inflection of those effects through the site of his scene of writing: indeed, it is my argument that the scene of writing is the source of the ultimate force in his work.

Melville's relation to the scene of writing is itself part of "history" and "culture" (to choose two particular points of focus in recent literary criticism), as well as, more specifically, part of a history of the thematics of writing. For a recent debate about situating a thematics of writing within literary critical discourses, see the exchange between Michael Fried and Bill Brown in *Critical Inquiry* (Fried, "Almayer's Face"; Brown, "Writing, Race, and Erasure: Michael Fried and the Scene of Reading," *Critical Inquiry* 18 [1992]: 387–402; and Fried, "Response to Bill Brown," *Critical Inquiry* 18 [1992]: 403–10. Walter Benn Michaels argues that the materiality of writing is a concern crucial to artistic representation in America from the end of the Civil War to the beginning of World War I (*The Gold Standard and the Logic of Naturalism: American Literature at the Turn of the Century* [Berkeley: U of California P, 1987]; see his introduction in particular). Mark Maslan provocatively explores a thematics of faces and writing in the case of Whitman's *Drum-Taps* ("Whitman's 'Strange Hand': Body as Text in *Drum-Taps*," *ELH* 58 [1991]: 935–55.

23. To Nathaniel Hawthorne [17?] Nov. 1851, L 212–13. The original letter has not been located.

24. Melville's wish to efface the material ("book") in this love letter to Hawthorne (see Edwin Haviland Miller, *Melville* [New York: George Braziller, 1975] and Caleb Crain, "Lovers of Human Flesh: Homosexuality and Cannibalism in Melville's Novels," *American Literature* 66 [1994]: 25–53) is reconfigured in *Clarel* as the interfering inef-

faceability of the material male body, which obstructs union between men. In the section "Vine and Clarel"—and I should add that scholars have long identified Vine as Hawthorne, an argument first made by Walter E. Bezanson and with which I concur—Clarel imagines Vine's "rebukeful dusking" (2.27.116) in response to the "inklings he let fall" (2.27.111) of his desire to "wed/Our souls in one" (2.27.106–7):

> But for thy fonder dream of love
> In man toward man—the soul's caress—
> The negatives of flesh should prove
> Analogies of non-cordialness
> In spirit. (2.27.124–28)

Putting words in Vine's mouth, Clarel imagines the "negatives of flesh" as a material blockage to the union of souls. I read this passage as a reversal of the gratifying dissolution and consequent union we find in the letter to Hawthorne in the present discussion.

25. My speculation that the phrase "turns over another page" signifies that the page of Melville's letter itself was turned at that point must remain speculation, since the original letter is unlocated.

26. To Nathaniel Hawthorne, [17?] Nov. 1851, L 212.

27. See Editorial Appendices to M 686 and to PT 652.

28. To Evert A. Duyckinck, 2 and 14 Dec. 1849, L 149.

29. Barbara Johnson, "Melville's Fist: The Execution of *Billy Budd*," *Studies in Romanticism* 18 (1979): 567–99.

30. Thus my assessment inverts readings that have been powerfully formative in their eschewal of the material components and force of Melville's writing. William Ellery Sedgwick's 1945 study proposes as "fundamental in Melville" the "sense of the interdependence of ultimate truth and inward realization"; Richard Chase argues that the "White Whale is for Ahab the mask which affirms, because of its horror and beauty, that all human, natural, and divine reality is concealed behind the masks of appearance"; Elizabeth S. Foster's introduction to *The Confidence-Man* comments, "Like Shakespeare, Melville was bemused with the falseness of appearances in this life, the oppositeness of appearance and reality." In the *Literary History of the United States,* Willard Thorp describes Melville's writing in terms of "his long quest for the ultimate truth. He would have an answer from the inscrutable mask of the universe. The appearance of things must be made to dissolve into the reality beyond." Charles Feidelson Jr. and Harry Levin place Melville in the context of "symbolism," an essentially antimaterial notion, as the crucial phenomenon in American writing. (I should add that both also see Ahab as a disappointed transcendentalist impatient with the material, a characterization with which I agree.) See William Ellery Sedgwick, *Herman Melville: The Tragedy of Mind* (Cambridge: Harvard UP, 1945), 12; Richard Chase, *Herman Melville: A Critical Study* (New York: Macmillan, 1949), 99; Elizabeth S. Foster, Introduction, *The Confidence-Man: His Masquerade,* by Herman Melville (New York: Hendricks House, 1954), xv; Willard Thorp, *Literary History of the United States,* ed. Robert E. Spiller, Willard Thorp, et al., 2 vols. [New York: Macmillan, 1948], 1:451); Charles Feidelson Jr., *Symbolism and American Literature* (Chicago: U of Chicago P, 1953), 4, 28; Harry Levin, *The Power of Blackness: Hawthorne Poe Melville* (New York: Knopf, 1958), 39, 166). In my account, the history of Melville criticism has largely valued Melville's writing (or, more recently,

devalued it) as a transcendental quest without seeing what, specifically, that quest itself seeks unsuccessfully to efface: his experience of sitting at his desk looking at a piece of paper, either blank or in the process of inscription.

Chapter One: Melville's Spell in *Typee*

1. Murray was not the only publisher who smelled fiction and disliked it. The house of Harper had compared the manuscript to *Robinson Crusoe*, but rejected it because "it was impossible that it could be true and therefore was without real value." Richard Tobias Greene, the man who had appeared as "Toby" in Melville's novel, announced through a Buffalo, N.Y., newspaper that he could testify to Melville's veracity. The controversy over the "authenticity" of Melville's narrative is particularly ironic since the book was published in two versions under five different titles. Leon Howard, Historical Note, *T* 278–80, 287, 288; Editorial Appendix to *T* 344.

2. Quoted in Sealts, Historical Note, *PT* 460.

3. Charles Roberts Anderson, *Melville in the South Seas* (1939; New York: Dover, 1966), 192.

4. Anderson, 126, 191, 166.

5. Hershel Parker, "Evidences for 'Late Insertions' in Melville's Works," *Studies in the Novel* 7 (1975): 413.

6. Nina Baym, "Melville's Quarrel with Fiction," *PMLA* 94.5 (1979): 911. On contemporary reactions to *Typee*, see Titus Munson Coan and J. E. A. Smith's remarks as quoted by Merton M. Sealts Jr. in *The Early Lives of Melville: Nineteenth-Century Biographical Sketches and Their Authors* (Madison: U of Wisconsin P, 1974), 44, 125, 127.

7. See Milton R. Stern's *Critical Essays on Herman Melville's "Typee"* (Boston: G. K. Hall, 1982) for a broad sampling of excerpts from the critical tradition. Some examples of the approaches I refer to include, on "civilization" v. "the primitive," D. H. Lawrence's *Studies in Classic American Literature* (1923; New York: Viking, 1961) and Lawrance Thompson, "Eden Revisited," in *Melville's Quarrel with God* (Princeton: Princeton UP, 1952), 43–55. Michael Rogin maintains that Melville "entered literature as a spokesman for the aboriginal victims of Manifest Destiny" (*Subversive Genealogy: The Politics and Art of Herman Melville* [1979; Berkeley: U of California P, 1985], 48). Mitchell Breitwieser argues that Tommo's "sympathy" toward the Typees is "unwittingly complicit in what it resents," and that in *Typee* Melville scrutinizes Tommo's sentiments toward this end ("False Sympathy in Melville's *Typee*," *American Quarterly* 34.4 [1982]: 396).

8. Stern, *Critical Essays on Herman Melville's "Typee,"* 1.

9. See, for example, Anderson, 146. Stanton Garner recapitulates this defense in his 1993 *The Civil War World of Herman Melville* when he addresses Melville's borrowings from *The Rebellion Record*. He writes, "What use Herman did make of the *Record* is defensible. *Pace* Edgar Allan Poe, it was not unusual or unprofessional, then or later, for an artist to exploit existing written materials in his imaginative work, providing he refashioned them. Through the power of his imagination, Herman made his borrowings his own property" (*The Civil War World of Herman Melville* [Lawrence: UP of Kansas, 1993], 390).

10. Jay Fliegelman argues that the plagiarism debate over Thomas Jefferson's "authorship" of the Declaration of Independence caught Jefferson between competing

aesthetics as the rhetorical agenda that valued "harmonizing" traditional thought gave way to a new aesthetic of authorship that valued originality and novel self-expression. See *Declaring Independence: Jefferson, Natural Language, and the Culture of Performance* (Stanford: Stanford UP, 1993). For another exploration of that plagiarism debate, see my "'Declaration-Men' and the Rhetoric of Self-Presentation," *Early American Literature* 24.2 (1989): 120–34.

11. Howard P. Vincent, *The Trying-Out of "Moby-Dick"* (1949; Kent, Ohio: Kent State UP, 1980), 6.

12. Gordon Roper, Historical Note, *O* 325.

13. Harrison Hayford and Walter Blair, Editors' Introduction, *Omoo: A Narrative of Adventures in the South Seas,* by Herman Melville (New York: Hendricks House, 1969), xx–xxi. Anderson had not detected how extensively Melville borrowed in *Omoo,* judging it to be "perhaps the most strictly autobiographical of all Melville's works" (197–99).

14. In a study that sees varieties of plagiarism as an important part of Melville's compositional technique in *Redburn,* Stephen Mathewson usefully points out, "Having Redburn read *The Picture of Liverpool* achieves the same end as plagiarizing it: Melville is 'swelling out' his 'volume' by using the book in two ways while writing." Mathewson also proposes that Melville is engaged in what he calls "self-plagiarism," by repeating material throughout the novel to flesh it out to the desired length ("'To Tell Over Again the Story Just Told': The Composition of Melville's *Redburn,*" *ESQ* 37.4 [1991]: 315, 314).

15. John Samson, *White Lies: Melville's Narratives of Facts* (Ithaca: Cornell UP, 1989), 53 ff., 56.

16. Howard points out Melville's equivocation here about having told the truth (Historical Note, *T* 293). Bryant notes that Melville's fundamental anxiety in *Typee* is that "he was publishing false goods and knew it" (*Melville and Repose,* 132).

17. Goldberg has demonstrated that debates about orthography in the English Renaissance were often based on the notion that orthography represented a realm of truth that the letter should transparently signify. John Hart wrote in his *Orthographie* (1569), "Orthographie is a Greeke woorde signifying true writing" (*Writing Matter: From the Hands of the English Renaissance* [Stanford: Stanford UP, 1990], 190 ff.). Goldberg also notes that spelling reform in English has always been based on the dream of reducing writing to a transparency. See especially "Letters Themselves: Inventions of the Hand," 171–229.

18. Stevenson is quoted by Anderson (444, n. 24) and Hayford and Blair (344, n. 2.28); Anderson, 80.

19. Broadly speaking, American spelling practices, particularly in the early national period, need to be contextualized as a social issue with important determinants and consequences growing out of notions of democracy and cultural independence. For an able discussion of this issue, see David Simpson, *The Politics of American English, 1776–1850* (New York: Oxford UP, 1986).

20. To Evert A. Duyckinck, 2 and 14 Dec. 1849, L 148 and 12 Feb. 1851, L 180; to Allan Melville, 10, 13, and 14 Nov. 1856, L 302; and to Evert A. Duyckinck, 13 July 1846, L 50.

21. To John Murray, 28 Jan. 1849, L 114.

22. Merton M. Sealts Jr., *Melville's Reading: Revised and Enlarged Edition* (n.p.: U of South Carolina P, 1988), 225.

23. Howard, Historical Note, *T* 280.

24. Howard, Historical Note, *T* 282.

25. Bryant, "Melville's L-Word," 125, and Note on the Text, *T* 303–25.

26. To John Murray, 15 July 1846, L 58.

27. Norman Eugene Jarrard, "Poems by Herman Melville: A Critical Edition of the Published Verse" (Ph.D. diss., University of Texas, 1960), 11. The Northwestern-Newberry edition's method for the treatment of spelling is "to correct spellings which were unacceptable by the standards" of the year of publication, but "to retain any acceptable variants." Any emendations made are cataloged in the List of Emendations to each text; thus, as the editors point out in the Note on the Text to *T,* by using the editorial apparatus anyone can reconstruct the copy-text in every textual detail (324). See the Treatment of Accidentals section in the Note on the Text in any of the Northwestern-Newberry volumes. Jacqueline Foulque, who published a French translation of *Omoo* (1951), "corrected" Melville's erratic spellings based on her familiarity with Polynesian languages. Hayford and Blair cite her *Omoo, ou le Vagabond du Pacifique* (Gallimard: Paris, 1951) extensively in their edition (xvi; Explanatory Notes). Davis and Gilman "silently" normalize Melville's spelling on some occasions, and on other occasions cite their spelling changes in the notes (Textual Notes, 321).

28. The spellings I discuss in this section and following are derived from my own reading of the original manuscript, which I had the good fortune to be able to study before its fragility necessitated denying access to it. (Gansevoort-Lansing Collection, Rare Books and Manuscripts Division, New York Public Library, Astor, Lenox and Tilden Foundations). I have numbered the draft pages found in 1983 sequentially, not including the leaf extant prior to that time, which sequentially speaking would come between pp. 22 and 23 in my numbering system. Since this single leaf extant prior to 1983 has not been inserted into its place in the narrative among the leaves found together, I have not numbered it with them.

What appears to be "KoKiri" appears on what I have numbered p. 10 of the draft; "Kiri Kiri" appears on p. 21. For additional readings, see also the genetic transcription in *T* 366–69; and John Bryant, "Melville, 'Little Henry,' and the Process of Composition: A Peep at the *Typee* Fragment," *Melville Society Extracts* 67 (1986): 1. See *T* 368–69 for reproduction and genetic transcription of the page on which the overscored "Fayaway" appears. Illustration 1 (of p. 20) shows the spellings "Tippii," "Tipii," and "Kiri Kiri"; illustration 2 (of p. 5) shows the spelling "Kori Kori"; and illustration 3 (of p. 7) shows "Kori Kori."

29. The fact that one letter may represent more than one sound or that more letters may be used than are required by a particular sound perturbed John Hart in his 1569 *Orthographie.* Goldberg points out that this "independence of letters from their truth function" was one Hart condemned as "corrupted" and "false" (*Writing Matter,* 192).

30. See, for example, pp. 13, 16, and 17 of the draft.

31. Bette S. Weidman, "*Typee* and *Omoo:* A Diverging Pair," *A Companion to Melville Studies,* ed. John Bryant (New York: Greenwood, 1986), 95; *T* 100.

32. Melville does not mention other works that may have been useful to him. See Anderson, 118–19.

33. Hayford and Blair, Editors' Introduction, xxii.

34. The text from "Among . . . subject" in the passage quoted was deleted in the AR

edition. See Howard, Historical Note, *T* 289 and List of Substantive Variants, *T* 346, 6.4–10.

35. Historical Note, *T* 289.

36. To John Murray, 15 July 1846, L 55; emphasis in original.

37. Hayford and Blair, Explanatory Notes, 345. They do invoke an aural argument when they argue that Melville's troublesome use of the letter *r,* for example in the word *Happar,* is attributable to the Northeastern American dialect of silent *r*'s constituting a long *a* sound (346). Their argument is complicated by the evidence in the manuscript that Melville did not spell *Happar* with the final *r* at this stage of production, so the invocation of sound reproduction as a ground again goes awry.

38. Hayford and Blair, Explanatory Notes, 344.

In J. Orville Taylor's *The District School* (New York: Harper, 1834), which was one of several books Melville's uncle Peter Gansevoort gave him while he was teaching, Taylor writes that the error at the root of so much bad spelling is that children in school "correct their spelling by the sense of hearing," spelling words the teacher pronounces. But outside the classroom people need to spell words that appear "not through the sense of hearing (the sense that has been educated, and always applied to as the corrective), but through the sense of seeing. The pupil has not been accustomed to judge whether words are spelled correctly or not by their appearance on paper, and the false spelling, not coming under the trial of the ear, escapes the unskilful observance of the eye" (147). Melville singled out Taylor's book as "of eminent usefulness" (to Peter Gansevoort, 30 Dec. 1837, L 8).

39. French spelling of Polynesian words was standard at the time (Anderson, Preface, 5). See, for example, L'Abbé Boniface Mosblech's 1843 *Vocabulaire Oceanien-Français et Français-Oceanien des dialectes parles aux Iles Marquises, Sandwich, Gambier, etc.* (Paris, 1843). Stewart uses "Tapii" and "Taipii," 224, 283; Reverend Robert Thomson, who wrote his account in 1841 although it was not published until the twentieth century, uses "Taipi" (*The Marquesas Islands: Their Description and Early History,* ed. Robert D. Craig [Laie, Hawaii: Institute for Polynesian Studies, Brigham Young University, 1980], e.g. 4); and contemporary orthography uses "Taipi" (see, for example, Robert C. Suggs, *The Hidden Worlds of Polynesia* [New York: Harcourt, Brace & World, 1962], 152).

40. Judging from the retrospective quality of the notes on the cover, "First Draught of 'Typee'—After which much was added & altered. Written in the Spring of 1845—Began in New York in the winter of that year & finished in Lansingburgh in the early part of the summer," this writing appears to postdate the draft itself. (This is my transcription of the manuscript at the New York Public Library; the cover also features what appears to be a large number *3* roughly centered below the title, whose meaning I have not determined.)

41. Quoted by Anderson, 444, n. 24.

42. Anderson, 101.

43. Captain David Porter, *Journal of a Cruise,* ed. R. D. Madison and Karen Hamon (1815, 1822; Annapolis, Md.: Naval Institute P, 1986), 322.

44. Quoted by Anderson, 91.

45. My thanks to Robert Schreur for first alerting me to the "type" in "Typee."

46. Leyda, *The Melville Log,* 1:281, and Leyda, *The Melville Log: A Documentary Life*

of Herman Melville, 1819–1891 . . . *with a New Supplementary Chapter,* 2 vols. (New York: Gordian, 1969), 2:919.

47. Langsdorff writes "popoi" (*Voyages and Travels in Various Parts of the World* [London, 1813], e.g. 125); Thomson also writes "popoi," e.g. 27; Willowdean C. Handy writes "popoi" (*Forever the Land of Men: An Account of a Visit to the Marquesas Islands* [New York: Dodd, Mead & Co., 1965]); Margaret Mead writes "poipoi" (*An Inquiry into the Question of Cultural Stability in Polynesia* [New York: Columbia UP, 1928], e.g. 74). Porter discusses breadfruit preparations under the rubric "breadfruit," but does not use the term in question. If the term "poi" appears elsewhere in his text in some form I have not been able to find it (344–46). Foulque writes "poé" (see Hayford and Blair, Explanatory Notes, 231.36, 411).

48. According to my numbering, p. 20, which corresponds to 103.7 in *T.*

49. *Typee*'s structural resemblance to *Pym* can be sketched quickly. Arthur Gordon Pym is a complex double for the author (Poe encoded his own name, for example, in the number and cadence of the syllables in the name "Arthur Gordon Pym"), just as "Tommo" doubles and differs from Melville; Pym teams up with a dark-skinned partner, Dirk Peters, as does Tommo with the "naturally dark" Toby (32); their adventures together include descending a dangerous precipice (an activity in which Pym follows the intrepid Peters, and Tommo follows Toby), searching for food, and hiding from the natives; and their goal is to escape by sea. For a discussion of *Pym*'s relationship to Poe, see John T. Irwin (*American Hieroglyphics: The Symbol of the Egyptian Hieroglyphics in the American Renaissance* [New Haven: Yale UP, 1980]). *Pym*'s sources include Captain Cook, J. N. Reynolds, Captain Benjamin Morrell, and others (Irwin, 151, 172). Irwin also argues that, as the narrative of the Jane Guy episode progresses, the polar world becomes more and more dominated by those oppositions that constitute the physical presence of writing (163). While Irwin argues that Poe's text explicitly thematizes the physical presence of writing, Melville's concern with that presence in *Typee* is different in that it is a source of anxiety and thus both disavowed and repressed.

50. C. S. Stewart, *A Visit to the South Seas in the U. States Ship Vincennes, During the Years 1829 and 1830,* 2 vols. (New York: John P. Haven, 1833), 1:261; Anderson, 144.

51. Editorial Appendix, *T* 320, 337.

52. T. Walter Herbert, *"Moby-Dick" and Calvinism: A World Dismantled* (New Brunswick, N.J.: Rutgers UP, 1977), 62, n. 12. By 1837, Herman and his mother Maria co-sign a bond both using the final *e* (Melville Family Papers, Gansevoort-Lansing Collection, Rare Books and Manuscripts Division, New York Public Library, Astor, Lenox and Tilden Foundations).

53. For example, to Catherine Van Schaick Gansevoort, 11 Oct. 1828, L 5; also to Evert A. Duyckinck, 13 Dec. 1850, L 172.

54. To John Murray, 25 Mar. 1848, L 105.

55. Philip Young, *The Private Melville* (University Park: Pennsylvania State UP, 1993), 151, 154.

56. See MSAm188 (369.4.1), "Daniel Orme," the Houghton Library, Harvard University. The page referred to is labeled *1,* followed by a circled *3* at top left.

57. Howard, Historical Note, *T* 284.

58. To John Murray, 15 July 1846, L 57; emphasis in original.

59. See, for example, Thomson, 18.

60. Thomson, 18; *OED*, "tapa" and "paper."

61. Melville's phrase is from one of the prose chapters of *The Marquis de Grandvin*, quoted by Vincent, Explanatory Notes, 484. See also Fliegelman on historically evolving notions of authorship.

62. For examples of the language of "art," see Ray Nash's bibliographical transcriptions of the title pages of George Thresher's *The Complete Penman's Repository* (1810); Eleazer Huntington's *The American Penman* (1824); Cooke and Hale's *Rules and Directions, in the Art of Penmanship* (1817); David Hewett's *Self-taught Penman* (1818); William Clark's *A Guide to Penmanship or the Art of Writing Simplified* (1824); and H. Anderson's *The Art of Penmanship* (1833) in Ray Nash, *American Penmanship, 1800–1850: A History of Writing and a Bibliography of Copybooks from Jenkins to Spencer* (Worcester, Mass.: American Antiquarian Society, 1969), entries #30, 96, 100, 106, 132, and 225. On the writing masters' other "arts," see Nash, *American Penmanship*, 53.

63. Fried, *Realism, Writing, Disfiguration*, 21; Ray Nash, *Writing: Some Early American Writing Books and Masters*, 2d ed. (n.p.: H & N, 1943), 22.

64. French's *The Art of Pen Drawing* was in fact a republication of William F. Stratton's 1840 *The Penman's Paradise*, which was itself largely copied from John Seddon's *Penman's Paradise* (c. 1695). See Nash, *American Penmanship*, 47–50, and #227 (179) and #290 (210).

65. See, for example, Nash, *American Penmanship*, 45–47 and #153; also 60, 123, 115, 100, 78, 53, 195, 210.

66. Henry F. Briggs, *Practical and Scientific Penmanship* [n.d.], cited in Nash, *American Penmanship*, #288, 48; also 60. See also his bibliographical entries for Dolbear and Brothers, *The Science of Practical Penmanship* (1837), and Briggs, *Practical and scientific penmanship* (191, #251; 209; #288).

67. Nash, *American Penmanship* #299 (215) and #362 (248); 3, 23.

68. Leyda, *The Melville Log*, 1:56. Family letters also show that Maria insisted that her children write to one another and that, at least on occasion, she scrutinized their letters to one another or opened their mail. Helen Melville writes to Augusta, reporting that Maria requested that she leave "half a page for her use. My obedience in this case brought only sorrow to me, for Mama having scanned the pa[ge] with a critic's eye, pronounced the chirography beneat[h] contempt, and insisted upon my copying the documen[t]. This I protested against, so my good lady, to close the conference, tore the unoffending sheet into a thousand pieces. The mood for composition is gone for the present, and if you consider its destruction a loss, as I certainly do, you must lay the sin at Mama's door.—" (Brackets record where the right margin of the sheet is torn; characters in brackets are my own supposition.) Maria wrote in the same letter, "Yours of the 8th Inst was duly received its being directed to Gansevoort did not prevent our opening it without compunction soon as the sight of the Post mark assured us it was from you" (Helen Melville and Maria Gansevoort Melville to Augusta Melville, 16 [?] Sept. 1841). (My transcription of a letter in the Melville Family Papers/Additions, Gansevoort-Lansing Collection, Rare Books and Manuscripts Division, New York Public Library, Astor, Lenox and Tilden Foundations.)

69. Leyda, *The Melville Log*, 1: 105, 110; Leon Howard, *Herman Melville: A Biography* (Berkeley: U of California P, 1951), 38.

70. Leo Marx, "Melville's Parable of the Walls," *Sewanee Review* 61 (1953): 602–27.

71. See "Chapter Eleventh" and "Chapter Twelfth [*sic*]." In both cases the words are ornamentally written and separated by a diamond design.

72. To Catherine Melville Hoadley, 28 Dec. 1881, L 477.

73. Anderson, 155–56.

74. For example, Anderson, 100; Herbie Butterfield, " 'New World All Over': Melville's *Typee* and *Omoo*," *Herman Melville: Reassessments*, ed. A. Robert Lee (London: Vision, 1984), 23.

75. If I am correct about the nature of the relation between Tommo and Melville, then it is all the more appropriate that, even at the level of the fiction, Tommo is presented as an autobiographical representation of Melville, but one who also operates under an assumed name, further rendering the "autobiography" a form of duplicity.

76. Other critics have also drawn this parallel. See, for example, Robert K. Martin, *Hero, Captain, and Stranger: Male Friendship, Social Critique, and Literary Form in the Sea Novels of Herman Melville* (Chapel Hill: U of North Carolina P, 1986), 28; Warwick Wadlington, *The Confidence Game in American Literature* (Princeton: Princeton UP, 1975), 64; Breitwieser, 413–14.

77. See Rev. Edward J. Pettid, ed., "Olive Ann Oatman's Lecture Notes and Oatman Bibliography," *San Bernardino County Museum Association Quarterly* 16.2 (1968). Olive Ann was tattooed on the chin. R. B. Stratton's *Captivity of the Oatman Girls* appeared in 1857.

78. See Alan B. Govenar, Introduction, *Stoney Knows How: Life as a Tattoo Artist*, by Leonard St. Clair and Alan B. Govenar (Lexington: UP of Kentucky, 1981), xi–xxxii, xv; see also C. H. Fellowes, *The Tattoo Book* (Princeton: Pyne, 1971), 7–8, and Albert Parry, *Tattoo: Secrets of a Strange Art as Practiced among the Natives of the United States* (New York: Simon & Schuster, 1933), 44–67. When Melville wrote *Typee*, tattooing was beginning to wane in the Marquesas because of missionary suppression. Conversely, it was just getting started as a profession in the United States. John Evelev discusses the career of James O'Connell, an ex-sailor who exhibited his tattooed body beginning in November 1840 (" 'Made in the Marquesas': *Typee*, Tattooing, and Melville's Critique of the Literary Marketplace," *Arizona Quarterly* 48.4 [1992]: 29–30). Girls claiming to have been tattooed by Indians became popular in circuses in the 1870s; often these "tattoos" were merely paint (Parry, 64).

79. Willowdean Chatterson Handy, *Tattooing in the Marquesas* (Bayard Dominick Expedition, Bulletin 1, No. 3 [Honolulu: Bernice P. Bishop Museum, 1922]), 24. Since the aboriginal culture died out quickly under the white man's encroachments, the roots of tattooing practices were already lost knowledge by the time Handy did her field work in 1920.

80. At the level of generality, I agree with Evelev that tattooing in *Typee* is "a place where Melville's attitudes toward writing get expressed," but my account of what the term *writing* means and of what those attitudes are differs from Evelev's. In his account, Melville's "conflicted reaction toward writing" in *Typee* is a function of his feelings about the marketplace: "Tommo's rejection of Typee culture in *Typee* is the sublimated and displaced textualization of Melville's own concern about being inscribed within the marketplace's demands for objectified exchange." Evelev reads the particular horror of facial tattooing as a threat to Melville's status because it represents his "transformation into an exotic 'object' " by his own text in a system of capitalist exchange (20, 27, 21, 26, 39).

81. Breitwieser, 412.

82. In *Redburn*, the narrator tells us that there is a "secret sympathy" between himself and the figurehead of a glass model ship that "perhaps more than any thing else, converted my vague dreamings and longings into a definite purpose of seeking my fortune on the sea" (7): "her figure-head, a gallant warrior in a cocked hat, lies pitching head-foremost down into the trough of a calamitous sea under the bows—but I will not have him put on his legs again, till I get on my own; for between him and me there is a secret sympathy; and my sisters tell me, even yet, that he fell from his perch the very day I left home to go to sea on this *my first voyage*" (9; emphasis in original). This figurehead stands (or falls) at the fore end of the career that is both Redburn's and Melville's. The corollary to this fallen figurehead is the late poem "The Figure-Head" from *John Marr and Other Sailors* (1888), in which the figurehead is cast aside in a wreck. Just as the now landlocked John Marr considers a life spent on the sea, Melville casts his eye over a career spent there. He places at the end of the career an emblem that alludes to and redacts the one he chose when his career was young, but the hope and determination of the early image have been converted to pathos and desolation. Thus the content of the figurehead image as a specifically writerly one for Melville is quite explicit.

83. I choose the term *disfiguration* throughout this chapter as one *Typee* itself invokes for the specter of facial mutilation, as I indicate in my discussion. Notions of disfiguration and defacement are also resonant in literary criticism. The notion of disfiguration I have proposed is partly compatible and partly incompatible with Paul de Man's notion of de-facement ("Autobiography as De-Facement," *The Rhetoric of Romanticism* [Ithaca: Cornell UP, 1984], 67–81). For de Man, disfiguration and de-facement are inherent features of language, ones to which he brings particular weight in the case of autobiography, with its premises of conjuring the author in the text. Such a notion of defacement is applicable to my argument that part of Melville's anxiety stems from his inability to produce the authentic worlds he promises. But my argument departs from the de Manian notion of the "illusion of reference" in which the figure is primary to the nominal referent, because, by my account, both the figure *as such* and the nominal referent are rendered secondary to the constitutive force of the materiality of writing, in this case, both printed pages open in front of Melville and his own inscribed pages. My operative notion of disfigurement here is thus closer to the one elaborated by Fried, who calls attention to "the thematization of writing as violent disfigurement and its association with effects of horror and repugnance but also of intense fascination" (*Realism, Writing, Disfiguration,* 121 and 185, n. 28).

84. See, for example, Anderson, 71.

85. Anderson, 146, 126.

Chapter Two: Fear of Faces

1. Raymond M. Weaver also notes that Pierre is haunted by faces. He believes that Herman's mother Maria is behind these (*Herman Melville: Mariner and Mystic* [New York: George H. Doran, 1921], 62). Dryden remarks that the "generative energy" of *Pierre* is "the story of the face" (*The Form of American Romance* [Baltimore: Johns Hopkins UP, 1988], 76).

2. I differ fundamentally from the important work of Rodolphe Gasché and Dryden. Gasché's analysis is primarily rhetorical, by which I mean that its focus is the

operations of language; it neither takes into account nor makes claims about Melville as a historical person with a particular set of habits and a particular relation to writing as an activity. Instead, Gasché traces metaphors of writing in *Moby-Dick,* disembodying this rhetoric from the material conditions that, I argue, give rise to it. Thus the effect of Gasché's deconstructive approach is to privilege figuration, a privileging that is, by my account, a blindness to the source of Melville's figures: specific material circumstances and practices. I have similar differences with Dryden's work on *Pierre.* For Dryden, *Pierre* is marked by the perception that "any act of speaking and writing is bound to be a repetition, a displacement or a representation of a purely textual entity," and the process of representation "points to the absence that all signs carry within them." Dryden's focus is representation as it destabilizes the ontology of the signified. I do not agree with Gasché and Dryden that the primary force in Melville's writing is the figural status of language; indeed, it is my claim that Melville's representations must be understood as products of material conditions. Thus although I share with Gasché and Dryden an interest in Melville's frequent figures of writing in particular, we differ in how we understand their origins and consequences. For them, such figures are a function of the ontology of written language; for me, they arise from specific material circumstances, practices, and relations in the case of a particular writer. See Rodolphe Gasché, "The Scene of Writing: A Deferred Outset," *Glyph: Johns Hopkins Textual Studies* 1 (1977): 150–71, and Dryden, *The Form of American Romance,* 105–6, 95.

3. Biographically speaking, the argument I make here helps to account for why *Moby-Dick* and *Pierre* were so hard on Melville. Charles Olson argued that writing *Moby-Dick* hurt Melville and *Pierre* made it worse (*Call Me Ishmael* [San Francisco: City Lights Books, 1947], 90).

4. One of the repeated formal complaints critics level against *Pierre* is that we suddenly find out that Pierre is an author midway through the book, a revelation that gives rise to the theory that Melville changed his writing plans after reading reviews of *Moby-Dick.* See Brian Higgins and Hershel Parker, Introduction, *Critical Essays on Herman Melville's "Pierre; or, The Ambiguities"* (Boston: G. K. Hall, 1983), 13 ff., for their theory about how reading reviews of *Moby-Dick* affected the composition of *Pierre.* It would also be useful to remember that, at the time of *Pierre's* composition, Melville had recently read Hawthorne's *The House of the Seven Gables,* in which Holgrave's career as a successful author of magazine pieces is just as suddenly revealed at the end of chapter 12, a possible model that could further problematize the Higgins/Parker theory that "very likely" Melville added the information, "arbitrarily and most belatedly, that Pierre had been a juvenile author" (13).

5. "Perhaps the violences, the distortions, the wrenchings in the versification of some of the poems are to be interpreted as the result not of mere ineptitude but of a conscious effort to develop a nervous, dramatic, masculine style" (Robert Penn Warren, "Melville the Poet," *Selected Essays* [New York: Random House, 1958], 186).

6. Eric Sundquist, "Suspense and Tautology in 'Benito Cereno,'" *Glyph: Johns Hopkins Textual Studies* 8, ed. Walter Benn Michaels (Baltimore: Johns Hopkins UP, 1977), 103–26. In *To Wake the Nations: Race in the Making of American Literature* (Cambridge: Belknap P of Harvard UP, 1993), Sundquist revisits the issue of tautology in "Benito Cereno" as a crisis of authority (155 ff.). I concur with Sundquist about the fundamental importance of tautology as an operation in Melville's prose, but differ in

how I position its stakes: my argument ultimately hinges on the tautological force of written characters and material text. See also chapter 4 herein.

7. Since I have mapped out in detail the positions of Pierre and the narrator, I want to specify where I place Melville the author in the series of oppositions I have been exploring. I read Pierre as Melville's autobiographical portrait of himself as the author of his prior novels; according to my account, his earlier relation to his own writing is one that he knows to be changing in crucial ways. The narrator's attitude toward Pierre and the narrator's crisis-in-progress with respect to the page are, I maintain, Melville's own. Thus I differ fundamentally from the critical tradition that places Melville the author at an objective and safe distance from the chaotic intensity of the novel (for an example of such a reading, see William B. Dillingham, *Melville's Later Novels* [Athens: U of Georgia P, 1986]).

8. See Fried's chapter on Eakins in *Realism, Writing, Disfiguration*.

9. I do not find existing attempts to identify Plinlimmon to be persuasive because they fail to account for this power in specific terms. He has been described, for example, as Melville's "most terrifying villain" and as a cynosure of self-knowledge; as a bitter picture of Hawthorne and of Emerson; as a moral zero and a moral center; as a Foucauldian representative of social supervision. See, respectively, Stern, *The Fine Hammered Steel of Herman Melville*, 194; Dillingham, 236; Henry A. Murray, Introduction, *Pierre, or, The Ambiguities*, by Herman Melville (New York: Hendricks House, 1949), lxxviii; Myra Jehlen, *American Incarnation: The Individual, the Nation, the Continent* (Cambridge: Harvard UP, 1986), 188; Carolyn Karcher, *Shadow over the Promised Land: Slavery, Race, and Violence in Melville's America* (Baton Rouge: Louisiana State UP, 1980), 15; and Wai-Chee Dimock, *Empire for Liberty: Melville and the Poetics of Individualism* (Princeton: Princeton UP, 1989), 172.

10. Dillingham, 235.

11. On the importance of pyramids in Melville's work more broadly, and indeed in nineteenth-century American literature in general, see Irwin.

12. Hayford et al., Editorial Appendix, *PT* 700.

13. This observation is based on my examination of the manuscripts at the New York Public Library (Gansevoort-Lansing Collection, Rare Books and Manuscripts Division, Astor, Lenox, and Tilden Foundations) and the Houghton Library, Harvard University.

14. I discuss these scenes of paper production in chapters 1 and 3.

15. Lawrence C. Wroth and Rollo G. Silver, "Book Production and Distribution from the American Revolution to the War Between the States," *The Book in America: A History of the Making and Selling of Books in the United States,* by Hellmut Lehmann-Haupt, Lawrence C. Wroth, and Rollo G. Silver, 2d ed. (New York: R. R. Bowker, 1952), 86–87. The Fourdrinier machine, patented in England in 1799, the Dickinson machine, patented in England in 1809, and the Gilpin machine, patented in America in 1816, all made use of the processes described although in other ways their designs differed. The Fourdrinier passed a revolving wire band or web through a vat of pulp; the Dickinson and the Gilpin utilized a cylinder covered with a wire web revolving through the pulp vat (86–87).

16. Fried discusses Peale's program in *Graphics* for achieving perfect perspective. Peale recommends viewing objects through an upright sheet of glass—"a plate of glass,

or window pane"—in order to trace them on it (Fried, and Peale as quoted by Fried, *Realism, Writing, Disfiguration,* 79–80). Melville's struggle with the conversion of three dimensions into two in writing, worked out through the face of Plinlimmon behind two windows, is thus importantly contextualized by roughly contemporary ideas of how to handle an analogous problem in drawing.

17. What I have called this newly configured position will result in the terms of *The Confidence-Man,* the subject of chapter 4.

18. My assessments are based on my examination of the manuscript of *Journal Up the Straits 1856* at the Houghton Library, Harvard University (MSAm 188 [373, 374]). One of Melville's entries on the pyramids is revised both in pencil and in ink, for example. Toward the end of the journal, Melville lays out a title page in ink, lead pencil, and colored crayon that reads in part, "Frescoes of Travel by Three Brothers."

19. Irwin calls Moby-Dick the "central hieroglyph" in the novel, with his pyramidi-cal hump and mystic-marked brow. He also notes that the brooding image of the pyramids saturated American culture of the period (285–86, 3–14).

20. I reiterate my debt to Fried.

21. Critics have long speculated about *Pierre*'s relation to *Moby-Dick.* Richard Brodhead, for example, puns that Pierre sorely lacks a Moby-Dick (*Hawthorne, Melville, and the Novel* [Chicago: U of Chicago P, 1976], 185). His observation is correct both in its sense of a fundamental emptiness in the novel (one Pierre himself eventually dis-covers and reacts to with terrified vertigo) and in its placement of *Pierre*'s particular effects as proximate to *Moby-Dick.* For an overview of theories and debates about the composition of *Moby-Dick,* see Robert Milder, "The Composition of *Moby-Dick*: A Review and a Prospect," *ESQ* 23 (1970): 203–16. See also James Barbour, " 'All My Books Are Botches': Melville's Struggle with *The Whale,*" *Writing the American Classics,* ed. James Barbour and Tom Quirk (Chapel Hill: U of North Carolina P, 1990), and Barbour, "The Composition of *Moby-Dick,*" *American Literature* 47 (1975): 343–60; Harrison Hayford, "Unnecessary Duplicates: A Key to the Writing of *Moby-Dick,*" *New Perspectives on Melville,* ed. Faith Pullin (Kent, Ohio: Kent State UP, 1978), 128–61; and the Historical Note to *MD.*

22. I disagree with previous critical assessments of the whale's absent face, includ-ing, for example, Paul Brodtkorb Jr., who argues that the whale "can have no true face" because it represents the formless process of contents of mind (*Ishmael's White World: A Phenomenological Reading of "Moby-Dick"* [New Haven: Yale UP, 1965], 25–27).

The face as a site of blockage in Melville's fiction appears in the context of a culture that directed enormous intellectual energy into developing systems of correspondence between surfaces and their meanings. Physiognomy specifically took the human face as its text, and attempted to come to interpretive terms with the variations of its outward form. John Casper Lavater, the most famous of the physiognomists, described it as "the science or knowledge of the correspondence between the external and internal man, the visible superficies and the invisible contents" (*Essays on Physiognomy: for the promo-tion of the knowledge and the love of mankind,* trans. Thomas Holcroft, 2d ed. [Lon-don, 1804], 19). Melville's impenetrable faces set themselves against systematizations like those Lavater's work fueled—explicitly so here in *Moby-Dick* as well as in *The Confidence-Man*—but at the same time they possess a signifying power compatible with the deep cultural investment in faces that allowed physiognomy to thrive. On physiognomy in *Pierre*, see Dillingham; on physiognomy's influence on the novel, see Graeme Tytler, *Physiognomy in the European Novel* (Princeton: Princeton UP, 1982); see also Irwin, 304 ff.

23. Barbour glosses the passages from "The Tail" and Exodus this way ("'All My Books are Botches,'" 31–32); see also Irwin, 305.

24. Sharon Cameron, *The Corporeal Self: Allegories of the Body in Melville and Hawthorne* (Baltimore: Johns Hopkins UP, 1981).

25. To cite only two examples, Sedgwick argues that "Moby Dick [*sic*] stands for the mystery of creation" (98), and that the horror of whiteness "is the soul's fear of itself" (122); indeed, Sedgwick's argument about *Moby-Dick* is that it served Melville's "headstrong preoccupation with truth" (86). For Chase, "Moby-Dick is God incarnate in the whale" (49).

26. Irwin notes that Moby-Dick is described as a "phantom" throughout the novel and is thus associated with the "ungraspable phantom of life" invoked in "Loomings" (291).

27. Hershel Parker, "*Moby-Dick* and Domesticity," *Critical Essays on Herman Melville's "Moby-Dick,"* ed. Brian Higgins and Hershel Parker (New York: G. K. Hall, 1992), 558. Parker "explores the possibility that Melville embodied some of his domestic comforts, compromises, and tensions in *Moby-Dick.*" Parker concludes that the novel can be said to be partly about "the rival—and incompatible—claims of creativity and marriage" (545, 561).

28. This connection is also legible, for example, in "The Blanket," in which "the visible surface of the Sperm Whale is not the least among the many marvels he presents. Almost invariably it is all over obliquely crossed and re-crossed with numberless straight marks in thick array, something like those in the finest line engravings" (306).

Chapter Three: Wife Beating and the Written Page

1. Walter D. Kring and Jonathan S. Carey, "Two Discoveries Concerning Herman Melville," *Proceedings of the Massachusetts Historical Society* 87 (1975): 137–41, rpt. in *The Endless, Winding Way in Melville: New Charts by Kring and Carey*, ed. Donald Yannella and Hershel Parker, intro. Walter D. Kring (Glassboro, N.J.: Melville Society, 1981), 11–15. Kring and Carey's reprinted article is hereafter cited as "Kring and Carey" by the new page numbers (11–15); the Yannella and Parker volume is cited as *EWW*; and Kring's introduction to that volume is cited as "Kring, Intro. *EWW.*"

2. Yannella and Parker, Foreword, *EWW*, v.

3. In addition to Kring and Carey, who first brought the letters to light, and Yannella and Parker, who solicited responses to them for the monograph on the subject, Parker discusses the letters in his Historical Supplement to *C* 649–50; Parker also includes the proposed separation of Elizabeth from Herman in his 1990 "Melville Chronology" based on *The New Melville Log*, in *Reading "Billy Budd"* (Evanston, Ill.: Northwestern UP, 1990), 186. Until the appearance of my "Herman Melville, Wife Beating, and the Written Page" (*American Literature* 66 [March 1994]: 123–50), other scholars had alluded, usually in passing, to the Kring and Carey discovery but no one had yet built an analytical case from the evidence. David Leverenz comments that Melville "probably beat" his wife (*Manhood and the American Renaissance* [Ithaca: Cornell UP,

1989], 179); Young sees the kidnapping plot as "evidence of how sick Melville became" and later comments without elaboration, "Mistreatment of his wife is established" (153, 157); Shurr takes the letters to indicate that "Melville may have threatened or even abused his wife" ("Melville's Poems: The Late Agenda," in Bryant, ed., *A Companion to Melville Studies,* 365); Bryant alludes to "severe domestic problems" (*A Companion to Melville Studies,* xxiii); Hennig Cohen's 1991 postscript to *Selected Poems of Herman Melville* notes "the recent discoveries regarding his estrangement from his wife" ([New York: Fordham UP, 1991], xvii); and Rogin ascribes the kidnapping plan to Elizabeth's worries about Herman's "insanity" (259). While he did not speculate about the nature of the marital difficulties the letters revealed, George Monteiro argued in a 1978 article that the letters contributed to our understanding of Melville's writing in the 1860s, specifically to his attitudes toward "womankind" ("Poetry and Madness: Melville's Rediscovery of Camões in 1867," *New England Quarterly* 51.4 (1978): 561–65). The Northwestern-Newberry edition of *Correspondence,* edited by Lynn Horth and published in July 1993, reprints the two letters in an appendix entitled "Two Letters Concerning Melville" (L 857–60). Clearly Melville scholars are once again challenged to assess this information.

Suggestions that Herman beat or otherwise abused Elizabeth have been circulating quietly for decades, and have been referred to in print in the ways my examples here and in the text indicate. What scholarship has not engaged is the question of how such information contributes to our understanding of Melville's writing. My own assessment differs from prior references in its direct and full treatment of the evidence of abuse and in its argument about how this information is central to understanding Melville's work.

4. Kring, Intro. *EWW* 1, 5–6.

5. I have not been able to determine how the particular term "ill-treatment" functioned rhetorically in the mid-nineteenth century, or if it was a euphemism for beating. Additional research in the area of wife abuse may demonstrate the cultural codes through which such behavior was discussed. Linda Gordon points out that late-nineteenth-century social workers who did not "see" wife beating often used the term "quick-tempered" to describe husbands who engaged in such behavior. See Linda Gordon, *Heroes of Their Own Lives: The Politics and History of Family Violence, Boston 1880–1960* (New York: Viking, 1988), 264.

6. All citations from Samuel Shaw's letter are from Samuel S. Shaw to Henry Whitney Bellows, 6 May 1867, Kring and Carey, 13–15.

7. Elizabeth Shaw Melville to Henry Whitney Bellows, 20 May 1867, Kring and Carey, 15; emphasis in original. All citations of Elizabeth Shaw Melville's letter are from this source.

8. Gordon, 271.

9. Samuel S. Shaw to Henry Whitney Bellows, 6 May 1867, Kring and Carey, 14.

10. Kring and Carey, 11.

11. Gordon, 259.

12. Elizabeth Pleck, "Wife Beating in Nineteenth-Century America," *Victimology* 4.1 (1979): 65; Gordon, 273.

13. Pleck, 67–68, 71.

14. See Gordon, 254; Pleck, 64–65; and Barbara Leslie Epstein, *The Politics of Domesticity: Women, Evangelism, and Temperance in Nineteenth-Century America* (Middletown, Conn.: Wesleyan UP, 1981), 106, 109. According to Pleck, by the late nine-

teenth century wife beating was prohibited by statute in eight states (Massachusetts, Tennessee, Nebraska, Georgia, Maryland, New Mexico, Delaware, Arkansas). All but the Massachusetts statute, which predated the others, were passed between 1853 and 1903. Wife beating was also prohibited by judicial decision in five states (New York, Texas, Delaware, Alabama, Kentucky; Pleck records Delaware on both lists). The absence of a specific statutory prohibition does not necessarily imply that wife beating was legal, since, for example, wife beaters were arrested for assault and battery in Maryland before it passed an explicit wife beating statute in 1882. But criminal penalties for those wife beaters who were convicted varied widely, sometimes amounting only to a fine. And many women who did bring complaints against their husbands then withdrew them or pleaded for their husbands' release lest they and their families be left without support (61, 63, 65, 67).

15. Gordon, 258–59.

16. Melville's letters frequently speak orgiastically of alcohol. Eleanor Melville Metcalf reports that in his desperation it became a "solace" to him. Edwin Haviland Miller reports that the family maintained "a conspiracy of silence" about the fact that "Herman at times leaned heavily on the bottle," especially after 1852. See Eleanor Melville Metcalf, *Herman Melville: Cycle and Epicycle* (Cambridge, Mass.: Harvard UP, 1953), 215, and Miller, 321.

17. E. Metcalf, family tree (paste-down endpaper and free endpaper); xv.

18. E. Metcalf, 293; xvi.

19. Weaver, *Herman Melville: Mariner and Mystic,* [vii]. On the history of the *Billy Budd* manuscript, see Parker, *Reading "Billy Budd,"* 43–50.

20. E. Metcalf, xvi; Leyda, *The Melville Log,* 1:xiii–xvi. Gaps in the extant family correspondence—for example, there appears to be a gap in Helen Melville's correspondence between 1847 and 1853, in Frances (Fanny) Melville's between 1848 and 1854, and in Augusta Melville's between 1851 and 1854—raise questions about what was preserved and why. Augusta's log of her own correspondence indicates ample exchanges with her mother Helen, Fanny, and Elizabeth from December 1849 to January 1854, yet correspondence in the period indicated above appears not to have been preserved. My analysis here is based on the materials discovered in 1983 and now in the Melville Family Papers/Additions, Gansevoort-Lansing Collection, Rare Books and Manuscripts Division, New York Public Library, Astor, Lenox and Tilden Foundations. Of course, as Horth points out in the Historical Notes to L, letters may continue to surface (790).

21. See Paul Metcalf's remarks in *EWW* 21–22. When it assists clarity I will refer to Paul Metcalf and Eleanor Melville Metcalf by their first names hereafter in the text.

22. Olson, 92.

23. Olson, 40.

24. See Braswell, *EWW* 19.

25. Paul Metcalf to Clare Spark, 30 June 1989, *Enter Isabel: The Herman Melville Correspondence of Clare Spark and Paul Metcalf* (Albuquerque: U of New Mexico P, 1991), 79–80 (hereafter cited as *EI*).

26. Quoted by E. Metcalf, 292; also checked at the Houghton Library, Harvard University, Frances Melville Thomas to Eleanor Melville Metcalf, 17 May 1926 [MSAm188 (347)]; P. Metcalf to Clare Spark, 15 Mar. 1988, *EI* 19; Weaver, 62.

27. *EWW* 19.

28. Clare Spark quoted by P. Metcalf, ed., *EI* 33.

29. Clare Spark to P. Metcalf, 18 May 1989, *EI* 77.

30. *EWW* 21.

31. P. Metcalf to Clare Spark, 3 Sept. 1988, *EI* 46.

32. Walker Cohen, Introduction, *Melville's Marginalia*, 2 vols. (New York: Garland, 1987), 1: xix.

33. Cowen, Introduction, *Melville's Marginalia*, 1: x–xlv, xxii, xx. See also Milder's comments in *EWW*, 46 on this issue. Chase comments that Melville is unable to represent "feminine love" and "could seldom picture a woman without terror," a problem he later links to his feelings for his mother (33, 19, 253). Newton Arvin maintains that Melville felt emotionally trapped between his mother and his wife, and that they had fused in his mind "into a single image of intrusive and oppressive hostility" (*Herman Melville* [1950; New York: Viking, 1957], 204). Lewis Mumford comments, "There was, one is driven to believe, something in Herman Melville's life that caused him to dissociate woman from his account of man's deepest experience" (*Herman Melville* [New York: Literary Guild of America, 1929], 201).

34. *EWW* 21; emphasis in original.

35. Olson, 40.

36. Harrison Hayford, "The Melville Society: A Retrospective," *Melville Society Extracts* Number 88 (1992): 6.

37. *EWW* 21.

38. Mumford, *Herman Melville*, 230. Whereas Mumford's biography was later proven wrong on a number of grounds (for example, his reading of *Typee* as fully autobiographical), he did write his study with access to persons who knew a great deal about the Melville family. Mumford places the period of Melville's domestic, physical, and mental crisis between 1852 and 1858. The Kring-Carey letters were, of course, unknown to him.

39. Murray was the co-founder of the Harvard Psychological Clinic and author of *Explorations in Personality* (Forrest G. Robinson, Preface, *Love's Story Told: A Life of Henry A. Murray* [Cambridge: Harvard UP, 1992], vii).

40. The letter from Hayford to Leyda was quoted by Spark in her 6 April 1990 correspondence with Hayford, and in turn quoted by Hayford in his discussion of Spark's work and of P. Metcalf's *Enter Isabel* ("The Melville Society," 5). For his 16 April 1990 gloss on the correspondence with Leyda, see "The Melville Society," 5–6. Hayford concludes his article with the words, "We 'Melville Society types,' as Clare Spark called us in that foreboding book *Enter Isabel*, are under scrutiny, our own ways and works becoming historical data" ("The Melville Society," 6).

41. Clare Spark quoted by P. Metcalf, ed., *EI* 8.

42. Amy Elizabeth Puett first published and discussed the letters in her 1969 dissertation, "Melville's Wife: A Study of Elizabeth Shaw Melville" (Ph.D. diss., Northwestern University, 1969), 87–91. See also Henry A. Murray, Harvey Myerson, and Eugene Taylor, "Allan Melville's By-Blow," *Melville Society Extracts*, Number 61 (Feb. 1985): 1–6. Young surveys the evidence of and scholarship about the illegitimate daughter.

43. P. Metcalf to Clare Spark, 22 Feb. 1988, *EI* 14–15.

44. Robinson, 370.

45. Murray, quoted by Robinson, 240–41; Robinson, 239, 240, 134. Murray's vig-

orous whipping sessions with his love "slave" Christiana Morgan ("slave" is their term) were understood by both of them as an integral part of Murray's work on the Melville biography. " 'Thou shalt be my slave until I have finished Melville to your utter satisfaction,' " Murray ordered Morgan. Robinson goes on: "In the months that followed there was much of Melville and, in return, much of the bruising sex that they both now craved" (257–58).

46. *EWW* 38.

47. Shneidman, "Some Psychological Reflections on the Death of Malcolm Melville," *Suicide and Life Threatening Behavior* 6 (1976): 40.

48. *EWW* 36–37; Edwin Haviland Miller, 319 ff. Miller calls forceful attention to Melville's enduring attraction to bachelorhood and male clubs in the context of his hostility toward marriage and family responsibilities, and his demeaning strictness toward Elizabeth and the children.

49. Eleanor Melville Metcalf to Frances Melville Thomas, 29 Aug. 1919 and 30 Aug. 1919, the Houghton Library, Harvard University [MsAm188 (272–73)].

50. Paul Metcalf, *Genoa: A Telling of Wonders* (Highlands, N.C.: Jonathan Williams, 1965), 75; Miller, 321–23.

51. Elizabeth to Catherine Gansevoort, 26 May 1873 (quoted by E. Metcalf, 228; emphasis in original).

52. E. Metcalf, 215; Edwin Haviland Miller, 345 (emphasis in original).

53. My sketch of the children is indebted to Spark as quoted by P. Metcalf, ed., *EI* 59. Others who have read the tragedy of the Melville children in terms of their father's influence upon them include P. Metcalf and Shneidman. In *Genoa,* Metcalf writes:

> And there were the children:
> Mackey,
> Stanny,
> Bessie,
> & Fanny,
>
> hovering at the edge of the storm, the vortex, and
>
> killed, crippled or withered, according to the order of birth, to how
> near in time (the father's *space*) they came
>
> to the eye of it.
> (73; emphasis in original)

Shneidman's case study of Malcolm's suicide cites this passage, which is indeed an especially apt one (238). See also Hennig Cohen and Donald Yannella, *Herman Melville's Malcolm Letter: "Man's Final Lore"* (New York: Fordham UP and New York Public Library, 1992).

54. Quoted by Shneidman, 237.

55. *EWW* 30.

56. *EWW* 20.

57. *EWW* 26.

58. *EWW* 29–30.

59. E. Metcalf, 98, 133.

60. Gordon, 260.

61. Shneidman, 231, 232. Melville scholars continue to blame Elizabeth and the Melville women for problems in the household and for interfering with Herman's writing. These scholars thus adopt Herman's attitudes of resentment and impatience. For example, blaming Elizabeth is a virtual reflex in Stanton Garner's *The Civil War World of Herman Melville,* in which, among other instances, Garner cites "the domestic tranquility of these days—always excepting Lizzie's pique" (240) and writes that "visiting in Boston allowed her to parade her marital grievances before her sympathetic family and to be reassured that she deserved better than life with Herman afforded her" (433).

62. P. Metcalf to Clare Spark, 16 Oct. 1989, *EI* 89.

63. See Hawthorne's notebook account of his visit with Melville soon after *The Confidence-Man* was completed: "Melville has not been well, of late; he has been affected with neuralgic complaints in his head and limbs, and no doubt has suffered from too constant literary occupation, pursued without much success, latterly; and his writings, for a long while past, have indicated a morbid state of mind. . . . I do not wonder that he found it necessary to take an airing through the world, after so many years of toilsome pen-labor and domestic life, following upon so wild and adventurous a youth as his was" (quoted in Branch et al., Historical Note, *CM* 314).

64. 20 Apr. 1853; quoted by E. Metcalf, 147.

65. 1 Sept. 1856; quoted by E. Metcalf, 159.

66. 7 Apr. 1856; quoted by Edwin Haviland Miller, 293.

67. *EWW* 41, 43.

68. Harrison Hayford, Alma A. MacDougall, G. Thomas Tanselle, et al., Notes on Individual Prose Pieces, *PT* 622.

69. Herman Melville, "Fragments from a Writing Desk," *PT* 191–204, 194; hereafter cited parenthetically as "Fragments."

70. I work out *The Confidence-Man*'s interest in "promising writing" and "poison writing" in chapter 4.

71. *Collected Poems,* 231.

72. Howard, *Herman Melville,* 134.

73. Rogin, 199; see chapter 1 herein.

74. Howard, *Herman Melville,* 161, 163.

75. [17?] Nov. 1851, *L* 212.

76. See, for examples, letters quoted by E. Metcalf, 7 and 171, and Weaver, 266. Edwin Haviland Miller also reads this *M* as a sign for "Melville" (47).

77. Of Maria and Allan Melville's eight children, four sons and four daughters, the three older sons (Gansevoort, b. 1815; Herman, b. 1819; and Allan, b. 1823) all struggled to earn a living in the wake of their father's death in 1832, in various short-lived and unsuccessful ventures away from home. In late 1838, Herman had returned home to Lansingburgh, after a brief attempt at teaching in a rural school. The family was in deep financial trouble; the Melvilles had moved from Albany to Lansingburgh in May 1838 because of their serious financial difficulties. Eleanor Melville Metcalf writes that despite the economic crisis of this period, "she [Maria] felt it necessary to keep a servant she could not pay, her wages being half the rent. The day had not come when she was to be

'energetic about the farm' in Pittsfield, and when her daughters would all lend a hand with the housework" (19). On June 5 Herman embarked on his first sea voyage, from New York to Liverpool. See Howard, *Herman Melville,* 7–14; E. Metcalf, 15–21; Leyda, *The Melville Log,* 1: 82–86; Hayford et al., Notes on Individual Prose Pieces, *PT* 622–23.

78. Howard, 93. The domestic arena that figures in such negative prominence for Howard includes both the household in which Herman grew up, presided over by his mother Maria, and the household in which he produced most of his writing, after his marriage in 1847, in which he was surrounded by wife and children in addition to mother and sisters. Thus, in the former case, Howard notes that Herman fled to New York City to write *Typee* since "writing could hardly have been easy in a household adjusted to an almost entirely feminine regime" (93); in 1846, Tom Melville, Herman's youngest brother, at age sixteen "had begun to show signs of manly restlessness in his feminine environment" and thus had determined to sail the South Seas before the mast (98); during the composition of *Omoo,* his sister Augusta was preparing to be a bridesmaid, "and the Melville household turned busily to dressmaking. The atmosphere was hardly productive of easy literary composition" (99). In the latter case, during the early stages of the composition of *Moby-Dick,* Herman and his brother Allan were sharing a household in New York City, "and a household consisting of a widow, two wives, three babies, and four spinsters would provide an impossible environment for a writer who was just hitting his stride" (153). D. H. Lawrence claims that Melville had pined in *Typee* for the two things he had run away from, and that were his damnation: home and mother (Lawrence, 136). In "*Moby-Dick* and Domesticity," Parker "explores the possibility that Melville embodied some of his domestic comforts, compromises, and tensions in *Moby-Dick*" (545).

79. Herman Melville, "The Paradise of Bachelors and the Tartarus of Maids," *PT* 316–35, 329; hereafter cited parenthetically as "Tartarus."

80. For an early example of this reading, see E. H. Eby, "Herman Melville's 'Tartarus of Maids,' " *Modern Language Quarterly* 1 (1940): 95–100; see also Lea Bertani Vozar Newman's summary of the critical history of the tale in *A Reader's Guide to the Short Stories of Herman Melville* (Boston: G. K. Hall, 1986), 283–305.

81. See Hayford et al., Notes on Individual Prose Pieces, *PT,* 709; Weaver, 303; Newman, 287; Parker, Historical Note to *MD,* section 3, p. 628. Prior to the marriage of Herman's other sister, Catherine (Kate), who married John Hoadley in September 1853, she too periodically lived at Arrowhead. In September 1853 Helen Maria became engaged to George Griggs, and subsequently moved out. Augusta and Frances Priscilla remained single (see E. Metcalf, 150; family tree, paste-down endpaper and free endpaper). As the correspondence among Maria and her daughters confirms, they all made frequent extended visits to a variety of homes, so it is difficult to establish exactly who was living at Arrowhead at any given time (Melville Family Papers/Additions, Gansevoort-Lansing Collection, Rare Books and Manuscripts Division, New York Public Library, Astor, Lenox and Tilden Foundations).

82. Edwin Haviland Miller, 260; Arvin, *Herman Melville,* 238; Newman, 287.

83. See Newman, 283–305.

84. Q. D. Leavis, "Melville: The 1853–6 Phase," *New Perspectives on Melville,* ed. Faith Pullin (Kent, Ohio: Kent State UP, 1978), 205–6.

85. This was probably the Carson mill in Dalton. See Hayford et al., Notes on Individual Prose Pieces, *PT* 710.

86. Judith A. McGaw, *Most Wonderful Machine: Mechanization and Social Change in Berkshire Paper Making, 1801–1885* (Princeton: Princeton UP, 1987) 335, n. 1.

87. While McGaw's history is enormously useful, I disagree with her account of why Melville changed what he would have observed at the mill. She argues that he meant the tale as a critique of the period's "well-known female textile mill employees as well as of the more general exploitation of women in industrializing America." She offers as further evidence the narrator's route in the story, which, she argues, is based on the route from Pittsfield to North Adams, a textile manufacturing center, rather than on the route from Pittsfield to Dalton, where the paper mill was located. Thus, her argument holds, he eliminated men from among the factory operatives at the paper mill in order to invoke textile mills and "women's employment generally" (335, n. 1).

88. Duyckinck to his wife, Margaret, 7 Aug. 1851 (quoted by E. Metcalf, 115).

89. See Foster, Historical Note, *M* 662; Parker, Historical Note, section 3, *MD* 619; Hayford, Parker, and Tanselle, Note on the Text, *CM* 362; Hayford, MacDougall, and Tanselle, Notes, *PT* 652, 574, and 700; Leyda, *The Melville Log*, 1:441, suggests that Helen copied at least part of *Pierre*.

Correspondence among Melville's mother and siblings illustrates a fascinating array of handwriting practices within a family economy of letter writing. Horth points out that the extant correspondence includes comparatively little correspondence by Herman; her valuable Historical Note to L maintains that "Melville seems always to stand on the periphery of this constant round of letters among the women" (779). Horth also stresses how partial our knowledge of the totality of Melville family correspondence is. As I indicate in my notes to chapter 1, Maria clearly scrutinized her children's correspondence for, among other things, penmanship and spelling, and the penmanship, spelling, and content of the letters are often subjects in the letters themselves.

Each correspondent has his or her own habits of hand, some of which are variations of a similar practice. If, for example, we consider the practice of turning the page sideways and writing up the margin, we can see that Frances (Fanny) implements this technique differently from the other siblings, writing her letters in two directions on the page in the greatest variety of spaces; of the sisters, Helen does this least, and her hand is much smaller than the others' hands; Tom writes only in one direction. The four sisters' hands bear some resemblance; the brothers' hands differ from the sisters' hands but resemble each other, similarities and differences that I suspect are a function of different schooling and therefore of different penmanship training. (My observations about the family hands are based on my examination of the Melville Family Papers/Additions, in the Gansevoort-Lansing Collection, Rare Books and Manuscripts Division, New York Public Library, Astor, Lenox, and Tilden Foundations.)

The particularities of Herman's hand thus emerge within a context of important cultural and family writing practices, but at the same time work out his own relation to the page, both in its peculiarities (for example, its chaotic obliteration of the page, whose particular features no other family hand doubles) and in the affect of those practices that are shared, such as, for example, abbreviations. That abbreviation (to take only one example) was a conventional writing practice in the period does not mean that all individuals bore the same relation to it. In fact, throughout this study I have been careful to make claims about Herman's particular relations to writing, relations that I do not believe are generalizable to all individuals, much less to an entire period.

The subject of the Melville women as copyists and writers with their own relations to the page certainly warrants further study, as Wyn Kelley has suggested ("The Mood for Composition: The Melville Family Letters," *Melville Society Extracts* 98 [Sept. 1994]: 12).

90. Weaver, 280–82, 272.

91. Elizabeth to her stepmother, Hope Savage Shaw, whom she addressed as "mother," 3 Aug. 1851, reproduced in my text as quoted by Weaver, 311. The letter at the Houghton Library, Harvard University, which I have cross-checked, reads, "I cannot write any more—it makes [paper torn] terribly nervous—I don't know as y [paper torn] n read this I have scribbled it so, but I can't help it—do excuse and burn it" (Houghton Library, Harvard University [MsAm188 (141)] Elizabeth Shaw Melville to Hope Savage Shaw, 3 Aug. 1851). I do not know if it was torn when Weaver saw it.

92. E. Metcalf, 76–77, 215.

93. Elizabeth Shaw Melville to Catherine Gansevoort Lansing, 7 Mar. 1879, extracted in *Family Correspondence of Herman Melville 1830–1904 in the Gansevoort-Lansing Collection*, ed. Victor Hugo Paltsits (Brooklyn, N.Y.: Haskell House, 1976), 57–58. See also Miller, 345, 320.

94. E. Metcalf, 26, 215, 55.

95. Edwin Haviland Miller, 320.

96. E. Metcalf, 213, 230, 185. I have confirmed this letter at the Houghton Library, Harvard University, in which "any one" is underlined [MsAm188 (145)], 9 Mar. 1875.

97. 2 Feb. 1876; quoted by E. Metcalf, 237; emphasis in original.

98. See Hayford, Parker, and Tanselle, Textual Record, *M* 686 and Hayford et al., Notes to *PT* 652.

99. Elizabeth to her stepmother, 5 May 1848, quoted by Hayford, Parker, and Tanselle, Historical Note, *MD* 619. See also Weaver, 271–72.

100. Herman Melville to Dix & Edwards, 24 Mar. 1856, L 288.

101. Based on my examination of the manuscript at the Houghton Library, Harvard University [MSAm 188 (386.B.2)].

102. To Evert A. Duyckinck, 2 and 14 Dec. 1849, L 149; emphasis in original.

103. William C. Woodbridge quoted in Nash, *American Penmanship*, 33.

104. Nash, *American Penmanship*, 64.

105. Pasteboard covers for books had become the rule by the late eighteenth century in America, replacing the wooden boards used prior to this. See Hannah Dustin French, "Early American Bookbinding by Hand," *Bookbinding in America: Three Essays*, ed. Hellmut Lehmann-Haupt (New York: R. R. Bowker, 1967), 14, 50, 95.

106. The name "Isabel" has also long been considered a form of the name "Elizabeth," suggesting another point of exchange between textual production in *Pierre* and in the Melville household. I do not thus mean to say that Isabel "is" Elizabeth Shaw Melville in any simple sense, but instead to indicate the complex ways in which *Pierre* invokes Melville's domestic scene of textual production, which needn't (and doesn't) function as a simple allegory. Elizabeth Shaw Melville's presence can also be felt in Lucy Tartan, for example. In light of the 1867 letters, *Pierre* newly confronts us with the scene in which Lucy's brother, Frederic, and Pierre's cousin, Glen Stanly, attempt to remove

her from Pierre's lodgings against her will (325). This scenario in *Pierre*, written at Arrowhead during the winter of 1851–52, powerfully anticipates the situation suggested by the 1867 letters. I am led to suspect that the 1867 incident was not the only or even the first time the family wanted to protect Elizabeth from Herman. As Samuel himself writes, Elizabeth's domestic case "has been a cause of anxiety to all of us for years past" (*EWW* 13).

Chapter Four: "Those mere phantoms which flit along a page" in *The Confidence-Man*

1. Quotations from the *Illustrated Times* and the *Critic* are cited by Watson Branch et al., Historical Note, *CM* 324, 325; see also Foster, introduction, xxxiv, xiii, xlvi, and Van Wyck Brooks, *The Times of Melville and Whitman* (n.p.: E. P. Dutton, 1947), 169. (Foster's introduction pointed me to this quotation [xxxix]). The novel's publication history illustrates something of its fortunes with readers: after publication in 1857, the novel was first reprinted in London in 1923, as volume 12 in the Constable edition of Melville's *Works*, and then not reprinted again until 1948 in England and 1949 in the United States (Branch et al., Historical Note, *CM* 330). See Foster's introduction and Branch et al., Historical Note, *CM*, 330 ff. for useful summaries of criticism of the novel; see H. Bruce Franklin, *The Wake of the Gods: Melville's Mythology* (Stanford: Stanford UP, 1963), and Watson G. Branch, "The Genesis, Composition, and Structure of *The Confidence-Man*," *Nineteenth-Century Fiction* 27 (1973): 424–48, for two clear and useful discussions of the novel's structure. (On Branch, see also Parker's response, "*The Confidence-Man* and the Use of Evidence in Compositional Studies: A Rejoinder," *Nineteenth-Century Fiction* 28 [1973]: 119–24.)

2. See Shneidman, "Some Psychological Reflections"; also Henry A. Murray, "Dead to the World: The Passions of Herman Melville," *Essays in Self-Destruction*, ed. Edwin S. Shneidman (New York: Science House, 1967), 16 ff. Stephen Railton comments that central to Melville's writing are the paradoxical impulses to court his readers' approval and to revolt against their assumptions, a "divisive uncertainty" about what he wanted from his audience (*Authorship and Audience: Literary Performance in the American Renaissance* [Princeton: Princeton UP, 1991], 157). Melville explored writing as an occasion for passive-aggressive behavior in "Bartleby, the Scrivener," in the wake of *Pierre*'s failure.

3. Branch et al., Historical Note, *CM* 285–86, discusses the tradition of identifying Winsome as Emerson.

4. Emerson's best-known expression of the necessity of inconsistency is perhaps "Self-Reliance," with its admonition, "A foolish consistency is the hobgoblin of little minds, adored by little statesmen and philosophers and divines. With consistency a great soul has simply nothing to do" (Emerson, 183). The style of Emerson's writing of course often enacts this principle of inconsistency.

5. J. Hillis Miller, *Ariadne's Thread: Story Lines* (New Haven: Yale UP, 1992), 60 (emphasis in original).

6. Karen Halttunen, *Confidence Men and Painted Women: A Study of Middle-class Culture in America, 1830–1870* (New Haven: Yale UP, 1982), 4. Halttunen studies advice manuals published in America between 1830 and 1870 and reads their primary concern

as that of ensuring the formation of moral character (28). Her larger argument situates middle-class concerns with hypocrisy and sincerity in that period with respect to a crisis of social identity arising from a new surge of social and geographical movement.

7. Johannes Dietrich Bergmann, "The Original Confidence Man," *American Quarterly* 21.3 (1969): 560–77.

8. Halttunen, xvii, 5, 25.

9. Halttunen, xvi, xvii.

10. My readings of Melville's revisions are based on my examination of the manuscript at the Houghton Library, Harvard University (bMSAm188 [365]). See also the reproduction of this page and the genetic transcription in *CM* 454–55. The first lines of the page, eventually struck through, seem to stutter over the word.

11. Chapter 14 is a pivotal chapter for understanding *The Confidence-Man*, particularly as Melville addressed the project in its final stages. He added the chapter midway through composition of the novel and revised it through four more versions after Augusta made the first-version fair copy. Adding chapter 14 necessitated making changes in chapters 13 and 33, and only after writing and placing chapter 14 among the other chapters did Melville draft the complete title list and establish the chapter numbers. He regarded the number, sequence, and contents of chapters as unsettled until the chapter was completed (Branch et al., Historical Note, *CM* 308–10). Melville systematically revised the word "characters" in this draft by striking out the *s*. He changed the phrases "consistency in the characters of fiction" to "consistency of character"; "inconsistent characters in fiction" to "inconsistent character in fiction" (then entirely deleted it); and "That fiction where all the characters can by reason of their obvious consistency be comprehended at a glance" to "That fiction where character can by reason of its consistency be comprehended at a glance" (see illustration 7, lines 10, 18, and 24 of the second paragraph), revisions that amend the specificity of the word from the level of literary "characters," like the good merchant whom the chapter is discussing, to the discussion of the "character" of fiction as such. Melville's extensive editorial engagement with this particular word in this crucial chapter indicates its centrality to his project and the subtleties of meaning he was concerned to draw from it. Irwin also stresses the centrality of chapter 14 to what he argues are the related issues of the self's inconsistency and the indeterminacy of signs (328 ff.).

12. Manuscript, the Houghton Library, Harvard University (bMSAm188 [365]). See also the genetic transcription, *CM* 422.

13. "Character"'s first, literal group of denotations includes a distinctive mark impressed or engraved; a graphic symbol standing for a sound, syllable, or notion, used in writing or printing; and writing, printing, or handwriting as such. The second, figurative group of meanings includes a distinctive mark, trait, or characteristic; the face or features as betokening moral qualities; the sum of the qualities that distinguish an individual or a race, viewed as a whole; and, in the more directly literary sense, a personality invested with distinctive attributes and qualities by a novelist or dramatist, or the part assumed by an actor (*OED*). The mark on a page that is the literal character becomes a figurative mark on a person or group of persons physically or morally stamped or engraved with attributes. J. Hillis Miller's incisive assessment of the *OED* on character works out how there is "much figurative play already among what the *OED* calls the literal senses of the word *character*" (56; emphasis in original).

14. See Goldberg's discussion of the graphic dimensions of character in the English Renaissance in *Voice Terminal Echo: Postmodernism and English Renaissance Texts* (New York: Methuen, 1986), 86–100; see also Halttunen, 4.

15. J. Hillis Miller, 58.

16. I am indebted here to Khalil Husni's attention to the motifs of color in *The Confidence-Man,* but I disagree with his conclusions. He reads the novel's attention to whiteness and blackness as a disruption of the polar archetypes of white as benevolent and good, and black as malevolent and evil ("The Confidence-Man's Colourful-Colourless Masquerade: Melville's Theatre of the Absurd," *Studia Anglica Posnaniensia: An International Review of English Studies* 17 (1984): 219–31). I also disagree with Foster, who argues that the deaf-mute is not one of the Confidence-Man's manifestations, and that the transition from this figure to the Black Guinea acts as a contrast between "Christ and Antichrist." In her argument, the white, fleecy vesture of the deaf-mute and the black fleece of the Black Guinea suggest "the pure ideal of Christianity and the black use made of it by the powers of evil" (Introduction, lii).

17. F. O. Matthiessen, *American Renaissance* (London: Oxford UP, 1941), 411. Matthiessen dislikes the book, and characterizes it as an "uncontrolled" work in which Melville was not fully engaged. He charges that Melville "was so far from having imagined a conclusion" that he could only break off the book as a distended fragment (412).

18. Two cases in point are Rebecca J. Kruger Guadino's "The Riddle of *The Confidence-Man*" (*The Journal of Narrative Technique* 14 [1984]: 124–41) and Henry Sussman's "The Deconstructor as Politician: Melville's *Confidence-Man*" (*Glyph: Johns Hopkins Textual Studies* 4 [1978]: 32–56). Both correctly identify a writing "theme" in the novel. While I am partly in agreement with one of Sussman's underlying notions, that the novel somehow "deconstructs" the realm of the ideal, I do not agree with his fundamental placement of this urge within the realm of the sociopolitical, which in effect reproduces a long-standing assessment of Melville as social critic. I ultimately locate the notion of the ideal with which Melville is so deeply engaged in a fundamentally different space: the realm of his own production whose material configurations produce a crisis of the transcendental (a term I use here synonymously with Sussman's "ideal"). Thus Melville as writer takes precedence in my assessment over Melville as social critic, and the terms of his fiction arise not from an ideological distance enabling critique, but rather constitutively from pressing material conditions as they impinge upon notions such as "the ideal." I bicker similarly with Guadino's assessment of the implications of the writing theme. Although incisive in her identification of manifestations of it—pointing out, for example, that materials for composition continually appear on the ship-desk of the novel, and that its invocations of whiteness become the blankness of the empty page (125)—she ultimately locates the importance of this "theme" in terms of Melville's concern with "the issue of fiction" (125), an assessment that stops short of articulating what kind of "issue" fiction is, or whether, for example, "fiction," "reading," and "writing" are to be understood as equivalent analytical terms.

19. Sundquist has argued that tautology is crucial to "Benito Cereno," in which oppositions that the tale nominally sets out (for example, between "master" and "slave") are then rendered "dangerously equal" by Melville's prose, a metaphor for the crisis of authority at the heart of the tale ("Suspense and Tautology in 'Benito Cereno,'" 108; see

also his recent revisiting of this issue in *To Wake the Nations*). Wai-Chee Dimock sees the importance of tautology in *The Confidence-Man*, and while I concur with her observations about the novel's delight in it, I disagree with her conclusions about its importance. She argues that tautology renders language "what Melville has always wanted it to be: a self-enclosed universe, untouched by the barbaric world, untouchable to barbaric readers," and that Melville's radically self-contained use of language produces freedom but also reduction to material signs, a reduction she characterizes as "inane" (*Empire for Liberty: Melville and the Poetics of Individualism* [Princeton: Princeton UP, 1989], 211–12). For Dimock these practices constitute what she calls an "imperial" gesture of freedom on Melville's part. I agree with Dimock's observation that the novel produces material signs, but disagree with her argument that the status of the material is "inane," since I see it instead embedded in Melville's relation to his writing in a constitutive and therefore crucial way. I also differ with her fundamental argument about Melville as a writer in the same terms in which I disagree with Sussman in the previous note. For Sussman, Melville writes from an ideological distance from the social that enables critique; for Dimock, he writes from complicity with prevailing ideology. I believe that both err in deriving the fundamental force of Melville's writing from the social.

20. Again, the crucial material bearings of Melville's case distinguish its trajectory from the "perpetual round of figure for figure" that Miller attributes to character.

21. For a summary of criticism taking these three chapters as a focal point, see Branch et al., Historical Note to *CM*, 345. Dimock also points out that these chapter titles are tautologies (211–12).

22. Melville's prose style in general features elaborate subordinate clauses and rhetorical devices such as litotes, a figure of speech in which an affirmative proposition is expressed by the negative of the contrary (*OED*), which create a dense resistance at the surface of his language. Irwin points out that Melville constructs sentences "of such ambiguous complexity that they function as syntactic mirrors in which an unselfconscious reader can always find his own prejudices reflected without ever being aware that he has projected them there in the process of interpretation and that the sentence could, with the same certainty, be interpreted to precisely the opposite effect by a reader of opposite mind" (335).

23. Foster, editorial apparatus, *The Confidence-Man*, xci–xcii. Branch also calls attention to the novel's balanced frame ("Genesis," 437).

24. Melville uses this technique again in the encounter between the cosmopolitan and the barber. The cosmopolitan begins to present the case "of the man with the averted face," asking the barber how he would judge the man's character. When the barber agrees that he would not automatically assume the man with the averted face to be a knave, the cosmopolitan replies, "You would, upon the face of him—," at which point the barber interrupts: "Hold, sir . . . nothing about the face; you remember, sir, that is out of sight" (228), conflating rhetorical and literal appearances of the face. The barber, whose trade, as the cosmopolitan says, of "handling the outside of men's heads" leads him "to distrust the inside of their hearts" (232), again opposes the face (the front "outside" of the head so conspicuously averted in the tale) and the heart, as in the passage I've been discussing.

25. Branch also points out that "half an hour" is the time elapsed between these two manifestations of the Confidence-Man ("Genesis," 431–33, n. 16).

26. See the genetic transcription of Fragment 21, a list of chapter titles, in Manuscript Fragments, *CM* 480–81.

27. I thus differ from Irwin because I construe these as word-based rather than concept-based equations (329).

28. Irwin, 337.

29. Irwin also points out that "P.W." could stand for pure or poison wine (337).

30. The first three words appear in capitals in the Northwestern-Newberry edition but in upper and lower case in the first American edition of 1857 (New York: Dix, Edwards & Co.).

31. For example, the terms "upper case" and "lower case," referring to capital and small letters, respectively, come from the arrangement of types in compositors' cases, capitals in the "upper case" and small letters in the "lower case"; to be "out of sorts" originally referred to the situation of a compositor who was out of a needed character, a "sort," in the midst of typesetting; and so on.

32. My thanks to Michael Winship for pointing this out.

33. See, for example, Stern, *The Fine Hammered Steel*, 179; Chase, 115; Franklin, 99–125; Saburo Yamaya, "The Stone Image in Melville's *Pierre*," *Studies in English Literature* 34 (1957): 31–57; and Richard Fleck, "Stone Imagery in Melville's *Pierre*," *Research Studies* 42 (1974): 127–30.

34. "In some words which we have borrowed from the Greek, *p* is mute, as in *psalm, ptisan*" (1847 Webster, entry under *p*; emphasis in original).

35. Reproduced in Manuscript Fragments, *CM* 483–86.

36. Reproduced in Manuscript Fragments, *CM* 484–86.

37. This observation is based on my assessment of the Melville manuscripts at the Houghton Library, Harvard University. For a valuable discussion of the *Billy Budd* manuscript that speaks to many of Melville's characteristic practices, see Harrison Hayford and Merton M. Sealts Jr., "Analysis of the Manuscript," *Billy Budd Sailor (An Inside Narrative). By Herman Melville. Reading Text and Genetic Text, Edited from the Manuscript with Introduction and Notes* (Chicago: U of Chicago P, 1962), 223 ff.

38. A. Robert Lee lists the book's key words as *confidence, charity, trust, charming,* and *shaving* ("Voices Off, On and Without: Ventriloquy in *The Confidence-Man*," *Herman Melville: Reassessments,* ed. A. Robert Lee [London: Vision, 1984], 159). Wadlington argues that *The Confidence-Man* manipulates a series of words related either etymologically or through "debased acquired meanings"—*original, genial, genuine, generous, genius, charity*—and that Melville explores an entire theme in considering the differences between the two (137).

39. Italics designate letters that differ in the two chains. As a candlemaker who wears a paper cap, China Aster is also associated with reading (paper) by light and with the extinction of light (snuff, char, the solar lamp at the end of the novel, the extinction of China Aster's life).

40. My observations about Melville's hand in this passage are based on my reading of the manuscript at the Houghton Library, Harvard University. To see a reproduction of Melville's inscription of "China Aster," see the reproduction of Fragment #22, *CM* 484.

41. Robert Sattelmeyer and James Barbour, "A Possible Source and Model for 'The Story of China Aster' in Melville's *The Confidence-Man*," *American Literature* 48 (1977): 578. I am grateful to Irmgard Schopen for calling my attention to *The China Aster*.

42. Robert Charles Ryan, " 'Weeds and Wildings Chiefly: With a Rose or Two' by Herman Melville. Reading Text and Genetic Text, Edited from the Manuscripts, with Introduction and Notes" (Ph.D. diss., Northwestern University, 1967), 14.

43. Vernon Lionel Shetley's fine study correctly points out that the asters resist the assignment of meaning (*A Private Art: Melville's Poetry of Negation* [Ph.D. diss., Columbia University, 1986], 169).

44. Manuscript Fragments, *CM* 470–71.

45. Twenty-six leaves and scraps from *The Confidence-Man* survive. All are worksheets, written on long sheets of blue paper, discarded between July and October 1856, when Augusta was making a fair copy. A sizable group of working manuscript leaves from *Billy Budd* survives as well (Branch et al., Historical Note, *CM* 308; Manuscript Fragments, *CM* 401).

46. Manuscript Fragments, *CM* 408.

47. Manuscript Fragments, *CM* 415.

48. Guadino, 131–33.

49. G. Thomas Tanselle, Historical Note, section 6, *MD* 663. Stereotype and electrotype plates were central to book publishing in this period. Jacob Abbott reported that Harper & Brothers did most of its printing from electrotypes (*The Harper Establishment; or, How the Story Books Are Made* [New York: Harper, 1855], 67). See also Philip Gaskell, *A New Introduction to Bibliography* (London: Oxford UP, 1972), 195 ff. Correcting plates necessitated cutting or punching out faulty letters, and soldering new ones in their place; the latter process was known as "botching" (Gaskell, 204; 204, n. 10). Melville's reference to this own books as "botches" is thus particularly intriguing, given the difficulties he and his publishers faced in driving his books through the press.

50. He changed the *e* in *rare* into an *a* and turned *o* into *a, n* into *vi,* and *e* into *s.* See discussion in Manuscript Fragments, *CM* 416–17 and reproduction of Fragment #3, 418; also reproduced in illustration 7, line 19.

51. Manuscript Fragments, *CM* 408, 432.

52. Nathalia Wright, *Melville's Use of the Bible* (Durham, N.C.: Duke UP, 1949), 154–55, discusses Melville's use of Proverbs 23:29–31, as does Foster, Explanatory Notes, 348.

53. Jacob Blanck, Preface, *Bibliography of American Literature* (New Haven: Yale UP, 1955), xxxiv. The herb-doctor's Omni-Balsamic Reinvigorator vials are encased in a paper wrapper water-marked with "capitals" spelling "confidence." "Wrappers" were also book covers made of single pieces of paper, sometimes with a printed label (Blanck, xxxix). The herb-doctor's other medicine, the Samaritan Pain Dissuader, features "a countenance full of soft pity" (83, 84). Since Winsome's doctrine of labels holds that inimical creatures are labeled "as an apothecary does a poison" (191), we can see that the herb-doctor's medicines are not only false (at the level of the plot), but also participate in an economy of "labels" that mark "poison writing."

54. Edgan Allan Poe, *Complete Stories and Poems of Edgar Allan Poe* (New York: Doubleday, 1966), 735. As Irwin has demonstrated, Poe is obsessively concerned with the materiality of text (often figured in his titles, e.g., *The Journal of Julius Rodman,* "MS. Found in a Bottle," "The Purloined Letter") and is particularly obsessed with the materiality of the text between the time of writing and publication, when it can be lost, a problem he often figures in tales of journeys to unexplored territory (as in "A Descent

into the Maelstrom" and *The Narrative of Arthur Gordon Pym.*) (Irwin, 64 ff.) The cave inscriptions in *Pym* include a *p*, ostensibly within a broken and disjointed chain of characters that in their perfect state, the Note at the end of the tale tells us, would no doubt have formed the full Egyptian word meaning "The region of the south" (Poe, 736). Within the context of the narrative, this *p* acts as a signature for "Pym" and for "Poe" (themselves encoded versions of one another). It also acts, as Irwin argues, as an alphabetical sign contrasted with the hieroglyphic signs that also comprise the inscription, raising the issue of "natural" v. "arbitrary" signs (168 ff.).

55. In 1846, Melville purchased the plates of the American revised edition of *Typee* from Wiley & Putnam and transferred them to Harper for subsequent printings (Howard, Historical Note, *T* 288). When Dix & Edwards, publishers of *The Piazza Tales* and *The Confidence-Man*, went bankrupt, Melville requested that the plates of his books be withheld from sale so that he could acquire them. What finally happened to these plates is unknown (see Melville's letter to George William Curtis of 15 Sept. 1857, *L* 314; also Historical Note to *CM* 316). In the case of *Moby-Dick,* Melville himself arranged and oversaw the typesetting and stereotyping of the manuscript, at the press of Robert Craighead in New York, before securing a publisher, although for his previous books the publisher had overseen these operations. As Tanselle points out in the Historical Note to *Moby-Dick,* while it had not been Melville's previous custom to arrange for the plating of his books, doing so was not uncommon for nineteenth-century authors; it gave authors greater control over costs and profits, as well as texts and typography. In Melville's case, it appears that he had the book plated before securing Harper & Brothers as publisher in order to speed up production, but the evidence is ambiguous (661–63). A provision in Melville's contract for *The Confidence-Man* stipulated that the stereotype plates were to be the joint property of publisher and author, and that Melville could buy them for 25 percent of the original cost after seven years or upon termination of the agreement (see Branch et al., Historical Note, *CM* 312).

56. Foster points out that "intelligence office" was a common term in the period for an employment bureau for domestic help. Melville mentions Hawthorne's story "The Intelligence Office" in "Hawthorne and His Mosses" (Foster, Explanatory Notes, 324, n. 129.3).

57. Manuscript Fragments, *CM* 476–77.

58. Abbott, 68.

59. See Foster, Explanatory Notes 2.7, 291–92; Hayford et al, Discussion of Adopted Readings 4.7, *CM* 376–77; and James Hall, chapter 27, *The Romance of Western History or, Sketches of History, Life, and Manners, in the West* (Cincinnati: Robert Clarke, 1885), which discusses the Harpes and Meason. See also Branch et al., Historical Note to *CM,* 281–82.

60. Howard, Historical Note, *T* 281, 288. See also Roper, Historical Note, *O* 329; Foster, Historical Note, *M* 664; Parker, Historical Note, *R* 319; Thorp, Historical Note, *WJ* 407; Hayford, Parker, and Tanselle, Historical Note, section 6, *MD* 669; Howard and Parker, Historical Note, *P* 378. *Israel Potter* was published serially in *Putnam's Monthly Magazine,* then in book form by G. P. Putnam & Company (Bezanson, Historical Note, *IP,* 205, 212); *The Piazza Tales* and *The Confidence-Man* were published by Dix & Edwards (Sealts, Historical Note, *PT* 498–99; 484 ff.).

61. Ezra Greenspan, "Evert Duyckinck and the History of Wiley and Putnam's Library of American Books, 1845–1847," *American Literature* 64 (1992): 690.

62. William Charvat, *The Profession of Authorship in America, 1800–1870,* ed. Matthew J. Bruccoli (1968; New York: Columbia UP, 1992), 183.

63. Michael Winship, "Critical Methods in the History of the Book in the United States" and "Bibliographical Approaches to the Nineteenth-Century Book in the United States," the Program in the History of the Book in American Culture, American Antiquarian Society, June 14–26, 1992. I am grateful to Winship and to the American Antiquarian Society for the enormous usefulness of these sessions to this project. Robert E. Mensel points out that late-nineteenth-century notions of "character" in the United States were understood to measure one's reliability in such matters as credit transactions, and were thus fundamentally economic (" 'Kodakers Lying in Wait': Amateur Photography and the Right of Privacy in New York, 1885–1915," *American Quarterly* 43 [1991]: 26).

64. Gaskell, 236

65. Rpt. in Sealts, *Early Lives,* 110. See also the Historical Notes to *WJ* (342), *MD* (688), and *P* (380). Many new impressions were made from the plates (see, for example, Historical Note to *WJ* 342). A 17 March 1854 letter from Augusta Melville to her sister Frances (Fanny) mentions that the Harpers, "owing to the two fires," are "not in a situation to publish" a manuscript of Herman's (Melville Family Papers/Additions, Gansevoort-Lansing Collection, Rare Books and Manuscripts Division, New York Public Library, Astor, Lenox and Tilden Foundations).

66. Foster also notes that Melville gives the two sharpers "Indian containers for their wine bottle and cigars" (Introduction, lxxii), which she takes to indicate that they are "the Indians of the argument." She reads the Indian figure as a metaphor—quite apart, she stressed, from Melville's beliefs about actual Indian people—for the figure who hides malice beneath a mask in order to betray men (Introduction, lxvii). I disagree that Melville uses the figure of the Indian this way, except to ironize such a reading, as he does in his insistence on its textuality. On Indians in Melville's work more generally, see Lucy Maddox, *Removals: Nineteenth-Century American Literature and the Politics of Indian Affairs* (New York: Oxford, 1991).

67. Foster, Explanatory Notes, 338. Maddox argues that the number of Melville's allusions in the Indian-hating chapters is a reminder that Hall constructed his stories out of bits and pieces from other writers (86–87).

68. Hall, 78, reproduced in Editorial Appendix, *CM* 506.

69. Halttunen, 30.

70. All Melville's irruptive faces, "racial" differences notwithstanding, are more continuous with one another than they are different in the signifying realm of Melville's work. To cite several examples: Babo's black face in "Benito Cereno" is one whose impenetrability fully participates in the structure of facial confrontations I describe, as do the tattooed faces of the Polynesians in *Typee.* The engagements in these fictions between white protagonists and nonwhite faces participate in a Melvillean signifying economy that, taken in its largest terms, is not primarily about racial difference.

For example, the specific impenetrability of Babo's face is of course deeply culturally resonant in terms of racist notions of blackness as impenetrable, inscrutable, and therefore opposed to cultural ideals of transparency (see Fliegelman on physiognomy and racist notions of the impenetrability of the black countenance, 192 ff.). In "Benito Cereno," Melville sees the problem of "black" inscrutability from a "white" position, a racialization of the facial confrontation that also characterizes *Typee.* Nevertheless, in

Melville's work nonwhite faces are more consistent with white, even (especially) appallingly white, faces than fundamentally different from them. The terms of Melville's work thus incorporate racially diverse faces within a larger structure of facial impenetrability; and that larger structure, understood from the standpoint of Melville's relation to his own production, ultimately speaks to the fundamental impenetrability of and struggle with his own scene of writing. I thus differ from much recent work on Melville and race in the ultimate location in which I place its power for him as a writer: the compelling force of race in his work is one whose power *for him* is configured by what are *for him* the more primary terms of composition and production.

Some examples of excellent recent work on the subject of race as a cultural configuration in Melville's work (which thus proceed from a different analytical ground than mine) are Toni Morrison, *Playing in the Dark: Whiteness and the Literary Imagination* (Cambridge: Harvard UP, 1992), and Sundquist, *To Wake the Nations.*

71. Marc Shell, *The Economy of Literature* (Baltimore: Johns Hopkins UP, 1978), 64.

72. Jean-Christophe Agnew, *Worlds Apart: The Market and the Theatre in Anglo-American Thought, 1550–1750* (Cambridge: Cambridge UP, 1986), 201, 14.

73. See Nash's entries #171 (153), 251 (191), 295 (210), and 300 (216) in *American Penmanship* for examples of penmanship manuals specifically advertising training in writing capitals.

74. Foster, Explanatory Notes 2.7, 291–92.

75. For information on Hall and Simms, see Branch et al., Historical Note, *CM* 282; I am also indebted here to Winship's description of Wiley & Putnam's Library of American Books for the Program in the History of the Book in American Culture at the American Antiquarian Society, June 14–26, 1992; Greenspan, 683–84, 685, 686; Charvat, 168–89. On Emerson's recommendation of *A Week* to Duyckinck and Thoreau's subsequent exchanges with Duyckinck on the subject, see Steven Fink, *Prophet in the Marketplace: Thoreau's Development as a Professional Writer* (Princeton: Princeton UP, 1992), 143–47. Emerson and Hawthorne both pressed Duyckinck to include *A Week* in the Library; Melville dined with Duyckinck just as he was deciding in the negative (Branch et al., Historical Note, *CM* 286). On the identification of Egbert as Thoreau and Mark Winsome as Emerson, see Branch et al., Historical Note, *CM* 285–86 and 332.

76. Greenspan, 691, n. 5.

77. Branch et al., Historical Note, *CM* 281; see also the appendix, "Melville's Indian-Hating Source," 501–10, for a reproduction of one of Hall's chapters.

78. I reiterate my differences with rhetorical readings of Melville such as Gasché's and Dryden's (see my notes to chapter 2). My emphasis here is not on the way in which language is always already figural, but rather on the force of the material in Melville's nominal figures. Printed sources here are not more language in an endless chain of representations, but physical objects whose ontology cannot be conflated with that of tropes.

79. Weaver, 128; on Coan, see also Sealts, *Early Lives,* 41–47.

80. I am indebted to Robert Schreur for suggesting this to me. Fried notes that poetry characteristically pursues effects of denaturalization (*Realism, Writing, Disfiguration,* 191, n. 43). Melville's *p* achieves a similar effect as it abstracts its graphic effects from "content."

81. Based on my analysis of the manuscript at the Houghton Library, Harvard University (MSAm 188 [363], leaf 158). See also the Hayford and Sealts genetic text, 349.

82. See Hayford and Sealts for the genetic theory that *Billy Budd* began with "Billy in the Darbies."

83. James Galvin, interview with William Marcus, *Morning Edition*, National Public Radio, WOSU, Columbus, Ohio, 3 Aug. 1992.

Chapter Five: Battle "Pieces"

1. I thus differ from the history of criticism about *Battle-Pieces*, which invariably accepts the Civil War as the volume's primary subject.

2. See the *OED* under *piece* and Hennig Cohen's introduction to *The Battle-Pieces of Herman Melville* (New York: Thomas Yoseloff, 1963), 14–15. Melville's 1857 journal records seeing Salvator Rosa's "Battle Piece" (see Cohen, Introduction, 4–15, and *J* 116, 496).

3. Cohen, Introduction, 15.

4. See Christopher Sten, "Melville and the Visual Arts: An Overview," *Savage Eye: Melville and the Visual Arts*, ed. Christopher Sten (Kent, Ohio: Kent State UP, 1991), 30; Robert K. Wallace, *Melville and Turner: Spheres of Love and Fright* (Athens: U of Georgia P, 1992), 3: 54–55; Cohen, Comment, 181. Sten sees "a new note" in *Battle-Pieces*, "a sudden openness to American art and artists that goes beyond the treatment of American themes one might expect to find in a carefully structured collection of poems on the American Civil War." He notes that Melville is working with analogies between poetry and painting, arranging his poems like pictures in a gallery and inviting his readers to consider them as a gallerygoer would (30, 31).

5. He includes on the list of such devices memory, reportage, tragedy, and the Aeolian harp. Timothy Sweet, *Traces of War: Poetry, Photography, and the Crisis of the Union* (Baltimore: Johns Hopkins UP, 1990), 169.

6. Unless otherwise noted, quotations from *Battle-Pieces* in this chapter are from the first edition, whose production Melville oversaw: *Battle-Pieces and Aspects of the War* (New York: Harper, 1866); here, [v]. Readers who don't have access to the first edition might want to consult the 1960 facsimile reproduction.

7. I transcribe these notes from the photocopy of the galley proofs of *JM* (pp. 4, 12, 13) (call number pAC85 M4977 888ja) and from the electroprint of the manuscript [MSAm 188 (370a)], both at the Houghton Library, Harvard University.

8. I derive this observation from my work with the manuscripts.

9. Nathalia Wright's examination of the poems in *Mardi* presents that novel as a combination of literary genres that she aligns to the later poems that contain prose ("The Poems in Melville's *Mardi*," *Essays in Arts and Sciences* 5.2 [1976]: 83).

10. See Hayford and Sealts on the genesis of *Billy Budd*.

11. Melville left ample poems in manuscript at his death.

12. William Bysshe Stein, *The Poetry of Melville's Late Years* (Albany: SUNY Press, 1970), 9.

13. Garner, 116.

14. Richard Harter Fogle, "Melville and the Civil War," *Tulane Studies in English* 9 (1959): 72; Cohen, Introduction, 15.

15. Both Fogle and Cohen have described these as poems of foreboding. Fogle deems the first three excellent and "Apathy and Enthusiasm" "less successful," an assess-

ment with which my discussion will differ. See Fogle, "Melville and the Civil War," 63, and Cohen, Introduction, 20.

16. Samuel Taylor Coleridge, *Coleridge: Poetical Works,* ed. Ernest Hartley Coleridge (1912; Oxford: Oxford UP, 1969), 101–2, ll. 39–43.

17. Coleridge, "The Eolian Harp," l. 47.

18. Joyce Sparer Adler, "Melville and the Civil War," *New Letters* 40.2 (1973): 100–101.

19. Garner, 50, 78 ff.

20. Garner 50, 284.

21. Garner, 397. Garner notes in his final chapter, "It has not been the purpose of this study to provide a foundation for a new evaluation of Melville's poetics, but rather to follow his biographical footsteps as he gathered his materials and made *Battle-Pieces,* to locate the source of the poems in his experiences, and to suggest what he intended them to accomplish. His achievement will become fully available only when the critical tools needed to measure it are forged by others" (443). Garner's study is an enormously useful collection of information with whose fundamental argument I strongly disagree. He consistently argues that historical events of the war determine Melville's actions, moods, and poetic images, while I see the importance of these historical events as secondary to Melville's relation to his own writing as such.

22. Daniel Aaron, *The Unwritten War: American Writers and the Civil War* (New York: Knopf, 1973), 78, and Cohen, Introduction, 15. Sweet points out that *Battle-Pieces* is mediated in its relation to the war by an apparatus of previously inscribed facts, and that it makes the conflicting assertion that it merely notes the airs played by the harp in the window (Sweet, 168), an observation that calls attention to Melville's conflicted relation to his own material.

23. This anonymous review from the *Atlantic Monthly* 19 (Feb. 1867): 252–53 is reprinted in Hershel Parker, ed., *The Recognition of Herman Melville: Selected Criticism since 1846* (Ann Arbor: U of Michigan P, 1967), 100–102, and the author is identified as Howells in Kevin J. Hayes and Hershel Parker, *Checklist of Melville Reviews* (Evanston, Ill.: Northwestern UP, 1991), 113.

24. Ryan, 136.

25. My assessment of the appearance of Melville's manuscript pages is based on my work with the manuscripts at the Houghton Library, Harvard University.

26. Newton Arvin, "Melville's Shorter Poems," *Partisan Review* 16.10 (1949): 1039.

27. Shetley discusses Melville's treatment of enthusiasts and enthusiasm in *Timoleon,* concluding that *enthusiasm* has a double-edged meaning for Melville: "It may indicate deluded fanaticism, and admirable energy and refusal to compromise, or it may hover undecidably between these alternatives" (92). Shetley points out that *enthusiasm* was generally pejorative throughout the eighteenth century (91) (as in the first of Webster's definitions). Samuel Johnson's definition of *enthusiasm* from *A Dictionary of the English Language* (6th ed.; London, 1785) is an almost verbatim source for Webster.

28. See Cohen, Introduction, 211–12, and "Comment on the Poems," 178.

29. Arvin, "Melville's Shorter Poems," 1037.

30. Warren, 186.

31. That arm also emerges in the domestically set poem "The House-Top. / A Night Piece. / (July, 1863.)" There Melville writes, "Hail to the low dull rumble, dull and dead, / And ponderous drag that shakes the wall" (ll. 17–18). In this poem, the "arm

drag" of *Moby-Dick*, here also set against "the wall" and attempting to break through it, oppresses a sleepless night. In his copy of *Battle-Pieces* Melville wrote "jars" in the margin to replace the prior word "shakes." (Based on my examination of this copy at the Houghton Library, Harvard University [*AC85.M4977.8666 (C)].) The sleepless narrator feels "a dense oppression" (l. 2) that makes him, through the simile of tigers, "apt for ravage" (l. 4). It is in this state that "fitfully from far breaks a mixed surf / Of muffled sound" (ll. 7–8).

32. Cohen, Introduction, 20.

33. 9 Dec. 1872, L 424, 425.

34. My analysis of the handwriting is based on my examination of the letter (Melville Family Papers, Gansevoort-Lansing Collection, Rare Books & Manuscripts Division, New York Public Library, Astor, Lenox and Tilden Foundations).

35. Garner, 393.

36. Warren, 189.

37. Cohen notes that the term "prison pen" was a neologism when Melville chose it for his title (Notes, 253).

38. James M. McPherson, *Battle Cry of Freedom: The Civil War Era* (New York: Oxford UP, 1988), 791, 796.

39. See, for example, photographs reproduced in McPherson (inset between 684 and 685).

40. Personal communication with Dr. Abbot Gaunt, Department of Zoology, Ohio State University, Columbus, Ohio, 30 June 1993. I am grateful to Dr. Gaunt for his illuminating discussion with me about the image of a pelican-beach in this poem, and its relevance to Civil War camps.

41. I examined these proofs at the Houghton Library, Harvard University [pAC85 M4977 888ja].

42. Blank pages also appear elsewhere in the 1866 edition, for example, in between some sections and on the reverse of section title pages. The features of "The Portent" stand out from the rest of the collection in the ways I have described.

43. For example, Vere advocates "measured forms" by telling "the story of Orpheus with his lyre," which he links to the political disruptions that will later determine the outcome of the tale (380); his nickname comes from a poem; and poetic terms inform such discussions as those of ships (306) and of Nelson (307).

44. William H. Shurr, *The Mystery of Iniquity: Melville as Poet, 1857–1891* (Lexington: UP of Kentucky, 1972), 16; Fogle, "Melville's Poetry," *Tulane Studies in English* 12 (1962): 81–86.

45. Darrel Abel, "I Look, You Look, He Looks: Three Critics of Melville's Poetry," *ESQ* 21.2 (1975): 117.

P.S.: Marks in "John Marr"

1. Jarrard, "Poems by Herman Melville," 325.

2. Quotations in this paragraph are from Jarrard, 173, 175.

3. The manuscript shows that he originally wrote "he was obstructed." See the electroprint copy of the manuscript at the Houghton Library, Harvard University [109 (MSAm188 (370a)]. See also Jarrard, 178.

4. Quotations in the paragraph are from Jarrard, 174, 173, 176.

5. Quotations in this paragraph are from Jarrard, 174, 173, 175.

6. Jarrard, 179a.

7. While my discussions of other manuscript pages of *John Marr* are based on the electroprint copy, I was able to look at this manuscript page in the original (Houghton Library, Harvard University [MsAm188 (370)]). The original manuscript was otherwise unavailable for study because of its fragility.

8. T. C. Hansard, *Typographia: An Historical Sketch of the Origin and Progress of the Art of Printing* (London: Baldwin, Cradock, & Joy, 1825), 431.

9. My transcription from the electroprint copy of the manuscript at the Houghton Library, Harvard University [MSAm188 (370a)].

Works Cited

Aaron, Daniel. *The Unwritten War: American Writers and the Civil War*. New York: Knopf, 1973.

Abbott, Jacob. *The Harper Establishment; or, How the Story Books Are Made*. New York: Harper, 1855.

Abel, Darrel. "I Look, You Look, He Looks: Three Critics of Melville's Poetry." *ESQ* 21.2 (1975): 116–23.

Adler, Joyce Sparer. "Melville and the Civil War." *New Letters* 40.2 (1973): 99–117.

Agnew, Jean-Christophe. *Worlds Apart: The Market and the Theatre in Anglo-American Thought, 1550–1750*. Cambridge: Cambridge UP, 1986.

Anderson, Charles Roberts. *Melville in the South Seas*. 1939. New York: Dover, 1966.

Arvin, Newton. *Herman Melville*. 1950. New York: Viking, 1957.

——. "Melville's Shorter Poems." *Partisan Review* 16.10 (1949): 1034–46.

Barbour, James. "'All My Books Are Botches': Melville's Struggle with *The Whale*." *Writing the American Classics*. Edited by James Barbour and Tom Quirk. Chapel Hill: U of North Carolina P, 1990.

——. "The Composition of *Moby-Dick*." *American Literature* 47 (1975): 343–60.

Baym, Nina. "Melville's Quarrel with Fiction." *PMLA* 94.5 (1979): 909–23.

Bergmann, Johannes Dietrich. "The Original Confidence Man." *American Quarterly* 21.3 (1969): 560–77.

Berthold, Dennis. "Melville and Dutch Genre Painting." *Savage Eye: Melville and the Visual Arts*. Edited by Christopher Sten. Kent, Ohio: Kent State UP, 1991.

Bezanson, Walter E. Historical and Critical Note. *Clarel: A Poem and Pilgrimage in the Holy Land*. By Herman Melville. Vol. 12 of *The Writings of Herman Melville*. Edited by Harrison Hayford, Hershel Parker, and G. Thomas Tanselle. 13 vols. to date. Evanston and Chicago: Northwestern UP and Newberry Library, 1968–. 505–637.

——. Historical Note. *Israel Potter: His Fifty Years of Exile*. By Herman Melville. Vol. 8 of *The Writings of Herman Melville*. Edited by Harrison Hayford, Hershel Parker, and G. Thomas Tanselle. 13 vols. to date. Evanston and Chicago: Northwestern UP and Newberry Library, 1968–. 173–235.

Blanck, Jacob. Preface. *Bibliography of American Literature*. New Haven: Yale UP, 1955. 1:xi–xli.

Branch, Watson G. "The Genesis, Composition, and Structure of *The Confidence-Man.*" *Nineteenth-Century Fiction* 27 (1973): 424–48.

Branch, Watson, Hershel Parker, and Harrison Hayford, with Alma A. MacDougall. Historical Note. *The Confidence-Man.* By Herman Melville. Vol. 10 of *The Writings of Herman Melville.* Edited by Harrison Hayford, Hershel Parker, and G. Thomas Tanselle. 13 vols. to date. Evanston and Chicago: Northwestern UP and Newberry Library, 1968–. 277–302.

Breitwieser, Mitchell. "False Sympathy in Melville's *Typee.*" *American Quarterly* 34.4 (1982): 396–417.

Brodhead, Richard. *Hawthorne, Melville, and the Novel.* Chicago: U of Chicago P, 1976.

Brodtkorb, Paul, Jr. *Ishmael's White World: A Phenomenological Reading of "Moby-Dick."* New Haven: Yale UP, 1965.

Brooks, Van Wyck. *The Times of Melville and Whitman.* N.p.: E. P. Dutton, 1947.

Brown, Bill. "Writing, Race, and Erasure: Michael Fried and the Scene of Reading." *Critical Inquiry* 18 (1992): 387–402.

Brown, Gillian. *Domestic Individualism: Imagining Self in Nineteenth-Century America.* U of California P, 1990.

Bryant, John, ed. *A Companion to Melville Studies.* New York: Greenwood Press, 1986.

——. "Melville, 'Little Henry,' and the Process of Composition: A Peep at the *Typee* Fragment." *Melville Society Extracts* 67 (1986): 1–4.

——. "Melville's L-Word: First Intentions and Final Readings in *Typee.*" *The New England Quarterly* 63.1 (1990): 120–31.

——. *Melville and Repose: The Rhetoric of Humor in the American Renaissance.* New York: Oxford UP, 1993.

Butterfield, Herbie. " 'New World All Over': Melville's *Typee* and *Omoo.*" *Herman Melville: Reassessments.* Edited by A. Robert Lee. London: Vision Press, 1984. 14–26.

Cameron, Sharon. *The Corporeal Self: Allegories of the Body in Melville and Hawthorne.* Baltimore: Johns Hopkins UP, 1981.

Carlson, Thomas C. "Fictive Voices in Melville's Reviews, Letters, and Prefaces." *Interpretations* 6 (1974): 39–46.

Charvat, William. *The Profession of Authorship in America, 1800–1870.* Edited by Matthew J. Bruccoli. 1968. New York: Columbia UP, 1992.

Chase, Richard. *Herman Melville: A Critical Study.* New York: Macmillan, 1949.

Cohen, Hennig. Introduction and Notes. *The Battle-Pieces of Herman Melville.* By Herman Melville. New York: Thomas Yoseloff, 1963. 11–28; 203–95.

——, ed. Postscript and Comment on the Poems. *Selected Poems of Herman Melville.* New York: Fordham UP, 1991. xvii–xviii; 175–259.

Cohen, Hennig, and Donald Yannella. *Herman Melville's Malcolm Letter: "Man's Final Lore."* New York: Fordham UP and the New York Public Library, 1992.

Coleridge, Samuel Taylor. *Coleridge: Poetical Works.* Edited by Ernest Hartley Coleridge. 1912. Oxford: Oxford UP, 1969.

The Compact Edition of the Oxford English Dictionary. 1971.

Cowen, Walker. *Melville's Marginalia.* 2 vols. New York: Garland, 1987.

Crain, Caleb. "Lovers of Human Flesh: Homosexuality and Cannibalism in Melville's Novels." *American Literature* 66 (1994): 25–53.

Davis, Merrell R., and William H. Gilman, eds. Introduction and Textual Notes. *The Letters of Herman Melville.* New Haven: Yale UP, 1960. xv–xxviii; 321–85.

de Man, Paul. "Autobiography as De-Facement." *The Rhetoric of Romanticism.* Ithaca: Cornell UP, 1984. 67–81.

Dening, Greg, ed. *The Marquesan Journal of Edward Robarts.* Honolulu: UP of Hawaii, 1974.

Derrida, Jacques. "Freud and the Scene of Writing." *Writing and Difference.* Translated by Alan Bass. Chicago: U of Chicago P, 1978. 196–231.

Dillingham, William B. *Melville's Later Novels.* Athens: U of Georgia P, 1986.

Dimock, Wai-Chee. *Empire for Liberty: Melville and the Poetics of Individualism.* Princeton: Princeton UP, 1989.

Dryden, Edgar A. *The Form of American Romance.* Baltimore: Johns Hopkins UP, 1988.

——. *Melville's Thematics of Form: The Great Art of Telling the Truth.* 1968. Baltimore: Johns Hopkins UP, 1981.

Eby, E. H. "Herman Melville's 'Tartarus of Maids.' " *Modern Language Quarterly* 1 (1940): 95–100.

Emerson, Ralph Waldo. *Ralph Waldo Emerson: Selected Essays.* Edited by Larzer Ziff. 1982. New York: Viking Penguin, 1985. 35–82.

Epstein, Barbara Leslie. *The Politics of Domesticity: Women, Evangelism, and Temperance in Nineteenth-Century America.* Middletown, Conn.: Wesleyan UP, 1981.

Evelev, John. " 'Made in the Marquesas': *Typee,* Tattooing, and Melville's Critique of the Literary Marketplace." *Arizona Quarterly* 48.4 (1992): 19–45.

Feidelson, Charles, Jr. *Symbolism and American Literature.* Chicago: U of Chicago P, 1953.

Fellowes, C. H. *The Tattoo Book.* Princeton: Pyne Press, 1971.

Fink, Steven. *Prophet in the Marketplace: Thoreau's Development as a Professional Writer.* Princeton: Princeton UP, 1992.

Fleck, Richard. "Stone Imagery in Melville's *Pierre.*" *Research Studies* 42 (1974): 127–30.

Fliegelman, Jay. *Declaring Independence: Jefferson, Natural Language, and the Culture of Performance.* Stanford: Stanford UP, 1993.

Fogle, Richard Harter. "Melville and the Civil War." *Tulane Studies in English* 9 (1959): 61–89.

——. "Melville's Poetry." *Tulane Studies in English* 12 (1962): 81–86.

Foster, Elizabeth S. Historical Note. *Mardi and A Voyage Thither.* By Herman Melville. Vol. 3 of *The Writings of Herman Melville.* Edited by Harrison Hayford, Hershel Parker, and G. Thomas Tanselle. 13 vols. to date. Evanston and Chicago: Northwestern UP and Newberry Library, 1968–. 657–81.

——. Introduction, Explanatory Notes, Textual Notes, and Appendix. *The Confidence-Man: His Masquerade.* By Herman Melville. New York: Hendricks House, 1954. xiii–xcv; 287–392.

Franklin, H. Bruce. *The Wake of the Gods: Melville's Mythology.* Stanford: Stanford UP, 1963.

French, Hannah Dustin. "Early American Bookbinding by Hand." *Bookbinding in America: Three Essays.* Edited by Hellmut Lehmann-Haupt. New York: R. R. Bowker, 1967. 1–127.

Fried, Michael. "Almayer's Face: On 'Impressionism' in Conrad, Crane, and Norris." *Critical Inquiry* 17.1 (1990): 193–236.

——. *Realism, Writing, Disfiguration: On Thomas Eakins and Stephen Crane.* Chicago: U of Chicago P, 1986.

——. "Response to Bill Brown." *Critical Inquiry* 18 (1992): 403–10.

Galvin, James. Interview by William Marcus. *Morning Edition.* National Public Radio. WOSU. Columbus, Ohio. August 3, 1992.

Garner, Stanton. *The Civil War World of Herman Melville.* Lawrence: UP of Kansas, 1993.

Gasché, Rodolphe. "The Scene of Writing: A Deferred Outset." *Glyph: Johns Hopkins Textual Studies* 1 (1977): 150–71.

Gaskell, Philip. *A New Introduction to Bibliography.* London: Oxford UP, 1972.

Goldberg, Jonathan. *Voice Terminal Echo: Postmodernism and English Renaissance Texts.* New York: Methuen, 1986.

——. *Writing Matter: From the Hands of the English Renaissance.* Stanford: Stanford UP, 1990.

Gordon, Linda. *Heroes of Their Own Lives: The Politics and History of Family Violence, Boston 1880–1960.* New York: Viking, 1988.

Govenar, Alan B. Introduction. *Stoney Knows How: Life as a Tattoo Artist.* By Leonard L. St. Clair and Alan B. Govenar. Lexington: UP of Kentucky, 1981. xi–xxxii.

Greenspan, Ezra. "Evert Duyckinck and the History of Wiley and Putnam's Library of American Books, 1845–1847." *American Literature* 64 (1992): 677–93.

Guadino, Rebecca J. Kruger. "The Riddle of *The Confidence-Man.*" *Journal of Narrative Technique* 14 (1984): 124–41.

Gurney, Cassius. *How to Read the Face.* New York: Mme. Gurney & Co., 1883.

Hall, James. *The Romance of Western History or, Sketches of History, Life, and Manners, in the West.* 1835. Reprint ed., Cincinnati: Robert Clarke & Co., 1885.

Halttunen, Karen. *Confidence Men and Painted Women: A Study of Middle-class Culture in America, 1830–1870.* New Haven: Yale UP, 1982.

Handy, Willowdean Chatterson. *Forever the Land of Men: An Account of a Visit to the Marquesas Islands.* New York: Dodd, Mead & Co., 1965.

——. *Tattooing in the Marquesas.* Bayard Dominick Expedition, Bulletin 1, No. 3. Honolulu: Bernice P. Bishop Museum, 1922.

Hansard, T. C. *Typographia: An Historical Sketch of the Origin and Progress of the Art of Printing.* London: Baldwin, Cradock & Joy, 1825.

Hawthorne, Nathaniel. *The House of the Seven Gables. The Complete Novels and Selected Tales of Nathaniel Hawthorne.* Edited by Norman Holmes Pearson. New York: Modern Library, 1937. 243–436.

Hayes, Kevin J., and Hershel Parker. *Checklist of Melville Reviews.* Evanston, Ill.: Northwestern UP, 1991.

Hayford, Harrison. "The Melville Society: A Retrospective." *Melville Society Extracts* Number 88 (1992): 2–6.

——. "Unnecessary Duplicates: A Key to the Writing of *Moby-Dick.*" *New Perspectives on Melville.* Edited by Faith Pullin. Kent, Ohio: Kent State UP, 1978. 128–61.

Hayford, Harrison, and Walter Blair, eds. Editors' Introduction and Explanatory Notes. *Omoo: A Narrative of Adventures in the South Seas.* By Herman Melville. New York: Hendricks House, 1969. xvii–lii; 341–438.

Hayford, Harrison, and Alma A. MacDougall. Manuscript Fragments. *The Confidence-Man: His Masquerade.* By Herman Melville. Vol. 10 of *The Writings of Herman Melville.* Edited by Harrison Hayford, Hershel Parker, and G. Thomas Tanselle. 13

vols. to date. Evanston and Chicago: Northwestern UP and Newberry Library, 1968–. 401–99.

Hayford, Harrison, Hershel Parker, and G. Thomas Tanselle. Historical Note. *Moby-Dick or The Whale*. By Herman Melville. Vol. 6 of *The Writings of Herman Melville*. Edited by Harrison Hayford, Hershel Parker, and G. Thomas Tanselle. 13 vols. to date. Evanston and Chicago: Northwestern UP and Newberry Library, 1968–. 581–762.

Hayford, Harrison, and Merton M. Sealts Jr. *Billy Budd Sailor (An Inside Narrative). By Herman Melville. Reading Text and Genetic Text, Edited from the Manuscript with Introduction and Notes*. Chicago: U of Chicago P, 1962.

Herbert, T. Walter, Jr. *Marquesan Encounters: Melville and the Meaning of Civilization*. Cambridge, Mass.: Harvard UP, 1980.

———. *"Moby-Dick" and Calvinism: A World Dismantled*. New Brunswick, N.J.: Rutgers UP, 1977.

Higgins, Brian, and Hershel Parker, eds. *Critical Essays on Herman Melville's "Pierre; or, The Ambiguities."* Boston: G. K. Hall, 1983.

Holden, Horace. *A Narrative of the Shipwreck, Captivity & Sufferings of Horace Holden & Benjamin H. Nute*. 1836. Fairfield, Wash.: Ye Galleon Press, 1975.

Howard, Leon. *Herman Melville: A Biography*. Berkeley: U of California P, 1951.

———. Historical Note. *Typee*. By Herman Melville. Vol. 1 of *The Writings of Herman Melville*. Ed. Harrison Hayford, Hershel Parker, and G. Thomas Tanselle. 13 vols. to date. Evanston and Chicago: Northwestern UP and Newberry Library, 1968–. 277–302.

Howard, Leon, and Hershel Parker. Historical Note. *Pierre*. By Herman Melville. Vol. 7 of *The Writings of Herman Melville*. Ed. Harrison Hayford, Hershel Parker, and G. Thomas Tanselle. 13 vols. to date. Evanston and Chicago: Northwestern UP and Newberry Library, 1968–. 365–410.

Howatson, M. C., ed. *The Oxford Companion to Classical Literature*. 2d ed. Oxford: Oxford UP, 1989.

Husni, Khalil. "The Confidence-Man's Colourful-Colourless Masquerade: Melville's Theatre of the Absurd 'in Black and White.'" *Studia Anglica Posnaniensia: An International Review of English Studies* 17 (1984): 219–31.

Irwin, John T. *American Hieroglyphics: The Symbol of the Egyptian Hieroglyphics in the American Renaissance*. New Haven: Yale UP, 1980.

Jarrard, Norman Eugene. "Poems by Herman Melville: A Critical Edition of the Published Verse." Ph.D. diss., University of Texas, 1960.

Jehlen, Myra. *American Incarnation: The Individual, the Nation, the Continent*. Cambridge, Mass.: Harvard UP, 1986.

Johnson, Barbara. "Melville's Fist: The Execution of *Billy Budd*." *Studies in Romanticism* 18 (1979): 567–99.

Karcher, Carolyn. *Shadow over the Promised Land: Slavery, Race, and Violence in Melville's America*. Baton Rouge: Louisiana State UP, 1980.

Kelley, Wyn. "The Mood for Composition: The Melville Family Letters." *Melville Society Extracts* 98 (Sept. 1994): 12.

Kemp, Peter, ed. *The Oxford Companion to Ships and the Sea*. London: Oxford UP, 1976.

Kring, Walter D., and Jonathan S. Carey. "Two Discoveries Concerning Herman Melville." *Proceedings of the Massachusetts Historical Society* 87 (1975): 137–41. Rpt. in Yannella and Parker, *The Endless, Winding Way: New Charts by Kring and Carey.*

Langsdorff, G. H. von. *Voyages and Travels in Various Parts of the World.* London, 1813.

Lavater, John Caspar. *Essays on Physiognomy; for the promotion of the knowledge and the love of mankind.* Translated by Thomas Holcroft. 2d ed. London: H. D. Symonds, et al., 1804.

Lawrence, D. H. *Studies in Classic American Literature.* 1923. New York: Viking, 1961.

Leavis, Q. D. "Melville: The 1853–6 Phase." *New Perspectives on Melville.* Edited by Faith Pullin. Kent, Ohio: Kent State UP, 1978.

Lee, A. Robert. "Voices Off, On, and Without: Ventriloquy in *The Confidence-Man.*" *Herman Melville: Reassessments.* Edited by A. Robert Lee. London: Vision Press, 1984. 157–75.

Lehmann-Haupt, Hellmut, Lawrence C. Wroth, and Rollo G. Silver. *The Book in America: A History of the Making and Selling of Books in the United States.* 2d ed. New York: R. R. Bowker, 1952.

——. *Bookbinding in America: Three Essays.* New York: R. R. Bowker, 1967.

Leverenz, David. *Manhood and the American Renaissance.* Ithaca: Cornell UP, 1989.

Levin, Harry. *The Power of Blackness: Hawthorne Poe Melville.* New York: Knopf, 1958.

Leyda, Jay. *The Melville Log: A Documentary Life of Herman Melville, 1819–1891.* 2 vols. New York: Harcourt, Brace, 1951.

——. *The Melville Log: A Documentary Life of Herman Melville 1819–1891 . . . with a New Supplementary Chapter.* 2 vols. 1951. New York: Gordian, 1969.

Maddox, Lucy. *Removals: Nineteenth-Century American Literature and the Politics of Indian Affairs.* New York: Oxford UP, 1991.

Martin, Robert K. *Hero, Captain, and Stranger: Male Friendship, Social Critique, and Literary Form in the Sea Novels of Herman Melville.* Chapel Hill: U of North Carolina P, 1986.

Marx, Leo. "Melville's Parable of the Walls." *Sewanee Review* 61 (1953): 602–27.

Maslan, Mark. "Whitman's 'Strange Hand': Body as Text in *Drum-Taps.*" *ELH* 58 (1991): 935–55.

Mathewson, Stephen. "'To Tell Over Again the Story Just Told': The Composition of Melville's *Redburn.*" *ESQ* 37.4 (1991): 311–20.

Matthiessen, F. O. *American Renaissance: Art and Expression in the Age of Emerson and Whitman.* London: Oxford UP, 1941.

McGaw, Judith A. *Most Wonderful Machine: Mechanization and Social Change in Berkshire Paper Making, 1801–1885.* Princeton: Princeton UP, 1987.

McPherson, James M. *Battle Cry of Freedom: The Civil War Era.* New York: Oxford UP, 1988.

Mead, Margaret. *An Inquiry into the Question of Cultural Stability in Polynesia.* New York: Columbia UP, 1928.

Melville, Herman. *Battle-Pieces and Aspects of the War.* New York: Harper, 1866.

——. *Battle-Pieces and Aspects of the War.* New York: Harper, 1866. Facsimile edition. Introduction by Sidney Kaplan. Gainesville, Fla.: Scholars' Facsimiles and Reprints, 1960.

——. *Billy Budd Sailor (An Inside Narrative).* Edited by Harrison Hayford and Merton M. Sealts Jr. Chicago: U of Chicago P, 1962.

———. *"Billy Budd Sailor" and Other Stories.* Edited by Frederick Busch. New York: Viking Penguin, 1986.

———. *Collected Poems of Herman Melville.* Edited by Howard P. Vincent. Chicago: Hendricks House, 1947.

———. *The Confidence-Man: His Masquerade.* Edited by Elizabeth S. Foster. New York: Hendricks House, 1954.

———. *The Confidence-Man: His Masquerade.* New York: Dix, Edwards & Co., 1857.

———. *The Letters of Herman Melville.* Edited by Merrell R. Davis and William H. Gilman. New Haven: Yale UP, 1960.

———. *Omoo: A Narrative of Adventures in the South Seas.* Edited by Harrison Hayford and Walter Blair. New York: Hendricks House, 1969.

———. *Pierre, or, The Ambiguities.* Edited by Henry A. Murray. New York: Hendricks House, 1949.

———. *Timoleon.* 1891. Facsimile edition. Introduction and census by Charles Haberstroh. Norwood, Pa.: Norwood Editions, 1976.

———. *The Writings of Herman Melville.* Edited by Harrison Hayford, Hershel Parker, and G. Thomas Tanselle. 13 vols. to date. Evanston and Chicago: Northwestern UP and Newberry Library, 1968–.

Mensel, Robert E. "'Kodakers Lying in Wait': Amateur Photography and the Right of Privacy in New York, 1885–1915." *American Quarterly* 43 (1991): 24–45.

Metcalf, Eleanor Melville. *Herman Melville: Cycle and Epicycle.* Cambridge, Mass.: Harvard UP, 1953.

Metcalf, Paul. *Genoa: A Telling of Wonders.* Highlands, N.C.: Jonathan Williams, 1965.

———, ed. *Enter Isabel: The Herman Melville Correspondence of Clare Spark and Paul Metcalf.* Albuquerque: U of New Mexico P, 1991.

Michaels, Walter Benn. *The Gold Standard and the Logic of Naturalism: American Literature at the Turn of the Century.* Berkeley: U of California P, 1987.

Milder, Robert. "The Composition of *Moby-Dick*: A Review and a Prospect." *ESQ* 23 (1977): 203–16.

———. "Herman Melville." *Columbia Literary History of the United States.* Edited by Emory Elliot. New York: Columbia UP, 1988. 429–47.

Miller, Edwin Haviland. *Melville.* New York: George Braziller, 1975.

Miller, J. Hillis. *Ariadne's Thread: Story Lines.* New Haven: Yale UP, 1992.

Miller, Perry. *The Raven and the Whale: The War of Words and Wits in the Era of Poe and Melville.* 1956. Westport, Conn.: Greenwood Press, 1973.

Monteiro, George. "Poetry and Madness: Melville's Rediscovery of Camões in 1867." *The New England Quarterly* 51.4 (1978): 561–65.

Morrison, Toni. *Playing in the Dark: Whiteness and the Literary Imagination.* Cambridge: Harvard UP, 1992.

Mosblech, L'Abbé Boniface. *Vocabulaire Oceanien-Français et Français-Oceanien des dialectes parles aux Iles Marquises, Sandwich, Gambier, etc..* Paris, 1843.

Mumford, Lewis. *Herman Melville.* New York: Literary Guild of America, 1929.

Murray, Henry A. "Dead to the World: The Passions of Herman Melville." *Essays in Self-Destruction.* Edited by Edwin S. Shneidman. New York: Science House, 1967.

———. Introduction. *Pierre, or, The Ambiguities.* New York: Hendricks House, 1949. xiii–ciii.

Murray, Henry A., Harvey Myerson, and Eugene Taylor. "Allan Melville's By-Blow." *Melville Society Extracts*. Number 61 (1985): 1–6.

Nash, Ray. *American Penmanship 1800–1850: A History of Writing and a Bibliography of Copybooks from Jenkins to Spencer*. Worcester, Mass.: American Antiquarian Society, 1969.

———. *Writing: Some Early American Writing Books and Masters*. 2d ed. N.p.: H & N, 1943.

Newman, Lea Bertani Vozar. *A Reader's Guide to the Short Stories of Herman Melville*. Boston: G. K. Hall, 1986.

Nickell, Joe. *Pen, Ink, & Evidence*. Lexington: UP of Kentucky, 1990.

Oatman, Olive Ann. "Olive Ann Oatman's Lecture Notes and Oatman Bibliography." Ed. Rev. Edward J. Pettid. *San Bernardino County Museum Association Quarterly* 16.2 (1968).

Olson, Charles. *Call Me Ishmael*. San Francisco: City Lights Books, 1947.

The Oxford English Dictionary. 2d ed., 1989.

Paltsits, Victor Hugo, ed. *Family Correspondence of Herman Melville, 1830–1904. In The Gansevoort-Lansing Collection*. Brooklyn, N.Y.: Haskell House, 1976.

Parker, Hershel. "*The Confidence-Man* and the Use of Evidence in Compositional Studies: A Rejoinder." Letter. *Nineteenth-Century Fiction* 28 (1973): 119–24.

———. "Evidences for 'Late Insertions' in Melville's Works." *Studies in the Novel* 7 (1975): 407–24.

———. Historical Note. *Redburn: His First Voyage*. Vol. 4 of *The Writings of Herman Melville*. Edited by Harrison Hayford, Hershel Parker, and G. Thomas Tanselle. 13 vols. to date. Evanston and Chicago: Northwestern UP and Newberry Library, 1968–. 315–52.

———. Historical Supplement. *Clarel: A Poem and Pilgrimage in the Holy Land*. By Herman Melville. Vol. 12 of *The Writings of Herman Melville*. Edited by Harrison Hayford, Hershel Parker, and G. Thomas Tanselle. 13 vols. to date. Evanston and Chicago: Northwestern UP and Newberry Library, 1968–. 639–73.

———. "*Moby-Dick* and Domesticity." *Critical Essays on Herman Melville's "Moby-Dick."* Edited by Brian Higgins and Hershel Parker. New York: G. K. Hall, 1992. 545–62.

———. *Reading "Billy Budd."* Evanston, Ill.: Northwestern UP, 1990.

———, ed. *The Recognition of Herman Melville: Selected Criticism since 1846*. Ann Arbor: U of Michigan P, 1967.

———. "Why *Pierre* Went Wrong." *Studies in the Novel* 8 (1976): 7–23.

Parry, Albert. *Tattoo: Secrets of a Strange Art as Practiced among the Natives of the United States*. New York: Simon & Schuster, 1933.

Pettid, Edward J., ed. "Olive Ann Oatman's Lecture Notes and Oatman Bibliography." *San Bernardino County Museum Association Quarterly* 16.2 (1968).

Pleck, Elizabeth. "Wife Beating in Nineteenth-Century America." *Victimology* 4.1 (1979): 60–74.

Poe, Edgar Allan. *Complete Stories and Poems of Edgar Allan Poe*. New York: Doubleday, 1966.

Porter, Captain David. *Journal of a Cruise*. 1815, 1822. Edited by R. D. Madison and Karen Hamon. Annapolis, Md.: Naval Institute Press, 1986.

Puett, Amy Elizabeth. "Melville's Wife: A Study of Elizabeth Shaw Melville." Ph.D. diss., Northwestern University, 1969.

Railton, Stephen. *Authorship and Audience: Literary Performance in the American Renaissance.* Princeton UP, 1991.

Renker, Elizabeth M. " 'Declaration-Men' and the Rhetoric of Self-Presentation." *Early American Literature* 24.2 (1989): 120–34.

———. "Herman Melville, Wife Beating, and the Written Page." *American Literature* 66 (March 1994): 123–50.

Robillard, Douglas. "Melville's *Clarel* and the Parallel of Poetry and Painting." *North Dakota Quarterly* 51.2 (1983): 107–20.

Robinson, Forrest G. *Love's Story Told: A Life of Henry A. Murray.* Cambridge, Mass.: Harvard UP, 1992.

Rogers, John G. *Origins of Sea Terms.* Mystic, Conn.: Mystic Seaport Museum, 1985.

Rogin, Michael Paul. *Subversive Genealogy: The Politics and Art of Herman Melville.* 1979. Berkeley: U of California P, 1985.

Roper, Gordon. Historical Note. *Omoo.* By Herman Melville. Vol. 2 of *The Writings of Herman Melville.* Edited by Harrison Hayford, Hershel Parker, and G. Thomas Tanselle. 13 vols. to date. Evanston and Chicago: Northwestern UP and Newberry Library, 1968–. 319–44.

Ryan, Robert Charles. " 'Weeds and Wildings Chiefly: With a Rose or Two' by Herman Melville. Reading Text and Genetic Text, Edited from the Manuscripts, with Introduction and Notes." Ph.D. diss., Northwestern University, 1967.

Samson, John. *White Lies: Melville's Narratives of Facts.* Ithaca: Cornell UP, 1989.

Sattelmeyer, Robert, and James Barbour. "A Possible Source and Model for 'The Story of China Aster' in Melville's *The Confidence-Man.*" *American Literature* 48 (1977): 577–83.

Scutt, R. W. B., and Christopher Gotch. *Art, Sex, and Symbol: The Mystery of Tattooing.* 1974. New York: Cornwall Books, 1986.

Sealts, Merton M., Jr. *The Early Lives of Melville: Nineteenth-Century Biographical Sketches and Their Authors.* Madison: U of Wisconsin P, 1974.

———. Historical Note. *The Piazza Tales and Other Prose Pieces, 1839–1860.* By Herman Melville. Vol. 9 of *The Writings of Herman Melville.* Edited by Harrison Hayford, Hershel Parker, and G. Thomas Tanselle. 13 vols. to date. Evanston and Chicago: Northwestern UP and Newberry Library, 1968–. 457–533.

———. *Melville's Reading: Revised and Enlarged Edition.* Columbia: U of South Carolina P, 1988.

Sedgwick, William Ellery. *Herman Melville: The Tragedy of Mind.* Cambridge, Mass.: Harvard UP, 1945.

Shell, Marc. *The Economy of Literature.* Baltimore: Johns Hopkins UP, 1978.

Shetley, Vernon Lionel. "A Private Art: Melville's Poetry of Negation." Ph.D. diss., Columbia University, 1986.

Shneidman, Edwin S. "Some Psychological Reflections on the Death of Malcolm Melville." *Suicide and Life Threatening Behavior* 6 (1976): 231–42.

Shurr, William H. "Melville's Poems: The Late Agenda." *A Companion to Melville Studies.* Edited by John Bryant. 351–74.

———. *The Mystery of Iniquity: Melville as Poet, 1857–1891.* Lexington: UP of Kentucky, 1972.

Simms, William Gilmore. *Charlemont; or, The Pride of the Village.* New York: A. C. Armstrong & Son, 1882.

Simpson, David. *The Politics of American English, 1776–1850.* New York: Oxford UP, 1986.

Sollors, Werner, ed. Introduction. *The Return of Thematic Criticism.* Harvard English Studies 18. Cambridge, Mass.: Harvard UP, 1993. xi–xxiii.

Stedman, Arthur. "Melville of Marquesas." *Review of Reviews* (4 Nov. 1891): 428–30. Rpt. in Sealts, *The Early Lives of Melville,* 110–15.

Stein, William Bysshe. *The Poetry of Melville's Late Years.* Albany: SUNY Press, 1970.

Sten, Christopher. "Melville and the Visual Arts: An Overview." *Savage Eye: Melville and the Visual Arts.* Edited by Christopher Sten. Kent, Ohio: Kent State UP, 1991. 1–39.

——, ed. *Savage Eye: Melville and the Visual Arts.* Kent, Ohio: Kent State UP, 1991.

Stern, Milton R. *Critical Essays on Herman Melville's "Typee."* Boston: G. K. Hall, 1982.

——. *The Fine Hammered Steel of Herman Melville.* 1957. Urbana: U of Illinois P, 1968.

Sterne, Harold E. *Catalogue of Nineteenth Century Bindery Equipment.* Cincinnati: Ye Olde Printery, 1978.

Stewart, C. S. *A Visit to the South Seas in the U. States Ship Vincennes, during the Years 1829 and 1830.* 2 vols. New York: John P. Haven, 1833.

Suggs, Robert C. *The Hidden Worlds of Polynesia.* New York: Harcourt, Brace & World, 1962.

Sundquist, Eric. " 'Benito Cereno' and New World Slavery." *Reconstructing American Literary History.* Edited by Sacvan Bercovitch. Cambridge, Mass.: Harvard UP, 1986.

——. *Home as Found: Authority and Genealogy in Nineteenth-Century American Literature.* Baltimore: Johns Hopkins UP, 1979.

——. "Suspense and Tautology in 'Benito Cereno.' " *Glyph: Johns Hopkins Textual Studies* 8 (1977): 103–26.

——. *To Wake the Nations: Race in the Making of American Literature.* Cambridge, Mass.: Belknap Press of Harvard UP, 1993.

Sussman, Henry. "The Deconstructor as Politician: Melville's *Confidence-Man.*" *Glyph: Johns Hopkins Textual Studies* 4 (1978): 32–56.

Sweet, Timothy. *Traces of War: Poetry, Photography, and the Crisis of the Union.* Baltimore: Johns Hopkins UP, 1990.

Taylor, J. Orville. *The District School.* New York: Harper, 1834.

Thompson, Lawrance. *Melville's Quarrel with God.* Princeton: Princeton UP, 1952.

Thomson, Reverend Robert. *The Marquesas Islands: Their Description and Early History.* Edited by Robert D. Craig, Laie, Hawaii: Institute for Polynesian Studies, Brigham Young University, 1980.

Thorp, Willard. "Herman Melville." *Literary History of the United States.* Edited by Robert E. Spiller, Willard Thorp, et al. 2 vols. New York: Macmillan, 1948. 1: 441–71.

——. Historical Note. *White-Jacket or The World in a Man-of-War.* By Herman Melville. Vol. 5 of *The Writings of Herman Melville.* Edited by Harrison Hayford, Hershel Parker, and G. Thomas Tanselle. 13 vols. to date. Evanston and Chicago: Northwestern UP and Newberry Library, 1968–. 403–40.

Tytler, Graeme. *Physiognomy in the European Novel.* Princeton UP, 1982.

Vincent, Howard P., ed. Explanatory Notes. *Collected Poems of Herman Melville.* Chicago: Hendricks House, 1947. 445–536.

———. *The Trying-Out of "Moby-Dick."* 1949. Kent, Ohio: Kent State UP, 1980.

Wadlington, Warwick. *The Confidence Game in American Literature.* Princeton: Princeton UP, 1975.

Wallace, Robert K. *Melville and Turner: Spheres of Love and Fright.* Athens, Ga.: U of Georgia P, 1992.

Warren, Robert Penn. "Melville the Poet." *Selected Essays.* New York: Random House, 1958.

Weaver, Raymond M. *Herman Melville: Mariner and Mystic.* New York: George H. Doran, 1921.

Webster, Noah. *An American Dictionary of the English Language, Exhibiting the Origin, Orthography, Pronunciation, and Definitions of Words.* Revised and enlarged by Chauncey A. Goodrich. New York: Harper, 1847.

Weidman, Bette S. "*Typee* and *Omoo*: A Diverging Pair." *A Companion to Melville Studies.* Edited by John Bryant. New York: Greenwood Press, 1986. 85–121.

Williams, Raymond. *Keywords: A Vocabulary of Culture and Society.* New York: Oxford UP, 1976.

Willis, A. E. *How to Read Character by the Face.* 5th ed. New York, 1888.

Winship, Michael. "Critical Methods in the History of the Book in the United States." Program in the History of the Book in American Culture. American Antiquarian Society. June 14–19, 1992.

———. "Bibliographical Approaches to the Nineteenth-Century Book in the United States." Program in the History of the Book in American Culture. American Antiquarian Society. June 21–26, 1992.

Wright, Nathalia. *Melville's Use of the Bible.* Durham, N.C.: Duke UP, 1949.

———. "The Poems in Melville's *Mardi.*" *Essays in Arts and Sciences* 5.2 (1976): 83–99.

Wroth, Lawrence C., and Rollo G. Silver. "Book Production and Distribution from the American Revolution to the War Between the States." *The Book in America: A History of the Making and Selling of Books in the United States.* By Hellmut Lehmann-Haupt, Lawrence C. Wroth, and Rollo G. Silver. 2d ed. New York: R. R. Bowker, 1952. 63–136.

Yamaya, Saburo. "The Stone Image in Melville's *Pierre.*" *Studies in English Literature* 34 (1957): 31–57.

Yannella, Donald, and Hershel Parker, eds. *The Endless, Winding Way in Melville: New Charts by Kring and Carey.* Introduction by Walter D. Kring. Glassboro, N.J.: Melville Society, 1981.

Yellin, Jean Fagan. *The Intricate Knot: Black Figures in American Literature, 1776–1863.* New York: New York UP, 1972.

Young, Philip. *The Private Melville.* University Park, Pa.: Pennsylvania State UP, 1993.

Index

LIBRARY OF CONGRESS CATALOGING-IN-PUBLICATION DATA

Renker, Elizabeth.
   Strike through the mask : Herman Melville and the scene of writing /
Elizabeth Renker.
      p.   cm.
   Includes bibliographical references (p.   ) and index.
   ISBN 0-8018-5230-7 (acid-free paper)
   1. Melville, Herman, 1819–1892—Authorship.   2. Authorship—Social
aspects—United States—History—19th century.   3. Literature and
society—United States—History—19th century.   4. Authors and readers—
United States—History—19th century.   5. Creation (Literary, artistic,
etc.)   I. Title.
PS2388.A9R46   1996
813'.3—dc20   95-31870

ISBN 0-8018-5875-5 (pbk.)